Duncan McNab, a former police detective, investigative journalist, TV producer and media advisor to government and the private sector, is the author of twelve books, including Australian bestsellers *Dead Man Running* (with Ross Coulthart), *The Snapshot Killer, Waterfront* and *Roger Rogerson*. Duncan was a producer on the Kennedy and Clarion award-winning *Murder Uncovered* series (7 Network) in 2017 and creator/ series producer of the groundbreaking *Australia Behind Bars* (9 Network/ITV). In 2017, his book *Getting Away with Murder* won the Ned Kelly Award for Best True Crime. He lives in Sydney.

Also by Duncan McNab and published by Hachette:

Waterfront
Roger Rogerson
The Snapshot Killer

RECIPE FOR MURDER

DUNCAN McNAB

WELBECK

First published in Australia and New Zealand in 2025 by Hachette Australia,
an imprint of Hachette Australia Pty Limited

First published in the UK in 2025 by Headline Welbeck Non-Fiction
An imprint of Headline Publishing Group Limited

1

Cataloguing in Publication Data is available from the British Library

Paperback ISBN 978 1 0354 4093 1

Offset in 10.62/11.9pt Simoncini Garamond Std by
Six Red Marbles UK, Thetford, Norfolk

Printed and bound in Great Britain by Clays Ltd, Elcograf S.p.A.

Headline's policy is to use papers that are natural, renewable and recyclable
products and made from wood grown in well-managed forests and other
controlled sources. The logging and manufacturing processes are expected
to conform to the environmental regulations of the country of origin.

Headline Publishing Group Limited
An Hachette UK Company
Carmelite House
50 Victoria Embankment
London EC4Y 0DZ

The authorised representative in the EEA is Hachette Ireland,
8 Castlecourt Centre, Dublin 15, D15 XTP3, Ireland (email: info@hbgi.ie)

www.headline.co.uk
www.hachette.co.uk

*'A false witness will not go unpunished,
and he who breathes out lies will not escape.'*

– Proverbs 19:5

CONTENTS

PROLOGUE

Beef Wellington is chef Gordon Ramsay's signature dish. Historically, the dish was supposedly created to celebrate the Duke of Wellington's victory against Napoleon at Waterloo in 1815. It's a special dish, usually made for a special occasion. It can be hard to get right, easy to get wrong and the meal is easily let down by soggy pastry or either undercooked or overcooked beef.

In the Ramsay version, you sear a nice lump of beef fillet, then fry off some finely chopped mushrooms to form a kind of paste, or duxelles. Next you lay out some prosciutto, smear the mushroom duxelles over it, then pop the beef on top and roll. Finally, you encase the rolled-up beef in puff pastry, glaze it with a little egg wash and pop it in the oven. The result is a golden brown, buttery, flaky pastry parcel that, when sliced, reveals gloriously pink beef and a fragrant waft from the mushrooms.

In late July 2023, beef Wellington made front pages around the planet – and it wasn't Gordon Ramsay's recipe.

This particular dish had been served at a family lunch held in the country town of Leongatha, Victoria. The lunch had purportedly been organised to help reconciliation between the host, Lego-loving true crime obsessive Erin Patterson, and her estranged husband, Simon, and his family. Erin also hoped her guests would provide counsel on how best to deal with some potentially serious medical issues she claimed to be facing.

According to Ramsay, 'Beef Wellington has to be the ultimate indulgence. It's one of my all-time favourite main courses and it would definitely be on my last supper menu.'

Sadly, it was to be the last supper for three of the four guests who sat down with Erin Patterson that day – husband and wife Don and Gail Patterson, and Gail's sister, Heather Wilkinson. Heather's husband, Ian, was also at the lunch, but after a long and brutal medical battle, Ian survived. Simon Patterson, Don and Gail's son, was also on the guest list that fateful day but prudently decided not to attend.

The lunch also proved to be Erin Trudi Patterson's Waterloo – an event that would have horrific consequences for all involved. After a lengthy investigation, Erin was charged with three counts of murder and five counts of attempted murder. Two of the five attempt charges arose from the beef Wellington lunch, but – in an intriguing development – three were for alleged attempts on Simon's life in the two years before that dreadful day.

In the lead-up to the trial, the attempted murder charges relating to the attempts on Simon were hived off, to be heard in a separate trial. This trial was to be held after the trial for the three counts of murder of Don, Gail and Heather, and the attempt on Ian Wilkinson. But just days before that trial started, those charges for the attempts on Simon's life were dropped.

The tragedy and bizarre nature of these crimes propelled these ordinary families, living quiet lives in the close-knit rural towns of Leongatha and Korumburra, onto the world stage. No-one could have anticipated the glare of global publicity that would ensue, and for the residents of these towns, that spotlight was unwelcome. Packs of journalists, reporters and film crews came knocking on the doors of those involved, their families, neighbours, friends and colleagues. They camped outside Erin Patterson's home in Leongatha, all hoping for a glimpse, a photo or a comment.

Each day brought more coverage, splashed on newspapers, TV and radio news bulletins and in the chat groups that were springing up on numerous social media platforms. First, they described the condition of those hospitalised, then the dreadful fate of the three decent, honourable people who lost their lives, before the focus shifted to Ian Wilkinson's months-long recovery and the careful, methodical work of the police.

Was it really the diabolical death cap mushroom that had caused the victims' fate? If so, was their inclusion in the dish an accident, a terrible, innocent mistake? Or was it something more sinister – a mother dedicated to her kids taking brutal retribution on her estranged family? And in the background was Simon Patterson's chilling suspicion that his wife had poisoned him before, and more than once.

There was a question we all wanted answered. Was Erin Patterson a person who had tried to commit mass murder?

1

WELCOME TO LEONGATHA

Murder is a crime that in one single devastating and usually unanticipated moment – at least for some – changes the lives of so many forever. The impact may become less vivid over time, the tragedy may soften, but it will always be there, lingering in a corner of the mind, waiting to be triggered. Those impacted include not only the victims' families and friends, but also the investigators, lawyers, and of course the perpetrator and those who know them. These crimes also leach into the community where the victim(s) and perpetrator(s) lived, worked, raised their families, walked their dog and lived out their day-to-day lives.

The death of three people put the towns of Korumburra, where the victims lived, and Leongatha, where the lunch took place, on front pages around the world. The bizarre events in this peaceful part of Australia, a place many of us needed a map to find, were a hot topic in discussions around both the nation and the globe, from true crime afficionados to the broader public. In the plentiful online chat groups that popped up, speculation was rife – was it an accident, misadventure or something more sinister?

Leongatha, the town that Erin Patterson and her deadly beef Wellington put on the map, is an easy 130-kilometre drive from Melbourne, with a population of around 6000 people. I'm a fan of the road less travelled, so when a road sign informed me I could turn off the main highway and enjoy a more scenic route to the scene of the crime, I jumped at the chance. First stop was Poowong, home to just over 700 people, a handful of shops, a petrol station and a pub – a sliver of bucolic bliss. But if you look past the houses on the main street, you'll see housing estates pegged out, presumably awaiting new residents escaping Melbourne in search of a quieter life.

Fifteen kilometres along the road, among rolling hills and verdant pastures, is Korumburra, population of around 4500 people. This close-knit town is home to the Patterson and Wilkinson families, and was also once home to Simon and Erin Patterson.

The main street of Korumburra boasts a pub spruiking vegan meals, a tattooist, a few cafes, a smart new craft brewery, a Thai massage parlour and a few greying tree-changers who've fled the city. A smattering of Marge Simpson-like hairstyles adds a little visual variety.

Korumburra was settled in the late 1800s, its development aided by the discovery of coal and the advent of the Great Southern Railway from Dandenong to Korumburra, which began construction in 1887 and finally opened in 1892. This work was spurred on by an 1889 Royal Commission that declared the rapid transport of coal from the mines to Melbourne should be an imperative.

Korumburra was the regional hub of a vigorous coal mining industry from the reign of Queen Victoria until the late 1960s, when it went into a rapid decline. The first profitable coal mine – the Coal Creek Proprietary Company – was established in 1889, and remnants of that era still linger in names like Mine Road, the Coal Creek Motel – the only motel in town – and the Coal Creek Miners Museum. The train line ceased operation a century later and is now a tourist attraction, the Great Southern Rail Trail. The last mine in Gippsland closed in 2015.

These days Korumburra remains a close-knit town with a strong sense of community, evidenced by over eighty local groups, mainly volunteers, working in organised sport, landcare, the arts, supporting senior citizens and simply helping each other. It's also a town devastated by the loss of Don and Gail Patterson and Heather Wilkinson, who, for decades, had worked hard for their community. Recovery will be slow.

Religion is a strong thread, with the churches not only significant as places of worship but also as social hubs that welcome the less religiously inclined. The town has a mix of the usual suspects, including a vigorous Pentecostal church and the Baptist church in Mine Road where the Patterson and Wilkinson families regularly joined the congregation. The Baptist church is a humble weatherboard building, painted a dark cream with dark green highlights and an ochre tin roof. It was built in 1895 during the town's thriving days, when the future looked rosy. In 1956, the church made history as the first Baptist church in Australia to induct a deaconess, Norma Barnett, to what Melbourne's *Argus* reported as taking 'full responsibility for a Baptist church'.

Fifteen kilometres along the picturesque A440 highway is Leongatha, the administrative heart of South Gippsland, and home to the South Gippsland Shire Council.

When motoring in from Korumburra, Leongatha – pronounced with a short 'a', rather than the drawn-out 'gartha' (like Martha) we city types were quickly schooled not to use – greets you with the not terribly welcoming sign 'Leongatha – Arrive Alive, Take A Break'. There's no suggestion of a warm country welcome, no proud claim of a 'tidy town', none of the signs announcing places to stay or to eat that are common on the outskirts of many Australian country towns.

The town was a key player in Gippsland's dairy industry, dating back to the late 1880s when the place was first settled. Today, many smaller producers have been taken over and consolidated by major global players like the Canadian conglomerate Saputo, who swallowed up well-known brands like Devondale, King Island Dairy and the sharp yet squishy cheeses of Mersey Valley.

Back at the close of the nineteenth century, Leongatha was also home to the first and probably only experiment in using a labour colony to help with unemployment in a time of recession. Spurred on by examples in Bismarck's Germany, a camp was set up to focus on clearing land and developing a self-sustaining community. It started with twelve men in 1893. They cleared the land, planted crops like silverbeet and corn, and started dairy production. Over the ensuing decade around 6000 men passed through the colony, and by 1914 it was closed, with some of the land sold to the Leongatha Butter and Cheese Factory, and other parcels to become soldier settlement farms in the wake of World War I.

These days, Leongatha is the service town for the region, home to the big shops like Woolworths and the wildly popular other note of German influence on the town, Aldi. There are traffic lights, more Thai massage parlours, and even a cafe offering a plant-based menu.

Locals who've lived there for generations now find themselves sharing the angle parking in the two main streets with middle-aged chaps sporting man buns and driving new-model SUVs that seldom see any offroad motoring.

On my visits, I found the locals weren't too keen to comment on the terrible crime that happened in their midst. Their reticence was perhaps a combination of coming to grips with the shock of it and the vigorous, and often intrusive, media attention that had stirred their lives a little too much. Having journalists, reporters and international stringers knocking on doors and loitering in the main streets for a vox pop can tax anyone's goodwill.

However, being politely persistent and turning the last remains of my ageing charm up to high did bring the occasional reward. Explaining why I was in town was always followed by a pause and the occasional grimace, then the consistent response: 'Erin Patterson? Well, she's not from around here really.'

2

FATAL FUNGI FORAGING

Britain's Woodland Trust describes the *Amanita phalloides*, commonly known as the death cap mushroom, as the 'silent assassin and killer of kings. The death cap has been used as a murder weapon for millennia.' The death cap is thought to have killed Roman Emperor Claudius in 54 AD and Pope Clement VII in 1534.

The Australian National Botanic Gardens and Australian National Herbarium, as part of a public information initiative, posed the question 'How dangerous is the death cap?' The answer? 'Deadly! The poisons in one cap are enough to kill a healthy adult and less will be enough to kill a small child.' In 2016, the *Guardian* reported that the death cap was responsible for more deaths than any other mushroom, adding, 'Worse still, death caps have been reported to taste quite pleasant.' The article went on: 'To make life even more difficult, it's easy to mistake the death cap for some edible mushrooms. They can be distinguished by a pale green cap, a bulbous ring at the bottom of the stalk and a ring-like collar at the top. But the cap can be white like an edible field mushroom, and the young unopened cap conceals its telltale white gills – a field mushroom has darker gills – and can also be mistaken for an edible young puffball.'

The internet provides a wealth of information on the death cap and its lethal ways, and it doesn't take a supersleuth to find numerous cases of poisoning by this fungi and the horrific consequences.

According to Royal Botanic Gardens Victoria, the first confirmed identification of a death cap in Australia was in Canberra in the 1960s, followed by Melbourne in the 1970s and Adelaide in 2008. Death caps have been spotted across suburban Melbourne, including the south-eastern suburbs where Erin Patterson grew up and kept a home. The death cap originated in Europe, but made its way to North America and Australia, probably through the transport of trees that had some of the fungus attached.

The mushrooms grow in autumn, often at the foot of an oak tree. According to South Australia Health, they're one of the deadliest mushrooms in the world and account for around ninety per cent of all mushroom poisoning deaths, which are thought to number around 100 per year. And according to Doctor Tom May, an expert from the Royal Botanic Gardens of Victoria and co-author of the 2021 book *Wild Mushrooming*, written to help people safely forage, the death cap is white when young, but as it ages the colours vary, including white, green, brown and yellow.

An amble around the internet reveals quite a few examples of the poor souls who've found themselves among that 100. Christina Hale, fifty-seven, and her husband,

Jocelyn Lynch, forty-nine, from the historic market town of Bridgwater in the United Kingdom, were rushed to hospital on 17 November 2012. On the night of 15 November, both had eaten mushroom soup that Mrs Hale had made using mushrooms she'd found in their garden. The couple had begun to feel unwell the next morning. Mr Lynch later said they'd eaten mushrooms foraged from the garden previously but had been fine. On this occasion he'd been at work when his wife picked the mushrooms, so he hadn't seen them, nor did he know how many she'd used.

With diarrhoea and vomiting persisting, Mrs Hale called an after-hours medical service and told them she'd 'eaten some dodgy mushrooms'. After examination, the doctor thought the cause was norovirus and the soup was unrelated. But he was wrong, illustrating the deceptive nature of death cap mushroom poisoning.

The couple stayed at home, hoping the symptoms would fade, but that evening Mr Lynch, who'd been sleeping, was woken by shouting and discovered his wife had called the paramedics. Both were taken to hospital. Mrs Hale's heart, affected by the toxins, stopped four times. She died of multi-organ failure on 19 November. Mr Lynch survived.

At the Inquest, Coroner Michael Rose described the toxins in the mushrooms as assaulting Mrs Hale, noting that the amount was too great to survive. The Inquest also heard expert testimony that the mushrooms had been identified from photos taken at the house, and the death cap could readily be mistaken for safe mushrooms. Chillingly, just half a mushroom could be fatal, and there was no antidote. The coroner's advice was, 'One should never pick mushrooms, particularly under trees, unless you know exactly what you're doing.'

In Australia there have been ample warnings about the danger of eating death caps. However, there have been a few recent cases of death by death cap, and in each instance the cause was accidental ingestion rather than someone with an intent to inflict harm.

The Australian Broadcasting Corporation (ABC) article of 19 November 2021 quoted Australian Capital Territory (ACT) Health Minister Rachel Stephen-Smith, who warned, 'While this is not the normal time of year for death cap mushroom growth in the ACT, it is a timely reminder to people not to pick and eat wild mushrooms.' The article also said that death caps usually grew in autumn, thrived in wet weather and were often found under oak trees, noting, 'Death caps are a very dangerous mushroom, causing liver damage, which can be fatal. The mushrooms are often confused for straw mushrooms, a commonly eaten variety in Asia that looks very similar.'

Other articles around that time outlined the symptoms of death cap poisoning, and reported the sad case of three people who ate them in Australia in 2012, two of whom died as a result. This event garnered publicity around the world.

An undated article in the online publication *Australian Food Timeline* said of the incident, 'Death cap mushrooms have been involved in the majority of mushroom poisoning deaths around the world including, in ancient times, that of Roman emperor Claudius.' The article went on to recount a New Year's Eve dinner in 2011/12 at Canberra's Harmonie German Club, which curiously had a Chinese bistro rather than the expected sauerkraut and sausages. The bistro's respected chef Liu Jun was a fan of foraging, and used some mushrooms he'd found to make a stir-fry at a private dinner for friends. Chef Jun and kitchen hand Tsou Hsiang died in hospital while awaiting a liver transplant, and a third diner recovered.

On 14 January 2012, the ABC reported that the chef had mistaken the mushrooms for a Chinese delicacy. This article also went on to note that death caps were often found under oak trees, and that five people in Canberra had died of death cap poisoning in the five years prior to this incident.

The article in the *Australian Food Timeline* noted also that a young woman had sued Woolworths in 2014, claiming that mushrooms she'd bought there contained traces of death cap. The woman alleged that she'd bought button mushrooms that had been contaminated by death caps from a Woolworths supermarket. The mushrooms were for her mother to make a family favourite – potato and mushroom curry. The woman, her mother and her housemate enjoyed the dish for dinner on 23 April 2014, but by 1 am the next day all three were violently ill and suffering from diarrhoea and vomiting. They initially passed it off as food poisoning but by late afternoon they were in the emergency unit of Canberra's Calvary Hospital, where staff quickly suspected death cap mushroom poisoning. Though her mother and housemate were stabilised, the woman endured multi-organ failure and was in a coma before a liver transplant saved her life. She was adamant the offending mushrooms came from Woolworths, and was reported in the *Sydney Morning Herald* of 14 June 2015 as saying, 'they don't believe me – they say [the] death cap didn't come from Woolies [that they] could be from anywhere. But I'm not stupid. Everyone knows that you don't pick mushrooms

from the forest. The mushrooms came from Woolies –
I remember.'

The investigation was complicated, because the
mushrooms allegedly used in the curry had been bought
two weeks before, so would most certainly be different stock
once investigations started. To further complicate matters,
the woman said she'd paid cash for her purchase and had
not kept the receipt. ACT's Chief Health Officer Paul Kelly
said it was an isolated incident and that no other reports of
poisoning by death cap had been received.

The case has an eerie similarity with the story first offered
by Erin Patterson after her lunch guests became ill.

The most recent death cap fatality was the May 2024
death of 98-year-old Loreta Del Rossi of Bayswater, Victoria.
Loreta grew her own vegetables and cooked with them, using
the wild grasses like dandelions that appeared in her garden,
and the mushrooms that also occasionally popped up.

In April that year she found a patch of mushrooms
growing in the front yard and told her son Nicola, who lived
with her, that she'd clean and test them. The pair then ate
them in a dish of rice and tuna to no ill effect. Nicola recalled
that the mushrooms were white in colour. On 15 May Loreta
found similar-looking mushrooms growing in the same part
of the yard. She collected them and included them in that
night's dinner. Both went to bed at their usual time and were
feeling fine.

Around 2 am, Nicola heard his mother in the bathroom.
Initially, he didn't think anything was wrong. However,
around 4 am he went to his mother, who told him she'd been
vomiting since around 2 am and that the mushrooms were
the cause. He wasn't feeling any ill effect so assumed she

had a simple case of food poisoning. But by 6 am Nicola was also unwell and vomiting. Hours later, they were so unwell they called 000. Mrs Del Rossi died seven days later of multi-organ failure following amanita poisoning. Her son survived.

3

MEET THE FAMILY

Erin Patterson, aged forty-eight at the time of the fateful lunch, lived with her two children – a boy and a girl – at 84 Gibson Street, Leongatha.

The Gibson Street property, then a vacant lot around one hectare (2.5 acres) in size, was bought by Erin in 2019 for around A$260,000. Simon later said that as they were separated at the time, he was puzzled as to why the property was in both their names. However, he also noted that Erin had used inheritances from her mother and her paternal grandmother to buy both that property and a property in Lyons Street, Mount Waverley, which had also been bought in joint names. At the time, Simon thought it might have been a sign of goodwill. That alleged goodwill wouldn't linger past early 2021.

According to one advertisement, the property boasted *a private, no-through setting, with lots of stately Eucalypts, Black Wattles, beautiful Blackwoods and more, including abundant birdlife. A permanent small creek meanders through the block,* offering *a private, natural setting at one with nature.*

It was an idyllic spot for a quiet family to enjoy their lives and for what Erin would tell her online friends would be her 'forever' home. Gibson Street is on the western fringe of the town, a well-made and maintained but unpaved street with new houses like Patterson's on one side and paddocks on the other. Her home is second along from the dead end. The house Erin had built for her family is an unpretentious two-storey dwelling surrounded by a deep verandah, providing welcome shade and shelter in the Mediterranean climate of South Gippsland. The design is practical rather than making an architectural statement.

With his engineering expertise and in-depth understanding of his family's needs, Simon was involved in the design of the house. It was built with the children in mind, intended as a 'good place to grow up' with plenty of space for them as well as spaces to share. Simon said Erin was very houseproud and, at the time the place was finished, she was committed to making them a family. Reconciliation, it seemed, was perennially on the cards.

The neighbours kept to themselves, and the Pattersons were unobtrusive. The location was both peaceful and discreet.

When I visited a few months after Erin's arrest and incarceration, the front gate was locked and sported a sign that appeared to have been produced using a home printer and then laminated. It looked like it had been there a while. The headline read 'Legal Notice', and the text basically said that all media had to keep out.

It went on to note that non-compliance would apparently constitute trespassing under section 9 of the *Summary*

Offences Act and police would be called. The section referred to has quite a bit of content, some not too relevant, suggesting the sign was likely the work of a bush lawyer rather than a qualified one.

The sign hadn't deterred burglars who, according to newspaper accounts, had broken into the house on three occasions in late 2023. The last was on Christmas Day, when Erin was in prison with bail refused. The intruders stole her car – a not-inconspicuous red MG – along with a vacuum cleaner and television sets. An unnamed friend of Erin's who had been keeping an eye on the place took to social media armed with CCTV. On 28 December 2023, Sky News reported the posts. '*We have had a friend's house broken into in Leongatha three times over the last month or so, last time being Christmas morning. This time they stole a car, TVs, vacuums. I have finally been able to retrieve CCTV footage from the second time they broke into the property and removed all the outside cameras.*'

She went on. '*Police caught a couple of offenders from the first burglary where they stole a heap of things and we are now thinking they took all spare keys, car keys etc. and were not retrieved by the police at the time. They have obviously passed the keys on to mates to come and go from the house as they please.*'

A 23-year-old woman and an 18-year-old man from the Melbourne suburb of Cheltenham, around 120 kilometres from Leongatha, were arrested around 1 am on 28 December 2023. It seems they were driving the stolen car at the time. Not criminal masterminds, evidently, just opportunists, probably hoping for some profit and bragging rights.

The house on Gibson Street speaks of Simon and Erin's comfortably middle-class upbringing. These are families of capable, decent people, succeeding modestly in their professions and communities. Good neighbours. No late-night parties, loud music or complaints of domestic disputes, alcohol and/or drug use, or undiagnosed or untreated mental illness. People who will lend a hand to those who need one and work hard for the betterment of their community. People with a firm commitment to caring and service.

For Simon's family, religion, particularly focused on the Korumburra Baptist Church in Mine Road, was a fundamental part of their lives. That included services on Sundays and participation in Bible study classes, usually held in the homes of the like-minded. Simon's parents, Don and Gail, had four children – Simon, Matthew, Nathan and Anna. They were salt-of-the-earth country people, their lives centred around family, church and community.

By contrast, Erin Scutter – she took her husband's surname when they were married – did not have a religious upbringing. Erin was born in 1974 to Eitan (who went by the name Hugh) and Heather Scutter. Hugh was a senior public servant, and Heather was a high-performing academic, holding a PhD and lecturing in English at Monash University. She wrote on young adult and children's fiction, and a short uncredited Monash review of her book *Displaced Fictions* described her as having 'an authoritative voice'. In addition to books and academic writing, she was a regular reviewer for the *Herald Sun* newspaper.

In a 1999 interview on the ABC's Radio National program, creatively titled *Book Talk*, Heather observed that writers for teens had 'tried to move away from what they see as the fairytale stories given to younger children and with a bit of bad logic, they've decided that if the fairytale has a happy ending, the realistic story must have a happy ending. The drive has been toward realistic stories with unhappier and grimmer endings and much more foreclosure of all possibilities.'

Hugh was a low-key, quiet man from an affluent Adelaide family and, according to neighbours, a pleasant chap with a good sense of humour who was always helpful with IT advice. The couple looked after guide dogs, with Hugh once quipping to neighbours that they were fostering 'recycled dogs'.

Erin has a sister, Ceinwen, about three years older, who is now a notable geologist, volcanologist and teacher. While some early media reports suggested the sisters were close, that seems unlikely, given comments Erin later made about her family to online friends, as well as what appears to be the total absence of Ceinwen throughout the investigation and trial.

Erin and Ceinwen grew up on Lagnicourt Street in Hampton, in Melbourne's staunchly middle class south-east. The house is a four-bedroom California bungalow, according to an enthusiastic real-estate agent who described the street as 'Hampton's prized period precinct'. In reality, Lagnicourt Street is a peaceful suburban street with nicely maintained houses, mainly pre-World War II – not loud or showy, just solid and comfortable. Neighbours became friends, dinners and barbecues were shared, locals always stopped by for a chat or to lend a hand.

According to *The Australian* newspaper, a family friend said, when asked about the Scutters' life in Hampton, that 'there were books everywhere. They were an educated family. A good family.' The same report noted that Heather was the dominant person in the house, and very proud of her home's presentation, though if you're cleaning the floors every day with Domestos – a very powerful bleach – as Heather is alleged to have done, the word 'obsessive' might creep into the description. The report also quoted a neighbour of the time as saying, 'They were good people. Everyone knew Erin was smart. She was singled out as bright from a very young age.'

Another neighbour recalled the Scutters lived in Lagnicourt Street between 1976 and 1994. They raised 'puppies for the blind' and they were a very quiet family, with the children seldom seen aside from when out walking the puppies. They also noted Erin's parents didn't own a car and used public transport instead.

Both girls went to the local primary school, Hampton Public, and then Erin entered an 'acceleration program', at University High School in Parkville, an inner-city Melbourne suburb over an hour's trip by public transport from Hampton. The *Herald Sun* reported on 24 August 2025 that a former student said the program was for 'super bright' students and they were nicknamed 'The Taskforce'. Erin was 'quiet, reserved and didn't get involved in the wider group. She really kept on the periphery and kept to herself.' The article also had a comment from a woman who remembered her sister saying Erin was 'brilliant but unhinged'.

After the girls left home, Hugh and Heather downsized in 1995, moving a few kilometres to Glen Tower Drive, Glen Waverley. It was a leafy suburb of '60s and '70s brick 'project homes', on bigger pieces of land with established trees and gardens. It was also closer to Monash University, where Heather was working.

One of the Scutters' Glen Waverley neighbours said the daughters were seldom seen, noting that the couple were 'lovely neighbours' who were hard-working, and had a strong sense of both humour and community. It was intriguing to find that when I door-knocked a few houses in the street in April 2024, the case of Erin Patterson was something they'd all heard about, but no-one had connected Erin Patterson to their former neighbours, who had retired to an oceanside home in New South Wales in the early 2000s but still kept loose contact for a good few years after.

The view of those who knew the Scutters was in sharp contrast to comments made by Erin in messages to friends in 2019, shortly after her mother had died. *'We had a horrible upbringing. Mum was essentially a cold robot. It was like being brought up in a Russian orphanage where they don't touch babies.'* She went on to say her dad tried to be 'warm and loving' but her mother would stop him. She added how she and her sister would hide in their room so they were out of the way.

Erin claimed she told this to her psychologist, who said she would have liked to have 'studied' Heather. As for her father, Erin summed him up in another message, saying, *'Dad was a doormat'*.

Both Hugh and Heather died of cancer, Heather in 2019 and Hugh in 2011. Their estate was shared between Erin and Ceinwen, and included their parents' retirement home at Eden, which was soon on the market, advertised as having 'uninterrupted water views that include the gentle curve of Aslings Beach, the dazzling blue of Twofold Bay, and beyond to the awe-inspiring expanse of the South Pacific Ocean'. The property sold for around $900,000.

Like their parents, both the Scutter girls were high achievers. One of Erin's earliest professions was as an air-traffic controller at Melbourne's Tullamarine Airport.

Airservices Australia confirmed that Erin Scutter was employed by them from February 2001 to November 2002. A colleague from those days, who preferred to remain anonymous, said he recognised her in the media storm that followed the Leongatha poisoning. He told the *Herald Sun* newspaper, 'She'd put [on] a bit of weight but she looked so familiar, and she had the same first name and we were 90 to 95 per cent convinced at that point that it was the same person, but then when we saw in the papers that her mother's name was Scutter we were completely sure.'

Erin, according to her former colleague, was highly intelligent and capable. He said, 'She was rated in the field and was actually responsible for running airspace for a while. She's very bright and much brighter than people might think ... she was very unkempt and she was abrasive.'

The colleague also observed that she could be quick-tempered, recalling, 'In the first week that she started in the job somebody walked behind her and tripped on a cord that was on the floor that was attached to her headset. She turned around and yelled, "You right, you buffoon?!" It was the head of the air-traffic control department. She didn't hold back.'

Another former colleague recalled an incident involving the space Erin was controlling – not in the air, but in the office. Air-traffic controllers had hot desks, meaning no-one had a space to call their own. Erin wasn't a fan of that sharing arrangement and had claimed a spot in the office for herself. One day she arrived for duty and found another controller at her preferred desk. She issued a sharp rebuke, but he declined to move. An uneasy shift ensued. A few days later, the colleague found that his locker had been opened and the contents – paper and clothing – shredded. While there was no evidence to identify the culprit, the timing was compelling.

On 8 July 2025, the day after the jury verdict in her trial, News.com.au reported that other former air-traffic control colleagues described Erin as a 'ritual, habitual and pathological liar, she would say anything just to get away with anything'. She was sacked for lying about her work hours, and when told there was CCTV of her comings and goings, she said, 'Ah, you've got me there'. Colleagues referred to her as 'Scutter the Nutter' and 'Crazy Erin' behind her back. She was, they said, 'manipulative' and 'aggressive' but still she managed to 'get guys wrapped around her little finger'.

This description was somewhat at odds with that given by Simon's brother, Matthew, who told a preliminary court hearing that in his view Erin was an introvert. Taking into account the different impressions of Erin, the picture that emerged was of a person with two faces, each distinctly separate.

After her departure from Airservices, Erin had her first brush with the law, described by the *Australian* newspaper as a 'high-speed drunken rampage', something considered out of character for the usually organised, in-control introvert. At the Dandenong Magistrates Court on 7 September 2004, Erin pleaded guilty to five charges arising from a car accident in which she was the driver. The scene of the accident was in her neighbourhood of Glen Waverley. According to reports, she'd been driving, had a collision and fled the scene in her car. While the details of the actual collision were scant, the charges that followed suggest she'd been driving fast while drunk, clipped a parked car or other object, then drove off – or, as police like to describe it, 'decamped from the scene'. When police caught up with her a few hours later it was still within three hours after the accident, a period in which police can demand a blood alcohol test.

Erin recorded a blood alcohol level of .14, nearly three times the legal limit. The charges included failing to stop after an accident, failing to give her details when property was damaged, using an unregistered vehicle, and driving at 95 km/hour in a 60 zone. The report noted the drink driving charge was dealt with as part of the other charges. Her penalty was an aggregate of $1000 in fines and loss of her licence for 30 months. The combination of an unregistered car, exuberant alcohol use and the decision to drive in that state suggest that Erin might have been in a messy state of mind at the time.

In 2006, Erin's grandmother Ora Scutter died in Adelaide, leaving a significant estate. She was from an émigré family living in Egypt, and married Edgar Scutter in Israel in 1943. Originally from Renmark in South Australia, Edgar had been serving in the Middle East in the Australian army during World War II. Corporal Scutter was a member of the famous Rats of Tobruk. Edgar brought his wife home with him and their son Eitan (Hugh) was born in Renmark in 1945. The family prospered, and Ora's bequests to her children and grandchildren gave them a financial boost – one that Erin shared with Simon's family, providing support in buying their homes to the tune of over $1 million. Erin's share of her grandmother's estate was reportedly around $2 million.

Simon and Erin met in 2005 when he was working as a civil engineer for the Monash City Council in Glen Waverley and she as an administrative assistant for the Royal Society for the Prevention of Cruelty to Animals (RSPCA), working out of the council offices. The RSPCA had the contract to deliver animal management services to the council.

For someone like Erin with a great fondness for animals, a job like this would be both challenging, dealing with the injured, and satisfying, to see the kindness of new homes offered for some. This care of animals was a character trait she'd inherited from her father.

Simon said he and Erin became friends through an eclectic group of people working at the council. With those friends, they travelled to Korumburra for at least one weekend away. Simon went to the Baptist church where his uncle Ian was pastor, and some of the group, including Erin, who'd told him she was an atheist, went along. While Erin appeared to be moved by the service, Simon later thought that it was the communion and its religious and spiritual aspects that had affected her. He recalled that she had looked upset and left the church.

Erin had a thirst for knowledge in diverse areas and loved travelling and reading. Simon said Erin was an avid reader, particularly of non-fiction – she had a penchant for true crime and politics along with autobiographies, and books about raising children and health. Simon reckoned she was an 'inquisitive and curious person'. She also loved Lego, though that didn't get a mention by her estranged husband – it was noted by her kids.

Erin's interest in true crime may be reflected in 2019 comments by journalist Michael Duffy, one of the founders of Australia's BAD Crime Festival. Duffy, also a crime writer, told me the genre 'is hugely popular and throws up a lot to discuss. Crime is much more than entertainment – it covers a huge range of human behaviour. In books, it is not restricted to crime novels. There's crime in the Bible, in Shakespeare and Dostoevsky. In the newspapers today, we see crime massively disrupting the Catholic Church, banking, and, of course, politics.'

Erin and Simon's friendship changed course and developed, leading to their engagement in February 2007 and their marriage five months later, not at the Korumburra Baptist Church but at St Paul's Anglican Church in Queen Street, Korumburra. Ian Wilkinson, then a Baptist pastor, didn't officiate, and didn't attend as he was unwell, but Heather was there. David Wilkinson, Simon's cousin, walked Erin down the aisle – her parents were travelling in Russia at the time.

4

TILL DEATH DO US PART

After a few nights honeymooning in Victoria's Dandenong Ranges, Simon and Erin moved into their first marital home, which was a small, very ordinary looking unit owned by Simon's parents. The unit was in North Road, Oakleigh – a busy major road – and had been used by the family for years as somewhere to stay when visiting the city or when the children were studying at university.

They stayed there for about a month before heading off to do something they both loved – travelling and camping. The newlyweds packed their four-wheel drive and hit the road, travelling around Australia for about three months. They visited the New South Wales coast, Sydney, then headed west to Broken Hill, Innamincka in north-east South Australia, and then across the Nullarbor to Perth.

By late 2007 they were living in Warnbro on the city's southern extremity, before moving closer to the city centre and the Swan River at Mosman Park. Around this time, Erin was studying science at university and had been accepted to study Veterinary Science at Murdoch. However, with the birth of their first child imminent, she decided to defer the course.

The baby, a son, was born in January 2009. Erin said it was a difficult birth, and very traumatic. 'It went for a very long time and they tried to get him out with forceps and he wouldn't come out and he started to go into distress and they lost his heartbeat, so they did an emergency caesarean and got him out quickly.' Her son then spent days in neonatal ICU. Erin recalled that after about a week the child was off oxygen and the feeding tube, and the doctors thought he was fine to be taken home by Simon. However, the doctors didn't think Erin had sufficiently recovered from the surgery and wanted her to stay in a little longer. She just wanted to go home with her child and, after discussions with Simon, decided to leave the hospital against medical advice. According to Erin, Simon said, 'You can just do it,' and so she did.

This incident was one of a few that showed her discomfort at being in hospital, even when leaving flew in the face of medical advice. In January 2015, after being admitted to hospital for bladder problems, Erin left after signing a 'Discharge at Own Risk' form from the Gippsland Southern Health Service. The discharge notes indicated that at around 10.30 pm on 24 January, 'Patient became fidgety and anxious stating she wanted to be discharged. Explained that she should at least have the first litre of fluid and needs to void before leaving. Offered Temazepam if that would help settle her to sleep. Refused. Patient was now out of bed walking around pacing and asked nurse to stop IV and disconnect so she could leave. Advised her to sign discharge at own risk form. Patient left at 22:35.'

Simon later said that Erin hated hospitals, and observed that 'she struggled a lot with mental illness, both post-natal depression, especially after X [her son] was born, and I believe that was real'.

Shortly after mother and son went home, which Erin described as a small inner-city flat they were renting from a friend, Simon's parents, Don and Gail, arrived to help for a week. Because the space was scant, Erin rented a holiday apartment south of Perth, where they all stayed for the duration of the visit. She recalled that it was 'lovely', and that Gail in particular was a great help. 'I remember being really relieved that Gail was there because I felt really out of my depth. I had no idea what to do with a baby and I was not confident and she was really supportive, and gentle and patient with me.' Gail gave advice on settling the child each night, interpretation of his cries and, most importantly, encouraged Erin to 'just relax and enjoy your baby'.

But parenthood didn't impede their adventuring, and in April, with the baby healthy, happy and settled, they packed a tent into their Nissan Patrol and set off on an epic journey across Australia, tracing the Western Australian coast, up across the top end to Alice Springs, then through Darwin and across to northern Queensland, travelling to Cairns, Townsville and Cape York. On the first leg of the journey they met up with Simon's brother Matthew, his wife, Tanya, and their kids in Broome and travelled the Gibb River Road, a 660-kilometre track across Western Australia's Kimberley region, from Derby to Kununurra. At the end, the others went home while Simon, Erin and their son pressed on, down the Tanami Track to Alice Springs.

It's a long, beautiful, sometimes risky and challenging trek through some of the most remote places on the planet. The travel gave Simon the opportunity to pursue his twin passions of nature and photography. He could aptly be described as a serious photographer, to the point of processing his own work.

Around November 2009, on the return leg, Erin decided to fly from Townsville back to Perth, with Simon and their infant son following in the four-wheel drive, driving straight through the middle of the continent. The massive trip took around a week. Erin explained her early departure by saying that she'd had enough. She wanted to sleep in a real bed, and it was becoming increasingly challenging to camp with their child, who was now sitting up, crawling, trying to stand and not sleeping as much as he had as a newborn. Though Erin and Simon agreed on the plan, it seems a little odd that Erin and the child didn't fly home together, leaving Simon to make the trip without the added challenge of looking after a very young child. Perhaps the decision speaks to the mental health issues Simon alluded to Erin enduring after the long and difficult birth.

During these early travelling years, Simon wasn't working and the couple were living comfortably on Erin's inheritance. Back in Perth, their marriage, still in its infancy, wasn't a bed of roses, and they had the first of a few separations. On returning to Perth, Erin and their son were living in the outer eastern Perth suburb of Roleystone, while Simon rented an onsite van in a nearby caravan park.

At Simon's initiative, they started counselling. During these sessions, they focused on how to be better at marriage, and identified the two drivers of their problems as being communication and Erin's mental health.

The separation lasted roughly six months. With the relationship patched together, the couple moved to the Shire of York, a bit over 100 kilometres east of Perth, in the wheat belt. Simon found work as the shire's engineer, and they lived in a house provided by the council.

Erin had also contemplated taking up her deferred Veterinary Science studies at Murdoch in Perth, but the combination of distance, a young child and Simon's long hours made the prospect untenable. Simon later opined that Erin's mental health 'challenges' may also have contributed to her decision not to resume study.

The family moved again when Simon began work as a civil engineer with the Shire of Manjimup. It's a peaceful and beautiful place of towering forests, on the coast about 300 kilometres south of Perth. In 2011 they bought a home in Karri Lane, Quinninup, an idyllic village set amid the ancient giant Karri forests. Quinninup is about a 25-minute drive to the town of Manjimup, where the shire has its offices. The purchase was funded in part by Erin's inheritance from her grandmother, as well as their combined incomes.

Like the house Erin would eventually build in Leongatha, the place was on a large block of partial bushland and quite private. It was described by the real estate agent as featuring four bedrooms, and 'a superb culinary centre' with bay windows overlooking 'the local four-legged residents feeding on the back lawn'. Wraparound verandahs 'keep the weather at bay and offer a charm that complements the environment to provide the ultimate lifestyle opportunity'. The price for this opportunity was $448,000.

With university off the agenda, Erin started her own business, Karri Books, in nearby Pemberton. It was a second-hand bookshop, stocked with books Erin had bought from book fairs, estate sales and old stock sold by libraries. She fitted out the store with carpet and shelves from Ikea and planned to attract both locals and visitors. The business was open for about a year. The town is a drawcard for wine-loving tourists, those keen to admire the national parks, forests and adventure options like hiking and trail biking. Others are drawn by the peace, the food and wellness options.

Their spacious new home was perfect for regular visits by Simon's family. It also provided a base for camping trips and long road trips deep into the state. Simon's brother Matthew and his family visited in 2011. Erin was the organiser for their stay, arranging a photo workshop and, as Matthew told a preliminary hearing, other arrangements to 'enhance the holiday experience'.

Erin also stepped up with some very generous and practical support for Simon's kin. She agreed to help Matthew and Tanya buy their first home, offering a finance deal they readily and wisely accepted – especially in light of Australia's aggressive property market. She helped them buy their home in Officer, a suburb on Melbourne's south-eastern fringe, about 50 kilometres from the CBD. It was an offer too good to refuse – $400,000, paying CPI rates on the principal, and making repayments at a time that suited them. Simon said that after their separation and asset split, Erin took over the loan, so repayments would go to her.

But a new house, Simon's visiting relatives and Erin's financial good deeds didn't equate to their marriage being in the best of shape. They were feeling the tyranny of distance, missing Simon's family and the support they offered, so in May 2013 they put their home on the market and moved back to Gippsland, ready to start the next chapter of their married life. The trip back was a bit of an adventure for the family. They drove across Australia, and for the first weeks of their return stayed with Don and Gail in Korumburra while Erin arranged a rental home in the village of Bena, about a five-minute drive away.

The closeness of the family was restored, and Erin quickly resumed her social management role, arranging holidays for the families at places like McCrae on Victoria's Mornington Peninsula, about 60 kilometres south of Melbourne's CBD, and with Erin's now-widowed mother, Heather, at her home in Eden, New South Wales. In late 2013 they went camping in New Zealand with Don and Gail, and a few months later, when Erin was heavily pregnant with their daughter, they bought a house in Nason Street, Korumburra. Interestingly, while the couple had a joint bank account and the Western Australian house had been jointly owned, the house they bought in Korumburra, where they lived until 2015, was solely in Erin's name. Thanks to Erin's inheritance and investments, Simon wasn't looking for work but instead was a stay-at-home dad, looking after their son. As usual, they were living comfortably but modestly.

5

UNHAPPY FAMILIES

The proximity, care and support of Simon's family, a new house, and the birth of their second child, didn't have the positive effect on Simon and Erin's marriage they may have hoped for. In 2015, they separated and by the end of that year Erin and the children had moved into a rental property in Korumburra. Simon was still perplexed about the reasons for the separation – he said Erin hadn't given him any reason for her decision other than 'she didn't feel able for us to live together'.

In the lead-up to the separation, Simon arranged counselling in an attempt to save a crumbling marriage that he later described, in something of an understatement, as 'strained, there was tension in it'.

'I was always keen to have a good relationship, have a good marriage and a good strong family to bring up the kids in,' Simon said. But Erin decided to leave anyway. She didn't give him a reason, Simon recalled, but told him in later conversations that she thought their relationship was toxic. Both claim they wanted it to work, but in Simon's view, Erin was always the one instigating the separations.

The two kept in regular communication by messaging, with the conversation spanning numerous topics, from daily life and their joint responsibility for the children through to what Simon said was 'banter and discussions about politics and interesting things'. They also continued to take family holidays overseas, interstate and to see Erin's mother in Eden.

While Erin maybe wasn't forthcoming with her true feelings to her husband, she was allegedly more talkative with friends online. Here she showed a different face, griping about Simon. Among the flurry of media reports following the poisoning was one disclosing a message purportedly from Erin. In September 2023, the *Daily Mail* published a message in which she wrote how she had hired a cleaner and they had been coming twice a week for nearly two years. She said, '*My husband has no idea …*' Erin went on about having someone else clean the '*bathrooms and dunnies*' and mop, vacuum and change the sheets, meaning all she had to resent Simon for was not doing the dishes. However, there was a problem with the story – Simon and Erin had been living separately since late 2015. Perhaps this colourful account was Erin creating a narrative for her credulous audience.

That said, the separation was, at least in those early days, amicable.

This was reflected in the detail of how the separation was formalised. Instead of involving lawyers, they resolved their affairs neatly, efficiently and without the animus so common in these situations. It was a very civil arrangement, at the beginning at least.

According to Simon, his assets in superannuation and shareholdings weren't part of the arrangements, with Erin noting she felt this was a fair deal. With some assistance from her mother, Erin bought a house in Anthony Court, Korumburra while Simon kept the family home in Nason Street. The Anthony Court property was a single-storey modern brick veneer house with four bedrooms and two bathrooms in a quiet, recently developed cul de sac on the edge of town – pleasant, spacious but bland. Simon later testified Erin paid cash for the property.

His access to the children was flexible; they were with Erin mainly during the week and Simon on the weekends. This arrangement allowed Simon to start his own civil engineering business, and he also registered the business names Karri Pix and later Simon Patterson Pictures – an outlet for his passion for photography. Meanwhile, Erin was a full-time mother – a role she relished.

The routine of life in a small country town ticked along, punctuated in 2017 by Erin's purchase of a property on Shellcot Road, Korumburra, a comfortable five-bedroom family home in a well-established secondary road on the fringe of the town, not far from schools and churches. Erin moved in with the kids. The following year Erin, Simon and the children took a trip together to southern Africa. The adventure spurred a reconciliation between the couple, but Simon noted that it only lasted a week and was marred by disagreements.

One issue that may have contributed was Simon's long hours working in his civil engineering business. On top of the long hours was travel, both to jobs and to the office, some 40 minutes away, but the money was good, at around

$200,000 per year. That said, relations between the separated couple still remained mostly cordial, with their children the focus for both.

With Simon's business kicking goals and both her children at school, Erin took the opportunity to involve herself in the Korumburra community. The *Burra Flyer* is a free community booklet produced by the Korumburra Community Development Association and funded by advertising from local businesses. It can be found in businesses around the town, in the library and online, and also has a Facebook page. It's published quarterly – March, June, September and December. The *Flyer* is the sort of publication that carries not only advertising but also reports on local happenings like school and sporting events, church news, community group news and events, along with an editorial and a few articles on a wide variety of subjects.

Don and Gail Patterson had been editors of the *Flyer* since 2013, with Simon, newly returned from Western Australia, lending his photographic skills to the publication. One particularly arresting picture made the front page of the June/August 2016 edition, showing vivid red toadstools growing on a lawn or nature strip in the town. Years later, that photo would raise a few eyebrows.

In early 2018, Don and Gail handed over the reins to Erin. Her first outing as editor was the March/May 2018 edition. In her maiden outing, she heaped praise on her predecessors, describing them in her Editor's Note as being 'extraordinarily generous' and supportive. She also thanked them 'for the enormous time and energy that they put into keeping the *Burra Flyer* going for the past five years'. Simon continued in his role as voluntary staff photographer, snapping pictures at sporting events, often where his children were participating, at basketball games and delivering catchy photographs for the front page. Erin continued as editor until the Summer 2020 edition, published in December 2019.

Another mushroom moment occurred during Erin's editorship. The September/November 2019 edition included details of a workshop where locals could be taught 'how to grow gourmet mushrooms at home using easy to source materials and low-tech methods'. Tantalisingly, 'the class includes making your own oyster mushroom grow bag to take home, teaching notes and a delicious afternoon tea'.

The event was part of what the *Burra Flyer* published as the Grow Lightly Winter Events, and was held, unsurprisingly, at the Grow Lightly Hub in Silkstone Road, Korumburra.

The event was held in September 2019, and was followed by other workshops including sourdough bread making – somewhat prescient, given the popularity of home-baked sourdough during the pandemic that was poised to strike – and cheesemaking. It isn't known if Erin attended any of these events.

The interest in the mushroom workshop was unsurprising. Gippsland has numerous mushroom farms, producing supermarket staples, exotic varieties and medicinal mushrooms. The local conditions are also conducive to mushroom growth in the wild, so many take to foraging with enthusiasm – and with an expert in tow, to make sure you don't get your slippery jacks or saffron milk caps confused with something that will make you decidedly unwell, or worse.

South Gippsland Councillor Nathan Hersey is a forager and told the media: 'I do it with my wife and friends. It's something that has increased over the years.' He said he'd been doing it for a decade, and gave the wise advice to 3AW's Neil Mitchell in August 2023: 'If you don't know what it is, don't even touch it.'

While Erin was thankful to her predecessors and looking forward to her time as editor, the lustre soon wore off. Erin was an habitué of Facebook groups, especially true crime groups, and while circumspect in person, she was candid with her views online. According to the *Daily Mail*, who published some of Erin's comments and apparently took screenshots of them – which turned out to be wise, as some groups disbanded and disappeared after Erin's arrest – her view of her fellow Korumburra residents wasn't flattering. In one alleged exchange with an online friend – or rant, as it was described – Erin referred to some of the people she dealt with as '*illiterate motherfuckers*'.

Anyone who works in print knows there are always going to be errors, and writing copy for a quarterly community booklet can be challenging, but labelling others 'illiterate motherfuckers' is particularly harsh.

January 2019 would bring both personal and financial changes for Erin. At the end of that month, her mother died. Heather's estate, including the gloriously sited home at Eden, passed jointly to Erin and her sister. The inheritance made Erin more affluent, but not enough to comfortably be considered 'wealthy', as was often bandied around in the months following the fatal lunch. One source also told me that Erin was thrifty, using the old Australian quip 'short arms and deep pockets'.

With the inheritance sorted, Erin invested in a property close to her old stomping ground in south-east Melbourne.

The property in well-established and steadfastly middle-class Lyons Street, Mount Waverley was handy when travelling in from Gippsland and overnighting in the city and, if Erin was looking ahead, a useful location for the children should they decide to go to university. Like her parents' old home nearby, it was close to transport, good schools and universities. And a familiar place for Erin if country life and a failed marriage became overwhelming.

With another eye to the future, she also bought the block of land in Gibson Street, Leongatha, to build a new home for herself and the children. As mentioned earlier, Simon later told the court he was somewhat surprised that both the Lyons Street and Gibson Street properties were bought by Erin, with her money, but in both their names. He reflected that, at the time of the purchases, he thought this was likely to be goodwill on Erin's part, but added, 'I thought so at the time.' While he didn't ask Erin the obvious question – why? – he believed then there was still hope of reconciliation and a return to a unified family. He thought Erin felt the same.

It's clear from their distribution of assets and Erin's recent inheritance from her mother that her life wasn't obviously extravagant, nor was it driven or motivated by money or its potential power to influence relationships. Simon's approach to money appeared to be similar – both led comfortable but not ostentatious lives. Erin wasn't one to show off her affluence.

That hope of reconciliation, at least in Simon's mind, was further stirred by the four of them holidaying as a family, Erin and Simon occasionally taking a camping break – just the two of them – and Erin asking for his help in the design and construction of her Gibson Street home. For Simon, the project was one focused on their children, with the goal of building a home for them to grow up in, with plenty of space of their own and to share. A home to be proud of, and one for all the family – perfect for the houseproud Erin. It was the first home they'd built from scratch.

There was, however, one dark cloud overhead – one that reflected how brittle the relationship was.

Building a house can be a stressful experience, and Simon was deeply involved in the project. The goodwill faltered when he asked Erin if the house was being built with reconciliation in mind or if she was just taking advantage of his expertise. The question didn't land well, and Erin became upset, which, given the question, shouldn't have been a surprise. Simon didn't share what prompted the question, but it may have been the catalyst for the further deterioration of their relationship.

In late 2020 and early 2021, Erin began working on their real-estate portfolio. In a flurry of activity, she sold the house at Shellcot Road, Korumburra, and bought another in the same street. She sold that home in 2022 for $545,000.

At Simon's request, the title of the house in Nason Street was transferred solely to his name. According to Simon, Erin 'demanded' transfer of ownership of the Gibson Street property to her – which was readily done. At this stage, while they were still reasonably amicable, the stresses were compounding, especially in Erin's mind.

And lurking in the background of these domestic cracks was the onset of the Covid-19 pandemic.

6

CRIME ONLINE

On 31 December 2019, the World Health Organization was told of multiple cases of pneumonia in the city of Wuhan in central China. Six weeks later, on 11 February 2020, the International Committee on Taxonomy of Viruses formally gave the virus the name Covid-19. A month later, Covid-19 was a global pandemic.

In the early hours of Thursday, 19 March 2020, cruise ship the *Ruby Princess* docked at Sydney's Circular Quay and nearly 2700 passengers disembarked to travel home, either locally or to connections around Australia and internationally. A day later, NSW Health authorities announced that some of those passengers had tested positive for the virus. Around 700 would eventually test positive, and twenty-eight would die.

Three days prior, Victoria's Premier Dan Andrews had declared a four-week state of emergency to help health authorities 'flatten the curve' of the virus spread.

Non-essential gatherings of over 500 people, such as sporting events and conferences were banned, and cultural institutions like libraries and museums closed. It was the first of many lockdowns in Melbourne and regional areas of the state. By the end of 2021 Melbourne had endured a world-beating 262 days in lockdown.

By September 2021, thanks significantly to vaccinations, lockdowns in regional Victoria were set to lift, but Melbourne would take a little longer. Impacts on the people were captured in a letter from Mendy Urie, the Mayor of East Gippsland, to the Premier early that month. She wrote, 'The cumulative impact of drought, the Black Summer fires (and previous fire events), pandemic lockdowns (including border closures and a decimation of our tourism industry), and the constant uncertainty is taking its toll on business, families and communities.'

The Mayor went on to say, 'We are seeing increasing states of stress and distress. Given the number of people seeking assistance for mental health issues and suicide rates in rural areas, pre-Covid, we are fearful that increased stress as a result of lockdowns and isolation will lead to a deterioration in mental health outcomes.'

A study by the University of Melbourne found that women in Victoria experienced a greater mental health decline during the lockdowns in 2020 compared to women around Australia. The University's Professor Mark Wooden, who co-authored the study, said it showed that lockdowns can exaggerate existing inequalities in the responsibility for household and caring duties. He said, 'If lockdowns and other policies intended to restrict population movement are to remain part of the policy toolkit for responding to pandemics, more attention needs to be given to providing support to alleviate the potential negative side-effects, including, for example, focusing on equitably delivering childcare services and schooling.'

In 2022, Doctor Jacqueline Jiang and colleagues published similar findings in the *Journal of International Medical Research*. 'We found that the general mental health of Victorians was negatively affected by Covid-19 restrictions during 2020.' They also found that 'Women, children, young people, carers, people who became unemployed owing to the pandemic, and those with pre-existing psychiatric conditions had a higher risk of adverse mental health consequences during the Covid-19 pandemic in 2020'. The conclusions of other experts looking at the mental health impacts were all similar. And then there was the unknown factor – the long-term mental health impact.

As the grip of the pandemic and lockdowns tightened, and communication with anyone other than immediate family was increasingly online rather than face to face, online communities thrived. Among the special interest groups that became rallying points was true crime. Erin Patterson was a true crime fan, and from the isolation of Korumburra, then her new home on the edge of Leongatha, her online relationships also thrived.

True crime has long been popular in various formats, including books and television programs, but it was the US investigative journalism podcast *Serial* that set the genre on fire. The podcast series started in 2014, digging into the cold case murder of American high school student Hae Min Lee. A review in *The Guardian* (UK) that year described it as 'the greatest murder mystery you will ever hear'.

By 2018, *Serial* had been downloaded over 340 million times. The 2015 Netflix series *Making a Murderer* added more fuel to that fire, with nearly 20 million views in the first thirty-five days after release.

Research by Pew University in 2023 found that American women were almost twice as likely to listen to true crime podcasts than men – a figure that didn't surprise me, having prepared true crime TV pitch documents. I was one of the producers and appeared in a two-part documentary (*Murder Uncovered*) on Kate Moir, the extraordinary young woman who escaped serial killer couple David and Catherine Birnie in Perth, Western Australia, and research showed our audience was around sixty-two per cent female, aged between 25 and 55 years old.

By 2024, the fascination and enthusiasm for true crime hadn't waned, with global measurement company On Device reporting that true crime was the most popular genre in Australian podcasting, captivating around forty-five per cent of the listening population – about fifty-three per cent of the country – who spend an average of 1.5 hours per day listening.

Allan Breiland, ANZ Research Director for On Device, said, 'Australia's podcasting landscape is evolving rapidly, with a significant preference for true crime content, suggesting narrative podcasts are a very strong medium for engagement.'

And the places people went to discuss these podcasts and the cases they explored were Facebook groups. This was where Erin Patterson shared her true crime podcast obsessions. She consumed these podcasts voraciously, listening while she worked around the house, transported her kids to the litany of commitments common among school-age children, and pottered around her kitchen. One former online friend told me that true crime podcasts were the soundtrack for Erin's day, and that she had strong opinions on a range of crimes that usually involved murder.

One of those groups was the Keep Keli Lane Behind Bars group, with around 2000 members, which started up in the wake of the ABC documentary *Exposed – The Case of Keli Lane*. Erin Patterson was a regular contributor. The group had plenty of media to whet their appetites – multiple podcasts, print media, and Lane's court cases, including appeals, applications and, more recently, her parole travails.

Erin joined the group around 2019 and was a random contributor until the group's administration had a clearance of the almost inert and fake profiles, which included Erin's, prompting her to become active. She went from random to regular and had plenty of opinions. For the reclusive Erin, who had no friends outside her estranged husband's family, it was a group in which she'd make close, long-term friends, even though they were unlikely to meet in person. It was where she could tell her real story – or at least the story she wanted people to believe.

The fascination of a case like Lane's is easy to see. Doctor Dean Fido, a lecturer in Psychology at the University of Derby, said in a piece in the university magazine titled 'Why are we so obsessed with true crime?' that 'They are the sort of stories you need to put your phone down and actually pay attention to. It's a big puzzle and we don't want to be left without a vital piece of information because we were checking social media.' He observed, 'As humans, we are always looking for something new and novel. Whether it's good or bad, we need something that creates an element of excitement. When we mix this desire with insight and solving a puzzle, it can give us a short, sharp shock of adrenaline, but in a relatively safe environment.'

His colleague Doctor Melanie Haughton said that people's fascination with criminals like serial killers and where they operated 'reflects the dark side of human curiosity'. Of the notable women's interest in the genre, Fido said, 'The majority-female audience of true crime could also have something to do with compassion for the victims – it might be easier for women to put themselves in the shoes of the largely female victims that these shows examine.'

Keli Lane's victim was her newborn child, Tegan – a story that would tug at anyone's heart, let alone those of a group of people isolated by a pandemic and mainly women, many of whom had children.

However, this group, as the name suggests, had no compassion for Keli Lane.

Keli, a teacher and elite Australian water polo player, was the daughter of a hospital worker and a former police detective. She was born in Sydney in 1975, and during the 1990s allegedly had five pregnancies, the first two of which were terminated. The third pregnancy, in 1995, ran to full term, and the child was put up for adoption.

Keli managed to keep her fourth pregnancy very quiet. At the time, she was living with her parents at Fairlight, on Sydney's northern beaches and she would allege a chap called Andrew Norris or Morris was the father, claiming that they'd had an affair in late 1995 and early 1996. But police investigations failed to identify anyone by that name.

On 12 September 1996, at thirty-six weeks pregnant, Keli was induced at the Auburn Hospital in Sydney's west and gave birth to a baby girl, Tegan.

The next day, both mother and child were examined and the doctors pronounced them fine to be discharged. That was the last anyone saw of Tegan. And from then on it was as if she had never existed.

Five years after her disappearance, social workers uncovered Keli's lies around how many children she had given birth to and police started to investigate. In 2005/2006 there was a coronial inquiry into the missing child, with the coroner finding that the baby was probably dead but not completely dismissing the hope she may be alive. Believing foul play was at the heart of the case, he referred it to the homicide squad for further investigation.

The absence of Tegan's body, of any witnesses to her fate, and of a crime scene or forensic evidence pointing to a crime, let alone a potential perpetrator, presented a challenge. Cases without a body are probably the most difficult to resolve, and history is well stocked with disappearances, often with a reasonable list of suspects but no arrests, let alone a conviction. Successful prosecution of such cases generally requires a weight of circumstances that prove the case beyond reasonable doubt. Most recently, one of the most infamous and high profile of these cases is that of Chris Dawson, convicted in 2022 for the 1982 murder of his wife Lynette. Lynette's body has never been found, and Mr Dawson's appeals have all failed. He's likely to die in prison.

Keli Lane is another who was charged with murder without a body found. Lane pleaded not guilty, and her trial in the NSW Supreme Court began in August 2010.

The trial lasted four months, and was before a jury of six men and six women.

After seven days of deliberations the jury found Keli Lane guilty on a majority of eleven to one. On 15 April 2011, Justice Whealy sentenced her to eighteen years in jail with a non-parole period set at thirteen years and five months, expiring on 12 May 2024.

It was a twisted story with much for a Facebook group to analyse and argue over. It pushed every maternal button in a group whose membership included many mothers, Erin Patterson among them.

7

ERIN'S ONLINE LIFE

As locked-down residents increasingly turned to Facebook groups for interaction, the topics of discussion broadened. Daniela Barkley, who met Erin online, said they'd talk about things such as lockdown issues and challenges, current affairs, royalty, their children and families, and cooking. Friendships flourished, and in smaller message groups they could be candid, even if – or perhaps because – they knew they were unlikely to ever meet face to face. These groups became places members could go for advice from their now trusted peers.

It was an intriguing move for Erin, who was described by one member, Lisa Tait, a journalist who'd go on to cover the trial in her *Mushroom Murder Trial* podcast, as being 'very insular, secretive and private' and someone who didn't need company. She said Erin 'didn't like people, and had said that while at playgroup she'd isolate herself, knit and hope no-one would speak to her'. But to her online friends,

Lisa recalled Erin could be 'funny, very bright and relished the gossip and drama that was part of the group'. Lisa said Erin was very active on social media but would also message frequently and could be demanding to the point of being coercive and controlling. Erin, Lisa suspected, was also an online troll with multiple fake profiles – a view that some of the other members concurred with.

Another member who preferred to remain anonymous thought Erin was 'reclusive and secretive' and was a 'pathological liar' – an opinion that was confirmed after her conviction.

The same member also said, 'Yet online, away from physical interaction, she thrived.' Erin, in what was becoming a common thread, definitely had two faces.

Disagreements became regular occurences in the volatile 'Keep Keli Lane Behind Bars' group – stirred, according to one member, by Erin and one other. This prompted some members, including Erin, to form a splinter group of around twenty or thirty members, imaginatively titled 'Ex Keep Keli Lane Behind Bars'. Erin started with the name, unsurprisingly, of Erin Patterson, and later changed her username to Erin Erin, then Erin Erin Erin.

The conversations covered the usual mix of topics. Five or so members also chatted outside the group via direct messages.

Erin quickly showed her research expertise in ferreting around cases. Her fellow group members described her as a 'super sleuth'. But her contributions soon broadened as she shared stories of her children and their lives, her fondness for Lego, news of buying the Leongatha property and building her house, and the challenges of being a mum.

Daniela Barkley listened to all the podcasts on the Erin Patterson case and followed media reports, and would later give evidence in Erin's trial, along with two of her online colleagues. She was part of the small group, which included Erin, who messaged each other privately. Daniela had never met Erin in person but, until the lunch, they would message daily.

She said that around Christmas 2022, Erin was talking about her relationship with Simon, observing that he'd bought her a shovel as a gift – perhaps more of a comment on how Simon's practical mind worked than on Erin's not unreasonable expectations of something more memorable. She also wasn't enamoured of his domestic skills – something the friends took at face value, only to later learn that the couple weren't living together. Erin had failed to mention they'd been estranged for years.

Erin had also expressed her concerns about Simon's illnesses, claiming he'd woken from a coma 'a changed man'. The coma followed Simon's admission to Monash Hospital in late May 2022 after suffering a mystery illness that led to an induced coma and life-saving surgery. In the lead-up, he'd been on a camping trip with Erin and eaten a chicken korma she'd prepared.

In other online chats, Erin had shown the group pictures of a dehydrator she'd bought and used to dehydrate mushrooms. She was quite the fungi fan, apparently. They also swapped recipes, with Erin observing that beef Wellington was a favourite and asking for advice on the best cut of beef to use. She revealed that the recipe she used was from Australia's bestselling book, *Dinner* by Nagi Maehashi of popular website RecipeTin Eats. The book was a favourite among the group.

Daniela at one point learned that Erin and Simon were separated and she said she thought Erin was 'a good mother, but very scared to lose her kids'. She got the impression that Erin's kids were all she had left in her life. As someone who'd been divorced, she couldn't fathom why Erin was so involved with Simon's family.

The Erin she got to know was 'funny and caring'. They shared photos and videos of their kids, including one of Erin's children playing the piano, and her new home in Gibson Street. From what she shared, Erin appeared to be content with her life and devoted to her children but, as a mother herself, Daniela was both intrigued and concerned that Erin's kids, according to Erin, always had health problems.

There were other things that stirred her concern. There was Erin's professed hatred of her sister, Ceinwen, and her sister's successful career, and what sounded like a smidgen of jealousy directed at Simon, who she nicknamed The Messiah. She complained that while he was recovering at her home after one of his hospitalisations, the cause of which remains a mystery, he'd been spoiled by ladies from the church popping by with soups for him, noting that he had the energy to drive to church but otherwise spent too much time in bed.

Daniela was troubled on hearing that one of Simon's bouts of illness happened shortly after he'd consumed a stew Erin had prepared for him, beef goulash, using a recipe she'd given her. Erin had asked her for help, saying she wasn't able to replicate her mother's dish. Daniela willingly shared her recipe, but she was surprised and disappointed when Erin sent her a picture of the completed dish, featuring mushrooms, which hadn't been in the recipe. Erin reckoned everyone loved it.

When chatting about their true crime interests, Erin had been enthralled by the Gregory Lynn murder case – Lynn was found guilty of the murder of Carol Clay in June 2024. She had also harshly (and falsely) accused the mother of missing four-year-old Cleo Smith, who'd been abducted in 2021 from a campsite in Western Australia, of shedding crocodile tears.

As for Keli Lane, Erin accused her of being a 'mental case' after seeing a photograph of her, taken two days after giving birth to Tegan, wearing a white pantsuit. Erin's reasoning was that white wasn't a sensible colour to wear after childbirth. In hindsight, it was an odd comment, given her choice to wear white pants the day after the lunch, when she was allegedly suffering from diarrhoea.

Other members of the groups shared some insights at the preliminary hearing in 2024. Jenny Hay, a semi-retired social worker, recalled that the original Keli Lane group started around 2019, but it fell apart, after which twenty to thirty members joined the splinter group that subsequently formed. Other groups that were common to members included one called GirlChat and, after the poisoning, the unfortunately named Mushroom Murder Meal, which dealt with the details of the case and the stresses of knowing some of the people involved, along with comparatively mundane conversations about their day-to-day lives – a very curious mix. The mushroom conversations apparently stopped when some of the participants were contacted by police. This was likely to have occurred after Erin's computers and other devices were seized and interrogated.

Jenny said she had a strong interest in true crime and was a member of other mainly US-based groups, including one focused on the Karen Read trial – a woman in Boston charged with the murder of her boyfriend, a police officer, in 2022. Read was acquitted of all charges after a jury declared her not guilty in June 2025. She said she'd often join a group, follow it for a while, then leave it.

When questioned on Erin, Jenny told the court that while they may have interacted in the original Keli Lane group, her recollection was that they didn't formally meet online until the following year. Erin, she recalled, would take breaks from the groups from time to time, and upon her return she'd share updates on her children and her life as a 'stay-at-home mum' – something she had in common with other members.

Simon also featured in her conversations, and Erin talked about his health challenges – presumably starting around the time of the first alleged attempt on his life by poison. Mushrooms, Jenny said, were also prominent in Erin's conversation. She talked about the dehydrator she used and even sent a picture to the group. Jenny said that Erin loved mushrooms and was keen to exchange recipes and cooking tips. She also corroborated Daniela's evidence about Erin's and the group's fondness for RecipeTin Eats.

Jenny also had a clear recollection of Erin asking the group about their preferred preparation of beef Wellington – a favourite dish for Jenny – and referencing the RecipeTin Eats version the group had discussed.

As an aside, the recipe Erin used was from Nagi Maehashi's cookbook, and the RecipeTin Eats website had a detailed, easy-to-follow video that ran for a shade over nine minutes. The video demonstrated the preparation of a large single beef Wellington, made using a duxelles of fresh mushrooms, and showcased that delicious moment of slicing through the crisp, buttery pastry to reveal a glorious pink piece of beef. As we will soon discover, Erin's interpretation of that recipe was somewhat different – for a couple of significant reasons.

In the aftermath of the July 2023 poisoning, Jenny recalled that discussion and speculation had been rife in the group. Members saw pictures of the house in Gibson Street, Leongatha, which confirmed that it was Erin's house where the lunch had taken place. They thought it was all 'a terrible mistake'. In those early days, with details still unfolding, Erin's online friends were akin to armchair detectives – something they shared with many others around Australia and the world as they tried to piece the case together based on media reports.

Jenny said that Erin had video-called her in early August to talk 'one to one' and she assumed Erin was calling from her home. The focus of the call was Erin's children, who she said were very distressed at being removed from her. Naturally, Jenny asked Erin questions about the day of the lunch, and about the mushrooms she'd used in the dish and where they'd come from. Erin said she'd been given legal advice not to talk about the lunch, and to be very careful what she said in any case. It was intriguing that her online friends, people she hadn't physically met, were the people she felt most comfortable speaking to in the most challenging of times. This didn't deter some, who pressed her for answers. Jenny said Erin became very distressed at this questioning, and even more so when asked about her children.

Another of the Facebook friends called to give evidence in the preliminary hearing was Christine Hunt from Brisbane, Queensland. She said she'd only met Erin online, not in person. They'd met around 2019 in the first Keli Lane group. Asked about her interactions with Erin in the group, she recalled Erin talking about her kids, observing that it was plain Erin was a devoted mother.

Christine had joined the Mushroom Murder Meal group after being told of a comment listing her as a friend of Erin's. She read the comments and then left the group but she thought Erin may have joined the group under a different name.

In the preliminary examination, none of the witnesses to Erin's online life had noted any hint of what might happen at that lunch in July 2023. What was notably absent from all the evidence was any insight into what made Erin Patterson tick. Not one of the members of this true crime group had been prompted to dig into the life of one of their own. For a group of chatterers and amateur sleuths, they weren't as inquisitive when the alleged murderer was someone they knew. The shock of what had unfolded was likely too close to home.

But there was one member, who requested to remain anonymous, not called as a witness, who offered a thoughtful account of Erin's online life – and it was a dim one, tinged with sadness. The member observed that Erin was both sneaky and jealous. At one point, Erin became aware of a relationship between two members. The discovery was a revelation to her, and her ignorance of it prompted feelings of both abandonment and hostility. Erin, the member said, was both paranoid and very upset, and they observed that Erin's biggest obsession was with Erin. When the first group 'blew up', Erin was devastated, but she responded by moving between both the old Lane group and the new, under fake memberships.

But that online behaviour only scratched the surface. Erin used her new life and new friends to rewrite her past, weaving fictions as she went. According to Erin, her mother's death wasn't from cancer but because she'd drunk herself into an alcoholic coma. Then there were fanciful stories of her work with Romanian orphans, and her near miss with the serial killer Ivan Milat.

According to the story Erin spun for her rapt online friends, in her youth she'd hitchhiked and backpacked in the outer south-western area of Sydney where Milat hunted his victims. Milat first came under notice as a teen, exhibiting antisocial and criminal behaviour, including attacking animals and minor to middling rank offences which led to stints in juvenile institutions. In his mid-twenties he escalated to violent crimes against people, including sexual assaults, brutal attacks and attempted murder. In the late 1980s and early 1990s he was back on the south-western fringe of Sydney, hunting backpackers. The first victims from his murder spree were found in the Belanglo State Forest – an eerie pine forest adjacent to the highway linking Sydney to Melbourne.

By the time of his arrest in May 1994, Milat was thought to have abducted and murdered more than seven people, and remains a suspect in many more disappearances. Milat died in prison in 2019 and, like most evil criminals, took his secrets to the grave. People like Milat get both power and pleasure from having secret knowledge.

In every crime, establishing the chronology is an imperative. Erin, born in 1974, would have been nineteen when Milat was arrested, meaning the time that she and Milat could have been in the same vicinity is quite short. But, as my source noted, Erin could be an 'unreliable narrator' and she never let the facts get in the way of a good story.

There was a similarly sceptical post-lunch view about the story Erin had told some of her online friends about a tragedy in her life. Before Simon came on the scene, she said there had been another young man in her life and they were poised to marry. That hope ended when the young man died in a motorcycle accident. To add to the tragedy, Erin said his family wouldn't allow her to attend his funeral. It was the saddest of stories, responded to by her friends with compassion, but in the light of Erin's other lies, was this true or just another fabrication?

Other intriguing snippets to emerge from our discussions were that Erin's true crime obsession ran to an allegedly large collection of true crime books – over 400 perhaps – and a fascination with fly-on-the-wall prison documentaries. I say allegedly because, as Erin didn't encourage visitors to her Leongatha home, it's difficult to confirm the size of the collection.

Psychologist Suzanne Degges-White, a professor at the University of North Illinois, has researched and written extensively about online friendships. In 2018 she wrote in *Psychology Today*, 'Face-to-face friendships are most frequently built on proximity, shared activities, or life events. Online friendships are similar in that they usually develop around the same three factors and in a way that's even more intense than it might be in real life. We connect with strangers online who show up in groups that centre around interests and activities.'

The professor said there was a broad spectrum of relationship quality – as evidenced by the disagreements in these groups – and that online we can project 'our best self' in ways that would be difficult to maintain in real life.

She went on to point out, 'We may actually be much more willing to expose our vulnerabilities and bring candid honesty and genuineness to the relationship. Research shows that it is "safer" to be open and honest about our struggles, deficits, and anxieties with "online buddies" than with people we see on a regular basis.' In a 2020 piece that was written while a chunk of the world was in Covid-19 lockdown, the professor said, 'While few of us are actually going to meet up with online friends/real-world strangers, there is less concern about "how others see them" and more about what they mean to us and what we gain from the relationship.' She also observed, 'Our "confessions" are limited to a containable space and shared with people we actually never have to engage with again, if we choose not to.'

Her observations put into perspective the rather withdrawn and not overly personable Erin Patterson's interest in online friends, people with whom she could share the joy of her children, along with pithy observations about her husband's shortcomings. Online, she lived another life, one separate from that of a stay-at-home mum and an estranged wife living in the small town community of Korumburra but not really a part of it. In real life, she was an outsider, but online, she belonged.

8

ATTEMPTED MURDER

Though Simon and Erin were separated, she was still part of the Patterson family. They'd enjoy weekends away, both with and without the kids, having no qualms about leaving the children with Simon's family while they travelled.

It was an adult and civil arrangement, and one that evidenced a strong but perhaps frustrating relationship – the idiom of 'can't live with them, can't live without them' seems apt here.

When the Covid-19 lockdowns started biting, the Patterson family stayed in touch via a chat group started by Don and Gail. Every Saturday morning they'd catch up online with their children, grandchildren, nieces and nephews. Not long after, the Korumburra Baptist Church embraced contemporary technology and began live-streaming their services. The triumvirate responsible for the streaming were Don, Simon and Erin, but Don liked to join in the service when possible, so the technical duties often fell to the estranged couple. It was an amicable arrangement, or so Simon thought.

Simon's brother Matthew concurred, recalling a 2021 lunch in Melbourne arranged by Erin. He thought she was sad and thought both wanted to reconcile, but they'd only do so if Simon agreed to attend marriage counselling – again. Erin wanted his advice on how to encourage Simon to participate. The couple also attended family gatherings and, as Matthew observed, were both respectful and cordial in their relationship.

Victoria's final lockdown – its sixth – ended on Thursday, 21 October 2021. The following day, the BBC reported, 'More than five million people are celebrating new freedoms, such as visits to cafes and other households. Melburnians have endured six lockdowns and more than 260 days under restrictions during the pandemic.'

As a result, Victoria's state capital was dubbed the 'world's most locked down city'.

Authorities said the city was well placed to reopen because seventy per cent of over-16s were now fully vaccinated. Around the state, bars, restaurants and cafes were full, congregations flowed back to churches, houses lit up with parties and people were, quite literally, cheering in the streets.

But that joy didn't last long in Korumburra, where just under four weeks later, on around 16 November, Simon Patterson's return to normality hit a hurdle. He became desperately ill and with no apparent cause.

In 2019, Erin had asked Simon if he'd accompany her on a trip to southern Africa. He later recalled thinking the request was a bit unusual. It was a trip of some significance and duration, and it was the first time she'd suggested something like that alone, since their children had been born. Plus, they were separated at the time. He recalled being fine with the idea.

The arrival of the pandemic put an end to those travel plans.

As an alternative, Erin suggested that when restrictions lifted, they leave the children with the family and drive around 100 kilometres south to Wilsons Promontory for two or three nights. Located at the southernmost point of the Australian mainland, it's a national park replete with walking trails, pristine beaches (for those who aren't averse to swimming in chilly water), camping sites – both family oriented and remote – and abundant wildlife.

There would be four bouts of illness for Simon, three of which resulted in the criminal charges, but, as explained earlier, they were dropped just before Erin's trial began.

The first started on the evening of 16 November 2021, when Erin arrived at Simon's house to pack for the trip. She'd brought some penne bolognese in a Tupperware container for Simon's dinner, which he ate around 9 or 10 pm – later than he usually ate – after Erin went home to sleep.

The next morning, Simon drove to Erin's to collect her. Simon's sister-in-law Tanya was there when he arrived. She'd always had a good relationship with Erin and the children, and would be looking after them while their parents were away.

The trip didn't get off to an auspicious start, with Simon vomiting in Erin's bathroom. He'd been feeling unwell, and looked rather grey. Both women expressed concern, but he assured them he was okay, and maybe just feeling stressed because it was just the two of them going away. With Simon not at his best, Erin drove. They got as far as Meeniyan, around 30 kilometres into the trip, before they had to stop. Simon's problems were increasing, with the onset of diarrhoea accompanying the vomiting.

They waited there for most of the morning to see if his issues subsided. Two options presented themselves – they could either return to Korumburra or press on for the remaining 70 kilometres to Wilsons Promontory and find an Airbnb rather than camping while Simon was unwell. They jointly opted for Plan B – they'd press on. In hindsight, it wasn't the best choice.

While Simon's recollections were somewhat hazy, he thought they'd arrived at a town starting with Y close to Wilsons Promontory, which is probably the coastal town of Yanakie. They settled into a house, and Simon took to bed in between bathroom visits. As he recalls, the vomiting declined but the diarrhoea persisted. Erin, he thought, spent her time in the lounge, reading, watching television and relaxing. She also nursed Simon, making him electrolyte drinks.

The next day or so was foggy for Simon. He couldn't clearly recall if he and Erin had discussed whether to go home or to a hospital, but thought Erin had suggested he ride it out, to which he agreed. However, his condition continued to deteriorate – he was seriously ill, and later said that he 'felt worse inside myself, I felt I was going downhill'. It was then he knew he had to go to a hospital. After discussion with Erin, who told him local hospitals were hard to get into, they decided to make the 40-minute drive to Leongatha Hospital.

He spent that night attached to a drip and was administered the anti-nausea drug Ondansetron. Though Simon didn't remember which doctor had treated him or their diagnosis, he thought he'd simply caught some sort of gastro bug, and no-one had disavowed him of that idea. He was released the next day, and believes Erin drove him back to his home in Korumburra. By that stage he was feeling better, and was relieved that the vomiting and diarrhoea had stopped. The following morning he was back at the hospital to have his creatinine levels checked. This test was to check kidney function, which may have been impacted by electrolyte deficiencies and dehydration.

The result wasn't what he'd been hoping for. Concerned about the impact on Simon's kidneys, the treating doctor at Leongatha had him transferred to Monash Hospital in Melbourne's south-east, where he spent the next five days on a drip. He was put in a room on his own, with a sign on the door warning medical staff to take care when entering the room. It was obvious they didn't know what was causing his illness and were being careful in case it was easily transmitted. He had no recollection of any discussions about it being a 'gastro bug', and knew he had been tested for 'lots of things'. However, despite their thoroughness, the medical team hadn't identified a specific cause. It was cold comfort to be told that sometimes gastro bugs don't show up in tests.

However, Simon did have an imprecise recollection of a member of the medical staff, either at Monash or Leongatha, raising the prospect of food poisoning and asking what Simon had eaten. He thought Erin had told him that he and the children had penne pasta, but the children hadn't been sick, so he assumed the pasta wasn't to blame. Given he'd eaten the dish after Erin had gone home for the night, questions such as when the children ate, how the food had been stored and for how long would have been useful to eliminate handling issues, thus leaving the possibility that Erin had added something to the dish – a question prompted by hindsight, not by any suspicions on Simon's part. Those would come later.

Simon was discharged when his creatinine levels had returned to normal. Reflecting on the incident, he said that Erin had been supportive and caring. He didn't notice anything out of the ordinary in her behaviour, and thought their relationship was okay.

That perception continued.

*

Meanwhile, in the lead-up to and during Simon's medical travails, Erin was having travails of her own.

She told her doctor, Cassie Zhou, in Leongatha in late 2021 that she was worried about ovarian cancer. She'd googled the symptoms she was experiencing and thought they were suspicious. After a battery of tests, she was referred on to a specialist physician, Doctor Ogilvie. The referral said she'd been experiencing extreme fatigue, along with a raft of other symptoms including poor appetite and weight gain, headaches, swollen feet, nausea, and an overactive bladder with incontinence. Though the list was a long one, the referral noted that she was otherwise in good health and not on any medications.

Erin's health concerns didn't preclude a school holiday trip to Tasmania with the children. She and Simon were messaging via Signal in early January 2022. She told him her back was improving (obviously something she had complained about to him previously), but she was now worried about heart issues, and Doctor Oglivie thought she might be suffering from right-sided heart failure. She told them she'd been online again, and all her symptoms fitted that diagnosis. She went on to tell Simon she had more tests scheduled for when she got home from their trip. Simon was solicitous, messaging, '*Holy crap that is [a] whole lot more than "low energy"*' and noting she was obviously counting the days until she got home and back to familiar surroundings and predictability.

In a medical history, Erin noted that her father, Hugh, had died of pancreatic cancer, her mother, Heather, and a maternal aunt from breast cancer, and both a paternal and maternal aunt from ovarian cancers. This history gave substance to her concerns, even if they were contrived.

With the spectre of Covid-19 receding, Korumburra and its residents settled back into a life with liberty restored. Family lunches were held at the Korumburra Middle Hotel in the centre of town, and the local hub was always busy. Bible study was also a weekly feature on the Patterson family calendar, and was sometimes held at the house of local doctor Chris Ford. The sessions ran for nearly two hours, with around four to eight attendees. It was through the church and Bible study that Doctor Ford got to know Erin and Simon Patterson. He was also their daughter's doctor and later, from around July 2022, Simon's doctor. He described Simon as a fit 47-year-old who didn't take regular medication and had no apparent medical conditions. In May 2022, Simon apparently weighed 115 kilograms and was a solidly built bloke.

But weight loss was imminent.

On 25 May 2022, Erin and Simon were on the road again – this time to Howqua, an historic gold-mining region around 300 kilometres drive due north of Korumburra and a rather circuitous drive via the outskirts of Melbourne. Simon said he'd readily agreed to go, as it was something they both wanted to do. Just as they had during the last ill-fated getaway, the children stayed with Tanya.

Their campsite in Upper Howqua was uncrowded. They chose a site near a stream, also fortuitously close to the ablutions block and some wooden picnic tables. As evening approached, Erin cooked dinner using the butane cooker they'd brought with them.

The menu on that first night wasn't exotic – sausages and bread – with leftovers doubling as lunch the next day. Simon said they'd brought their own drinking water, around 40 to 50 litres. He didn't recall any taps or tank water supplies at the campsite, nor drinking from the stream. They spent the day motoring around, sightseeing, enjoying each other's company and simple pleasures.

On the second night of the trip, Erin cooked, this time doing her food preparation on one of the wooden picnic tables. On the menu was a chicken korma and rice she'd made at home, which had travelled with them in Tupperware containers in the esky. In the lead-up, Simon had been at Erin's when she'd been experimenting with the heat levels in curries. He had helped with a taste test. The kids apparently didn't like spicy food, and their father preferred somewhere between mild and spicy. Simon reckoned all of them were 'very mild'. He recalled Erin telling him the purpose of the test was to 'customise future curry production for our respective tastes'. It was a similar curry that Erin had packed for the camping trip. Simon couldn't recall if the curry had been packed in individual serves or if they were both eating from the same container – he later said he hadn't really been paying attention. He was certain that he ate all of his serve but couldn't recall if Erin had eaten all of hers.

And then history repeated. Simon began vomiting during the night, though he didn't recall any diarrhoea. With the problem not abating, by late morning they drove around 30 minutes to the nearest hospital, in Mansfield, where he was put on a drip and again given the anti-nausea drug Ondansetron.

The next morning, the vomiting having abated, it was back to Korumburra. Simon said he had little recollection of the next few days, noting he probably missed a family birthday gathering in the town's Coleman Park on the Saturday. He couldn't recall if Erin had sent their children to the party and stayed to care for him.

The next day, Simon woke when it was still dark. He needed to get to the toilet, but needed help, so he called Erin, who came straight over. Simon was in dire straits when she arrived and couldn't recall if they exchanged greetings. 'I was sitting at the end of the bed, I laid back and that's the last thing I remember.' Simon later learned that during the time he'd blanked out, Erin had called 000 and he'd been taken to hospital by ambulance. His next recollection was of lying on a trolley in the hospital hallway while Erin tried to get the attention of medical staff. She was 'brushed off', he recalled, by a female staff member who was 'quite abrupt'. He recalled thinking that Erin was upset at the way she'd been treated.

Simon's illness was too complex and perilous for local treatment, so he was taken by ambulance to Monash Hospital. With Simon unconscious and his condition precarious, doctors sought Erin's permission to perform what could be life-saving surgery, as she was still his next of kin. After seeking counsel from her father-in-law, Don, she gave the doctors permission to operate. Even with surgery, it would be touch and go. The surgery removed a large portion of his bowel. Fortunately, Simon survived the ordeal and had a good chance at making a full recovery.

But a mystery remained. In one of the few interactions with doctors he could recall, he was told they'd done extensive tests to try and identify the cause of his illness, but it remained elusive. When asked about Erin's demeanour throughout all this, he said she was always caring and that there was nothing unusual or out of the ordinary about her behaviour. She made sure that his family and friends were kept up to date about his condition and were informed of the success of the surgery. For someone who wasn't known for being a great communicator, Erin had excelled, using the app Signal to give updates and coordinate visits.

As Simon's condition improved, Erin again stepped in, arranging rehabilitation for him at the St John of God Frankston Rehabilitation Hospital, where he spent over a week. She still coordinated his visitors, cleaned his home, organised gardeners and paid his bills. Simon also thought she may have had his car serviced and his tyres changed.

On release, he didn't go back to his now spotless home but instead took up Erin's offer to recuperate at her just-completed home in Gibson Street. She'd just moved there, and had set up a bedroom downstairs for him, as well as a space for physiotherapy.

When Simon arrived he was still quite weak and experiencing occasional diarrhoea. He couldn't get upstairs, so the downstairs bedroom and bathroom were ideal. He spent a chunk of time in bed working, and as his strength slowly returned, he gradually made it out of the house and into the grounds. When not working, he played computer games with the children, watched television and chatted. He and Erin cooked family meals together, but the clean-up was usually left for Erin. On the face of it, a happy family.

By the end of June he was able to get up the stairs and to drive, but his progress stalled in late July, while he was still at Erin's. Though they usually had lunch together, he thought it was 'unusual' when one day Erin made a stew especially for him. While they ate together at the table, he couldn't recall if she'd eaten the stew or something different. The stew was Erin's take – with the addition of mushrooms – on the beef goulash recipe provided by Daniela.

The afternoon passed normally, the kids came home and Simon bought some fish and chips for dinner. Around midnight, his nightmare began playing out again. He'd been in bed for about 30 minutes when he started vomiting. Not long after, he felt like diarrhoea was about to add to his fears and misery. He called out for Erin and she swiftly came downstairs. They called Don and Gail to come and look after the children, and they were at the house by 1.30 am. Erin drove Simon to Leongatha Hospital, where he spent the night, before being transferred to Monash and was once again put on a drip and anti-nauseants. By the afternoon he was improving, and by the next day he felt he was recovering quickly, though he was apprehensive that it was false confidence. His medical travails were having an impact on both his confidence and his mental health.

Fortunately, his recovery continued and he was discharged. Back to Gibson Street he went, but to a very different reception than he'd enjoyed the first time around. The solicitous Erin had disappeared, and instead he described her as giving him 'the cold shoulder'.

That shoulder got colder as the days passed. One morning while Simon was still in bed, Erin gave voice to her feelings. She came into his room, obviously very upset, and came straight to the point. She accused him of spending too much time in bed, not helping with domestic chores, and not getting up in time to take the children to school. He was also in the habit of making toasted ham and tomato sandwiches and failing to clean up the kitchen adequately. While in hospital she thought he'd been 'dictatorial' over a minor issue with a phone charging cable, and she was, in his view, generally frustrated with him.

Simon got the point – he was no longer welcome at Gibson Street. He recalled: 'I paused for quite a long period, unsure how to respond, then said, "I'm sorry to hear you feel that way." Then she stormed out and I thought it wasn't wise to stay there.' Simon was beginning to think that something was seriously wrong in his relationship with Erin.

Not long after his release from hospital, Simon was back at his home in Nason Street, Korumburra.

Though distressed about the direction his relationship was going in, and with a growing unease about the still-unknown cause or causes of his illnesses, he hadn't begun to entertain the dark thoughts that the woman he still loved may be trying to kill him. But that reality was soon to dawn.

9

DARK THOUGHTS DAWN

Despite the disastrous history of their recent weekends away, when Erin proposed a return to Wilsons Promontory for a few days in early September 2022 for 'just the two of us', Simon said yes. Perhaps he was still clinging to the hope of reconciliation.

This time, Simon, who was in good health, unlike on their last trip to that location, drove. But, like the last trip, Erin did the catering, in this instance Simon's lunch was a pita-bread wrap, and he thought it may have contained curry and some vegetables. He thought that Erin had similar, only minus the pita bread. He recalled he may have 'possibly' eaten some of Erin's meal but was confident she hadn't eaten any of his.

After lunch Simon again became unwell with symptoms that were all too familiar. It was 6 September 2022. The nausea, diarrhoea and vomiting increased and the pair decided it was best to head home, and fast, with Erin at the wheel. Back in Korumburra, they drove straight to

Simon's parents, Don and Gail. Simon recalled that when they arrived, his son was also there, looking concerned. That concern would not have been eased by Simon's first words to them: 'I'd like a bed and a bucket, please.'

Given his health concerns over the past year and his obviously precarious condition, his parents weren't taking any chances. They called an ambulance. Simon recalled that he was feeling very weak and that his symptoms were getting worse. He thinks he may have had a few fits. His strength had waned so much, he had to be helped onto the ambulance trolley. By the time he was in the back of the ambulance, he was alarmed to find that he was slurring his words and losing muscle function, to the point where he could only move his neck. He was taken straight to Monash Hospital, where he was sedated.

On waking, he was still nauseous, feeling decidedly unwell and very weak. Though his symptoms persisted for a day or so, he was improving steadily and was soon released. Again, batteries of tests and the finest of medical minds hadn't been able to pinpoint the cause.

This time, he didn't head to Gibson Street, choosing to recuperate at his parents' home instead. Dark thoughts about the possibility that Erin could be the cause of his illness were growing in his head. As someone with a background in the logic of civil engineering, a man who had, until recently, been in robust good health, he couldn't ignore the fact that there was one common denominator – he only got sick when he went away with Erin and she'd been cooking for him. It's not a leap anyone would readily make, but the chronology and circumstantial evidence were all pointing in one direction. Most criminal prosecutions based on this type of evidence are circumstantial, as it's very rare to find a smoking gun. More often, it's the weight of the circumstances, when linked, that make the case.

It was around this time that he shared his suspicions with two of his relatives, sister Anna Maree Terrington and cousin Tim. Anna Maree was an interesting choice as she'd been close to Erin, with the two pregnant at the same time – in Erin's case, with her daughter. Their babies had been born three days apart and were also close, referred to by the family as 'the twins'. Erin had done a Bible reading at Anna Maree's wedding, and Anna Maree had been the recipient of Erin's largesse when she'd loaned her and her husband, Josh, $400,000 to help buy their home in Melbourne's Blackburn South.

Anna Maree couldn't recall precisely when the conversation took place, but it had been by phone while she was at home and he was recuperating at their parents' house. Nor could she offer a reason why Simon was confiding in her. He told her he thought Erin may have been putting something poisonous in the food she made for him, that it was the only explanation for what had happened to him. However, he thought he was the only one at risk. The only person Anna Maree told was her husband.

Simon recalled telling Tim of his suspicions in around September 2022, saying it was a turning point for him. He told his cousin he'd been thinking about the possibility of being poisoned during the first half of 2022, but that he'd treated it as a bit of a joke, even suggesting before they left on the Howqua trip that Erin might have put something poisonous in his food. He didn't recall whether Erin was amused by the joke.

At that point the suspicion remained a very tightly held secret, and one that no doubt haunts them, in light of what happened nine months later. But it was just a suspicion, with no credible evidence aside from the chronology to support it.

Following his hospitalisation, Simon also changed doctors – that was when he began seeing Doctor Chris Ford. Ford was a logical choice as the two had a personal relationship already, and they'd talked about Simon's hospitalisations. Ford had discussions with the admitting intensive care doctor at one of Simon's admissions, and with the gastroenterologist who'd also seen Simon as a patient. Ford had been told of Simon's various tests, and the possibility that his second admission had been due to a bacterial infection of some kind. What Ford wasn't yet aware of was Simon's suspicion – that would come later.

But, as Ford later told a preliminary hearing, he'd considered what had happened to Simon. Like any good investigator, he knew that if there wasn't a conspicuous reason then a process of elimination was the best option. In this instance Ford, an experienced medical practitioner, couldn't think of a single reason other than poisoning that could account for Simon's multiple hospital admissions. Poisoning, he thought, was feasible, but the how – and possibly the who – wasn't something he could confirm. In the absence of any objective evidence, it was a suspicion he kept to himself.

Months later, Simon's worst fears were confirmed.

10

NO RETURN FROM THE TAX

Toward the end of 2022, members of the Patterson family noticed that Erin and Simon's previously amicable relationship was deteriorating. Tanya Patterson observed that Simon's stay with Erin while he recuperated from illness hadn't been as long as they'd expected, and that Simon's hopes of reconciliation seemed to have been dashed. She'd also noticed their lack of interaction at family gatherings, and the paucity of even basic niceties like saying goodbye to each other. Family members' invitations to Erin's new home at Gibson Street had also been elusive, to the point where Simon couldn't remember the last one, and his visits had been solely to collect or return the children.

Around early November 2022, the chill between Erin and Simon deepened. The cause was Simon's tax return. He recalled dropping one of the children at Erin's house when Erin emerged and said she wanted a chat. By her demeanour, Simon could tell that it was something serious. She slipped into the passenger seat and told him she'd discovered that his tax return for the previous financial year stated that they were separated. How she made this discovery wasn't canvassed.

This was the first time he'd done this, and it was a surprise to Erin. She wasn't pleased, pointing out that the change of status impacted their family tax benefits. She told him that, as a consequence, he'd have to pay child support. Curiously, Simon didn't ask how she'd found out, but he thought the change of status was the result of a miscommunication with his accountant. To placate Erin, he offered to change the document, but the damage had been done and he said Erin 'rejected that possibility and said she wasn't happy with that', insisting that the next step was child support. Simon thought they'd parted on good terms and that Erin would apply for child support. But he was being optimistic.

She became colder toward him after that. During their years of separation they'd exchanged frequent texts, which had been chatty and responsive, but after this revelation, he said that chattiness was gone, and conversations became purely functional, focusing primarily on the logistics of sharing two children. Like most if not all married couples, there'd been disputes in their life together, and Erin had often responded by being cold, sometimes rude and 'not very nice', but this felt different to him. He felt she was more distant, rather than what he said had been 'aggressive emotion' in years past. Sometimes she did not respond at all, relegating him from the cold shoulder to the freezer. Simon began to realise that, this time, there would be no healing of the rift.

Following the formality of separation in the tax return, Erin filed for child support and told him to expect a call, which duly came, followed by a series of invoices. Child support, as Simon found out, involved the government as the intermediary, who assessed, collected and disbursed the money.

The formality increased, with Erin asking him to sign a form from the children's school, agreeing to pay half the fees. Simon, to his recollection, had already been paying half but declined to sign the form, telling her he thought that was a matter for the child support people, who had told him not to sign anything. To complicate matters, these discussions were mainly via the encrypted Signal app, not face to face. While messaging isn't the greatest way to gauge the feelings of others, Simon could tell that Erin wasn't happy.

Erin ignored Simon's requests to meet and sought counsel from Don and Gail, initially also via Signal. Her in-laws both encouraged cooperation rather than confrontation. Despite Don and Erin's closeness and mutual respect, Erin wasn't pleased with Don's advice, and made that clear in a long message to Simon and his parents on 5 December 2022. She told them all she was not happy with Simon and his actions:

> 'I foolishly trusted him to do right by me and the kids when it came to the crunch but I was wrong to do so it seems.'

The message went on to rail against Simon not paying school fees and to let Gail and Don know she thought it 'unconscionable' that he was refusing to help after she claimed child support. She saw his actions as a punishment of her.

Money had finally entered the fray. With Simon's family owing Erin over a million dollars and relations between them deteriorating, it wasn't a surprise.

Don replied an hour later, making apologies and hoping Erin got a *'reasonable sleep'*.

Erin was back just before 10 am the next day with another long message, which in part nailed her ongoing issues with Simon. She told them she would continue messaging to keep Simon accountable, even though Gail and Don did not want to be involved.

But on that same day, Erin was showing her other face to her online friends. Under her Erin Erin Erin persona, she posted a rant about her in-laws and the fact that they weren't going to help her. She wrote, *'So Don said they can't adjudicate if they don't know both sides. This family I swear to fucking god.'*

She went on to query whether they had *'any capacity for so-called self-reflection'* and called them a *'lost cause'*.

She wasn't finished offering her views of Simon and his parents. Don had called her to suggest they all talk and pray together and that there was a suggestion that she withdraw her child support claim. *'My head nearly exploded and I was like what??* She told her friends she wanted nothing more to do with her in-laws because she was *'so sick of this shit'*.

Obviously the close and warm relationship Erin had purportedly enjoyed with her in-laws was also in turbulent waters, and perhaps headed for the rocks.

The next day, 7 December, Erin was still wound up. She messaged her online friends again, saying that she wasn't reading the messages from Simon or his parents, *'I don't need anything from any of these people. Simon's parents say they don't want to take sides but by their very action they have.'*

Erin was on a roll, going on to describe how she thought Don and Gail would definitely get involved if their daughter was faced with a similar issue. And she noted he was still going to their place for tea but they hadn't thought about her.

One of her online friends asked if Erin would still go to *'that church'* [Korumburra Baptist]. She said that the kids went there with Simon on his weekends with them, otherwise they went with her to Leongatha. She said she hadn't been to that church for months. She didn't elaborate on which church or denomination she allegedly attended.

That evening Erin Erin Erin was back online and still unhappy, telling her friends that Gail was 'horrified' she'd asked for child support. She went on to wonder why that was an issue and not her 'dead beat' son not contributing.

Though matters were unresolved when Erin took the children to New Zealand in December 2022, the messages from there had a softer tone, focusing on the kids' adventures. On 16 December, Simon responded to some vision Erin had sent of their holiday, thanking her for sharing and commenting on the 'expert' camera operation.

Erin responded minutes later, telling Simon they were having a 'great time' and told him about their daughter's adventures.

Two days later, Erin messaged Simon from New Zealand about the goats and lambs she had grazing at her Gibson Street home. A tree had fallen across a fence dividing her place from the neighbours, and an enterprising goat had used the moment to get into the adjoining property. The neighbour was unwell and couldn't resolve the issue.

Erin messaged Simon to ask for his help and Simon responded swiftly letting her know that he was away but back the next day and made a point of saying, *'I'm always your husband no matter how we're doing so no probs with you asking.'*

Erin replied, *'Much appreciated'*.

Again, a simple, civil and caring exchange, in stark contrast to the bickering over school fees.

The issue of school fees did resolve when the first invoice for child support arrived and Simon discovered it was around $40 per month. Noting that 'it was hardly anything', Simon agreed it wasn't appropriate and said he'd pay half of the school fees. At the time he was earning a good income, and the children were at a private school, but one where the fees weren't too exorbitant. His grandmother was also contributing toward the fees, as she apparently had done for all her grandchildren and now great-grandchildren.

The conflict with Erin affected Simon's relationship with his children. He had what he described as a positive but difficult relationship with his daughter – they did activities together but not life. His son was more problematic. Simon thought he'd started to 'disengage' after his second major illness, and the distance between them was deepening. One positive note was that their son had a strong relationship with his grandfather, Don, who was tutoring him in maths and encouraging his dreams of becoming a pilot.

Amid all this turmoil, Simon decided it was time to have a serious conversation with his doctor and mate, Chris Ford. He'd seen him professionally a few times before deciding to share his suspicion that his illnesses may have been caused by poison, and that Erin may be responsible. Ford acknowledged the allegation but said little more. He didn't record Simon's suspicions in his clinical notes because he didn't have 'objective evidence', which he thought was a reasonable course to take but he remembered what Simon had said.

For a general practitioner in a country town, Ford's response was unsurprising – intentional poisoning was a major step away from the usual fodder of colds, flu, childhood illnesses and the medical needs of an ageing population. Simon thought Ford may have suggested drawing up a timeline, to which he responded, 'Spreadsheets are my thing.' He then set about creating one, based on memory and diary references and didn't share this document with anyone.

However, he did share his misgivings with his father around the same time. He said Don was very thoughtful when confronted with this astounding allegation, and then said, 'I suggest you don't tell too many people about that'. Simon recalled, 'I thought I had a reasonable sense of why he would say that, probably because it could create issues in the way people relate, especially with Erin and our family and outside too.'

The exchange prompted a subsequent discussion regarding the matter of Simon's next of kin for the purpose of an advanced care directive – an important document, particularly given his medical track record. Erin, as he observed, had been the decision-maker during the illnesses he'd experienced, which he now strongly suspected she'd caused, and while the decisions she'd made weren't inappropriate or harmful, it was an arrangement that needed to change. In February 2023 Simon changed the directive, giving his father, Don, and brother, Matthew, the power to act on his behalf should he again be incapacitated. Ford recalled the directive was signed by Simon at a Bible study class on 21 February 2023, and witnessed by Ford's wife, Bethany.

Ford also said that at some point, Simon had expressed concern about some cookies that his daughter had baked for a trip they'd taken to Sydney. Simon, he said, had been apprehensive to eat them, and after a small nibble had discreetly thrown them out. His daughter was living with Erin at the time and, while Ford had not asked a specific question, it is likely Simon was wondering if Erin had slipped something into them. Simon told him that Erin had rung a few times while father and daughter were on their trip, inquiring if he'd eaten any. Later, Simon conducted some online research into which poisons you could inconspicuously slip into a cookie, but there were too many options to pinpoint.

11

LUNCH IS SERVED

Simon Patterson declined his invitation to the lunch Erin had planned for 29 July 2023.

Erin had extended an invitation to him at the Korumburra Baptist Church on 16 July. Simon was there most weeks, and he and Erin were still running the live-streaming of the service, which they'd continued after Covid lockdowns had been lifted.

After the service, Simon was at the desk where the laptop and sound mixing equipment were positioned when Erin approached. She said she'd invited his parents and Ian and Heather to lunch at Gibson Street for what Erin called a 'serious chat', and she wanted him to be there too. She had some important medical news and wanted advice on how best to tell their children. The kids wouldn't be there. Simon was reluctant but acquiesced.

While Simon didn't discuss the event with his aunt and uncle, he spoke to his parents about it several times, including that Sunday afternoon. They didn't know the reason for the lunch either but were intrigued, especially because Heather and Ian would be there, which was their first invitation to Erin's new home. Don said Erin had recently confided that she'd had some medical tests because of a potentially cancerous lump on her elbow. He thought that might be what she wanted to discuss.

The day before the lunch, Simon messaged his parents to let them know he wouldn't be going, then messaged Erin to let her know. This message was sent by SMS, not Signal. At 6.54 pm on 28 July, Simon texted to say he felt '*too uncomfortable*' to come to lunch. He added that he was happy to talk about her health another time. By phone.

Erin responded a minute later that she was very disappointed and had spent '*many hours*' over the previous week preparing to make things special. And she said she had '*spent a small fortune on beef eye fillet … as I may not be able to host a lunch like this again for some time.*' She told him everyone was coming at 12.30 and hoped he'd change his mind and come.

While beef Wellington does have some technical challenges, Erin's claim of having spent 'many hours' in preparation over the preceding week was clearly exaggerated. In any case, Erin's entreaty didn't sway her estranged husband, who by that time was staying well clear of her cooking.

Curiously, in the week or so before the lunch, no-one mentioned Simon's concerns of earlier in the year. While Simon had discussed his misgivings about Erin with his father and siblings, the Wilkinsons were unaware. While not a family secret, Simon's fears were, understandably, not widely known, and any sense of apprehension may have abated as Simon's health had improved.

*

Ian, seventy years old at the time, later recalled that the arrangements were made between Erin and Heather, and his wife had made a diary note of the event – common practice in the Wilkinson household. Ian said his wife was 'meticulous', noting that she'd made an adjacent diary entry of 'fruit' as a reminder that they'd be taking a fruit platter. Both, he recalled were 'very happy' to be invited, but he was mildly curious about the reason for his invite, as one hadn't been offered previously.

Initially, he thought that he and Heather were the only invitees, but later learned that Don, Gail and Simon were also on the guest list.

The Wilkinsons had quite a social few days in the lead-up to the lunch. The day before, they'd taken an old friend to lunch at the Korumburra Middle Hotel for his birthday; Ian recalled he'd had a schnitzel. That night they enjoyed another birthday celebration at their daughter Ruth's home, this one for her husband, Brad, who was an avid smoker of meats. They enjoyed the fruits of his smoky toils along with roast vegetables. Breakfast the next morning wasn't memorable, with Ian observing he'd had his usual 'nice bowl of porridge'. He wasn't sure what Heather had that morning but thought it might have been a slice of toast. The couple had coffee with neighbours mid-morning at a local cafe, and Ian has a lingering memory of them enjoying a pastry.

All very useful in establishing their menus leading up to the lunch, and thus eliminating other possibilities in their subsequent fate.

Don drove them all to Erin's house, where they arrived around 12.30 pm. Upon arriving, Ian was surprised by the absence of Simon's car. It was at this point that he was told Simon wouldn't be attending. Erin's two children were not present either; they had gone to the movies in Leongatha.

The visit started with a brief tour of the house and surrounds, then they gathered in the kitchen, chatting comfortably – family from a small community, catching up. The conversation was relaxed – family, the kids, the new house. Ian recalled that Heather and Gail were driving the conversation, and Erin told them she also had a pantry behind one of the walls in the kitchen. This prompted an enthusiastic response from Heather, who'd just had one built in their home and wanted some ideas on setting it up. She headed for the pantry with Gail on her heels, and called for Ian to follow. Ian noticed that Erin appeared very reluctant, prompting him to think the pantry might have been a bit of a mess. Erin finally joined the two in the pantry, leaving the two men standing at the counter. They then adjourned to the verandah for an inspection of the garden.

Simon's absence wasn't mentioned.

They chatted for about half an hour as Erin finalised the food. Gail and Heather offered to help – both women were always keen to lend a hand – but in this instance, Erin politely declined. She was organised, Ian recalled, and had most of the meal prepared before they arrived. The menu was individual beef Wellingtons – 'pasties', both he and Erin's defence barrister Colin Mandy SC called them, which would no doubt horrify purists – along with mashed potatoes and green beans. Ian thought there might have been some gravy on the table. The pastry completely enclosed the beef and mushrooms.

Ian recalled that Erin stood on the kitchen side of the island to plate the food. He saw five plates laid out on the bench – four were large mid-grey coloured matching plates, while one was a smaller orangey tan colour – the 'odd man out' that the host would get when the dinner set wasn't big enough. It didn't strike Ian as unusual that, despite living in a new and well-managed house with three residents, Erin only had four matching dinner plates. While Erin plated the meal, Heather and Gail stood opposite her at the bench, ready to take the plates to the table.

As Ian later told the court – unprompted – 'they [Gail and Heather] didn't put anything on plates for example'.

Seating at the table wasn't prearranged. Ian, the pastor and a naturally dominant personality, took a seat at the head, with Don and Gail on his right side, and Heather and Erin on his left. Gail and Heather delivered the matching plates to the table and took their seats. Erin followed, carrying the odd plate, and sat beside Heather. The only beverage on offer was water.

The chat around the table didn't broach the topic of reconciliation between Simon and Erin. Instead, Erin had bad news about her health. She delivered this news after they had finished eating.

She told the group she'd had a recent possible – not confirmed – diagnosis of ovarian cancer. Erin told them it was potentially life threatening, and sought their counsel on how to deal with the children. 'Should I tell them or shouldn't I?'

It was news that came as a blow to them all, particularly given the prominence of cancer in Erin's family. Immediate reactions around the table were to offer compassion and support, and their consensus was to be truthful with the children. Depending on the diagnosis, Erin was potentially at the beginning of a long and challenging time, and one where the support of her children and that of her estranged in-laws would be imperative.

The discussion was cut short by the return of Erin's son and a mate. Knowing the conversation would be curtailed, Ian said, 'I suggested that we pray and I prayed a prayer asking God's blessing on Erin, that she would get the treatment that she needed, that the kids would be okay, that she'd have wisdom in how she told the kids.'

Simon had dropped the boys at the house and noted that his parents' car was parked outside, but he didn't go in. Instead, he and his daughter returned to Korumburra and spent the afternoon together. When the two boys were inside, focus quickly shifted to Erin's son and his studies to be a pilot. He proudly showed the guests his instruction books and talked avidly. The two boys also spied some dessert – either a muffin or cake, according to Erin's son's friend – and they helped themselves before heading upstairs to play games on the PC. The boy couldn't recall if the dessert had been eaten by the adults or what flavour it was.

Meanwhile, back at the table, the beef Wellington had been a hit. Ian and Heather had cleaned their plates. Don, whose appetite was on the hearty side, had finished his own and also despatched half of Gail's – her appetite was the opposite of her husband's, as noted by a few good-natured quips. Ian had no recollection of what Erin had done with her meal, but recalled that they were all quite full. The fruit and cake, which were served family style in the centre of the table, were nibbled at rather than demolished.

The gathering ended not long after, as Ian had a 3 pm appointment to discuss church business. He reflected that aside from Erin's news, there had been nothing out of the ordinary about the lunch.

Erin and her son dropped the son's friend home and on the way the boys chatted about school, and while Erin wasn't part of the chat, the friend said he thought she was just her normal self.

Ian couldn't recall what they'd had for dinner that night, but said he had worked in his study preparing for church on Sunday, noting that he and Heather went to bed a little later than their usual time of 10–10.30 pm. That night, the Pattersons and Wilkinsons began suffering severe gastro-like symptoms – vomiting, nausea, abdominal pains and diarrhoea.

The Wilkinsons hadn't yet fallen asleep when those terrible symptoms first struck. Ian said, 'Heather got up abruptly out of the bed and made her way to the laundry and I could hear her vomiting. She was vomiting into the laundry trough.' Ian was feeling alright at this point, but soon after he was also vomiting, and then diarrhoea hit. These symptoms lasted all night, and by morning they were both feeling 'washed out'. Ian recalled that as morning neared, the symptoms abated slightly, which he put down to both of them being empty. Neither had made it back to bed, with Ian spending the cold winter night camped outside the laundry, which had a toilet connected to it, while Heather stayed in the lounge room, where she had quick access to the bathroom.

Around dawn, Heather rang her sister Gail and found that she and Don were also very unwell. Ian, ever practical, rang a fellow church member to let them know he'd be unable to attend church that morning, and sent his sermon notes so the service could go ahead in his absence. Around 8.45 am Simon got a call from his father, telling him they'd been up all night vomiting and with diarrhoea, and had called emergency services. They were awaiting patient transport.

Simon then tried to call his uncle and aunt, but they weren't answering, so he drove to their house. Ian answered the door, looking 'sick', as Simon recalled. 'He looked grey, I suppose, and stooped. He was struggling.' Simon wanted to call an ambulance as his parents, who were by now en route to the hospital, had done, but Ian and Heather resisted, insisting, 'It's only a case of gastro and in a few hours we'll be right.'

They were both terribly wrong.

In a moment alone, Heather told Simon, with a puzzled look on her face, 'I noticed Erin served herself her food on a coloured plate, which was different to the rest.' Simon didn't ask any follow-up questions, and Heather didn't offer anything more.

Simon was adamant that his aunt and uncle needed to go to hospital, and they finally relented. Rather than wait for an ambulance, he drove them to Korumburra Hospital, but a staff member said they were full and directed them to the larger Leongatha Hospital.

On the way, Heather, in spite of her condition, clearly had Erin's choice of serving plates nagging at her. She said to Simon, 'Is Erin short of crockery? Is that why she would have this different kind of coloured plate that she served herself with?' Simon said, 'Yes, Erin doesn't have that many plates and that may be the reason.'

Simon helped them with the documentation required for examination and admission, waited until their daughter Ruth and Ruth's husband Brad arrived, then headed back to Korumburra Hospital to check on his parents. He was shocked by what he saw. The couple were in separate beds in the same room. He said, 'Dad was substantially worse than Mum. He was really struggling. He was lying on his side, he was hunched quite noticeably. A really discoloured face and struggling.' Don was having trouble speaking, and was obviously in a lot of pain. In hindsight, one reason for Don's dire condition may have been his enthusiasm for the beef Wellington and his decision to polish off his wife's leftovers.

Despite their poor condition, Don and Gail were still thinking of the welfare of others. They wanted to tell Simon what Erin had disclosed to them and asked if Simon was okay with that. He was. They explained that Erin had some tests done on her elbow – an issue that Simon was aware of – and the tests had come back with a cancer diagnosis, for ovarian cancer, curiously enough. Erin was expecting to undergo chemotherapy and possibly surgery. Don and Gail told Simon they had advised her to be honest with the children.

Perhaps it was the circumstances surrounding these revelations, but no-one stopped to question the oddity of an elbow issue leading to an ovarian cancer diagnosis.

That night, Don and Gail, with their condition deteriorating, were transferred to Dandenong Hospital in Melbourne. Doctor Chris Webster, with food poisoning topping a list of possible causes, quizzed Ian and Heather about what they'd been eating, but Ian couldn't recall anyone asking about or mentioning mushrooms. As Heather and Ian's conditions further deteriorated, they were also transferred to Dandenong Hospital.

Medical staff decided that the best option was to transfer the four to Melbourne's Austin Hospital in the suburb of Heidelberg for specialist care. While there were nearer hospitals, the Austin is home to the state's poison specialists. With poisoning – not the most common of medical challenges – expertise is sometimes ahead of speed.

However, even with the best of care, the patients' conditions continued to worsen. On 4 August 2023, Heather Wilkinson and Gail Patterson died in the Austin Hospital. Donald (Don) Patterson died the next day. Ian Wilkinson spent weeks in an induced coma, fighting for his life. He was finally discharged from hospital on 22 September 2023, nearly two months later, the only one of the four to survive the ordeal.

*

Amid this dramatic and sad time, Erin put her online life briefly on hold. One of her online friends told me that the usually chatty Erin had gone quiet in the last days of July 2023, but returned around the Wednesday after the special lunch, for which she'd sought cooking tips. However, she returned under a new profile name, 'Croissant', saying nothing about the lunch, food poisoning, mushrooms, in-laws in peril, or her children spending a night in hospital. When her friends asked about the name change, she claimed it was to avoid Simon, but didn't offer anything further.

The horrible reality of Erin's special lunch didn't hit her online friends until the following Sunday, when news of the deaths hit the media. Her friends recognised the house from Erin's online tours, and when they heard that the chef was a 48-year-old mother of two, they realised they'd just stepped into their own online hell. The revelation caused a tempest in the small group – some were stunned that someone so close to them may have done something so terrible, while others refused to believe their mate Erin could be involved, insisting it was all just a terrible accident.

Over the next few months, they discovered that what had been pitched as a convivial lunch to help Erin was, in fact, mass murder.

12

THE COOK'S TALE

Erin, according to Erin, had shopped at an Asian grocery store not far from her other home in Mount Waverley in April 2023. She recalled buying some dried mushrooms for a dish she was planning but, as they were 'very pungent' and not compatible with her plans, she put them into a container and left them in the pantry. The container and its contents later travelled with her back to Leongatha.

She said that in May and June 2023 she was also dehydrating mushrooms in her kitchen at Gibson Street. She said 'generally, I would put them into a container that I already sort of had going with Woolies mushrooms and whatnot in there. So I would just dry them and put them in a container and if there was no container, I'd start one.' She remembered putting the dehydrated mushrooms into the same container as other dried mushrooms. Erin would later deny at her trial that she'd foraged for mushrooms around the nearby Outtrim and Loch areas in April/May 2023.

In June 2023 Erin thought that her relationship with Don and Gail was 'very good' but she was a little worried there might be a 'growing distance' between her and Simon's family and that she might not have been invited to a few family gatherings. By May/June 2023 she thought she needed to be 'more proactive about that social contact, to make sure I didn't lose that connection'. Those thoughts prompted her to hold a lunch at Gibson Street on 24 June 2023. On the invitation list were Simon, his parents, their children and a friend of her son's and on the menu was shepherd's pie. While Simon didn't attend, Erin said the lunch was a hit and while Don and Gail 'really liked' the pie, Erin later thought it 'wasn't special enough'. She was also chuffed that Gail had said the garden looked 'really nice' and thought her sister Heather would 'probably like to see it'. This prompted Erin to think she'd have another lunch and invite the Wilkinsons too, but this time with an upgraded menu. She said her mother 'on really important occasions' would make a beef Wellington and so for her next lunch, 'I thought I'd do that too, I'll give it a go'. While she hadn't made the dish before, she had RecipeTin Eats to guide her, along with cooking tips from her online friends.

Erin recalled that she was at church and talking to Heather and Gail when she suggested they come to lunch and they said, 'we'd love to'. She didn't give a reason for the gathering, but when inviting Simon she foreshadowed she wanted to talk to him about 'some medical things'.

Preparation started with a visit to Woolworths Leongatha on 23 July 2023, and it would be one of a few shopping trips through to 28 July, as she assembled the menu – beef fillets, potatoes for mashing, more puff pastry (Pampas butter puff), packs of gravy, filo pastry as a substitute for the crepe in the recipe, which 'looked too hard' and pre-cut and packaged green beans. She said she ran into a problem with the beef and couldn't find the large cut, so she took pictures of beef fillet steaks in a twin pack and sent it to her online friends to ask if it was 'the right thing' and 'one or two said yes'. The glory of a whole beef Wellington was amended to individual Wellingtons or, as a few lawyers and Ian would later observe, 'pasties'.

On Friday, 28 July, Erin did her last-minute shopping and then it was into the kitchen to start her preparations. She said she read the recipe, did some 'Googling for tips on how not to stuff it up' and then salted the steaks 'to try and get some juices out of them'. Simon rang around 7 pm that night to tell her he wouldn't be coming to the lunch, and she was 'a bit hurt and I felt a bit stressed' but pressed on with getting ready.

Saturday morning around 9.30/10 am, she was back in the kitchen, making the mushroom duxelles, which required some chopping in the Thermomix, then cooking for about 45 minutes on a low heat to 'get all the water out so it won't turn your pastry soggy'. She thought the duxelles of mushrooms she'd bought from Woolworths were 'a little bland' so she added dried mushrooms she'd bought 'from the grocer' that were in her pantry. They were rehydrated with a little water 'to get the crispness out of them' then chopped and added to the duxelles. At trial Erin conceded that the dried mushrooms might have contained some she'd foraged.

Erin said she'd made six beef Wellingtons and they were out of the oven resting when the guests arrived at 12.30 pm. The lunch that followed was convivial, the food a hit and she said she ate about half of her Wellington. When her guests had departed she said there was one Wellington leftover, and quite a lot of fruit and around two-thirds of Gail's orange cake – but the latter didn't last. She said, 'I kept cleaning up the kitchen and putting everything away and I had a piece of cake and then another piece of cake and then another' until there was none left. She reckoned this eating binge made her feel sick and 'over full', so she went to the toilet and 'brought it back up again'. We're not likely to ever find out if Erin had deliberately served herself a death cap–free Wellington, or if she'd eaten some and had planned to vomit at the first possible opportunity to rid herself of the deadly mushroom before it could start its poisonous work.

Erin said after vomiting she felt better, and that later that afternoon, around 5 or 5.30ish, she was back in the bathroom where she had 'some sort of loose stool'. Loose stools notwithstanding, she took her son and his friend to his friend's home in Korumburra then, on the way home, stopped at Subway in Leongatha where she waited in the car while her son was inside. Later that night, around 10 pm she began to suffer from diarrhoea. With frequent visits to the toilet ruining any chance of sleep she took some Imodium tablets – treatment for occasional diarrhoea – and finally dozed off around 5 or 6 am.

What Erin didn't mention, and we'd only find out about after the trial, was that on the afternoon of the lunch, when the guests had gone, she'd driven to the Koonwarra tip, where she'd paid to dump some cardboard and the contents of a 120-litre bin.

Erin was up around 10 am and said she started the day with a herbal tea but was still nauseous and had diarrhoea that was 'not as bad as the early hours of the morning but it was still fairly regular'. They skipped church but not the trip to Tyabb – around 100 kilometres and bit over an hour's drive west of Leongatha – for her son's flying lesson. With her symptoms receding, and the lesson pushed back by the instructor to a little later than the original 2 pm appointment, Erin decided she was okay to make the journey.

With both her son and daughter in the car, she headed off. Erin said about half an hour into the trip nature called loudly, so she stopped and went into the bush on the roadside, attended to business, then cleaned herself up with tissues, which she put into a dog poo bag she had with her, then put that into her handbag. About 3.20 pm she stopped at a BP service station in Caldermeade, where she got rid of the dog poo bag in the toilets, and the children bought some food. This stop was captured on CCTV and Erin was wearing white trousers – something quite startling for anyone watching when the video was publicly released during the trial; it was not the most astute colour choice for someone allegedly suffering from diarrhoea and motoring along a road offering bushes rather than toilets if the need struck. In the end, the trip proved to be a dud when the instructor cancelled the lesson because of weather issues. They were close to Tyabb, turned around and motored back to Leongatha, a return trip where the only stop was at a Koo Wee Rup food van for the kids and where Erin had a coffee.

That night she had a bowl of cereal for dinner, the diarrhoea continued and she felt 'a little off in the tummy'. The diarrhoea became more vigorous during the night and around 5.30/6 am she gave up hope of getting any sleep so she got up, prepared lunches for the children, sorted their bags and around 7.20 am dropped them at the bus stop to catch the school bus.

Not long after, she said, she called Simon and told him that she thought she should go to the Leongatha Hospital to 'get some fluids'. The call, she said, was because 'I didn't want to go by myself'. Simon, however, told her he was tired, still in bed and she should drive herself, which she did, arriving at the hospital around 8 am. She saw Doctor Chris Webster and, after telling him she had 'a bit of gastro', followed him into Urgent Care. She said, 'I remember feeling a little bit unsettled because when I said my name, his reaction communicated that he knew who I was or was aware of me, like, that name triggered something for him which threw me quite a bit'. After the trial, we'd hear a lot more about the doctor's reaction to Erin.

Erin said they chatted about the source of the mushrooms she'd used for the lunch, telling him they were from Woolworths, and was 'shocked and confused' when Doctor Webster said 'we're concerned you've been exposed to death cap mushrooms'. She reckoned she'd been expecting some saline for gastro and not a chat about deadly fungi. She said she was 'overwhelmed' because she'd arrived at the hospital anticipating being there for a few hours and was now being told she faced transportation to a hospital in Melbourne. Erin said the reality of her situation caused her brain to be 'stuck' and 'it was like trying to turn a really big ship' and she told the doctor she had to go home and sort a few things first, including packing for her daughter's ballet event that afternoon, feeding the dog and lambs and making sure they were all safe and with shelter on a winter night.

According to Erin, she said she'd discussed leaving with hospital staff and agreed she'd be back in around 20–30 minutes. That trip was a bit longer, and she was back at the hospital at around 9.28 am. There she had a conversation with the staff about leftovers and was also handed a phone to direct police to where the leftovers could be found at her home.

It was a very busy morning for Erin. She also spoke with her brother-in-law Matthew, who was with Don in hospital, and the doctors wanted to know where the mushrooms came from, which is when the alleged Asian grocery purchase was given its first outing.

Her children were also on the doctor's agenda. He wanted them brought to the hospital for examination. Erin was reluctant. She recalled she was the one who wanted to get them, but there was 'pushback on that from the medical people'. On the prospect of Simon collecting them, she said, 'My first thought was, I had rung him already that morning and he wasn't prepared to drive 10 minutes to help me.' She then said she didn't think he would pick up the kids. But that was resolved with Simon agreeing to collect the children and take them to Monash Hospital, where Erin would be heading to soon.

Later that day, Erin was taken by ambulance to Monash. She recalled that the next day she was feeling better when she awoke and that the children were in the same hospital, in the paediatric wing where they'd also spent the night. Simon had spent the night close to them.

On her initial reluctance to have the children brought to the hospital, Erin said, 'It wasn't that I didn't want them to be treated, but more, the drastic step of putting them in hospital.

I wanted to understand that that was really necessary, because of their anxieties about being in hospital.' There was an alternate view though – with the assumption Erin hadn't been concerned about her children because she knew she hadn't put their lives at risk by feeding them poisoned food. While the children had eaten what Erin had billed as leftovers, she was the only one who knew if their food had been anywhere near a death cap mushroom.

Oh, what a wicked web …

13

THE INVESTIGATIONS BEGIN

Before police started their investigation, public health officials were already on the case. Doctor Conor McDermott was working as a toxicology registrar at the Austin Hospital when, on the morning of 31 July, he got a call from a female doctor at the Leongatha Hospital.

McDermott was an emergency specialist who'd also worked as a registrar in intensive care. Toxicology was a six-month placement for him. In this role he saw patients coming through the hospital's toxicology unit and consulted with people who'd called the Victorian Poisons Information Line, generally healthcare practitioners and the occasional member of the public.

The doctor who called McDermott wanted some advice on a patient, Erin Patterson. Erin was the last of five people to present with symptoms akin to those of mushroom poisoning. By that time, McDermott had been made aware of the other four cases, who were to be transferred to the

Austin. He asked about Erin and was told that the patient was stable other than having a heart rate of 140, but she looked well, and their investigations so far were unremarkable. This observation was supported by blood tests, which had returned normal results.

McDermott was told that Erin had complained of having diarrhoea for the last thirty-six hours, but that this hadn't been observed by the doctor. He said he'd questioned Erin about the mushrooms and was told she thought they'd been sourced from Woolworths in Leongatha and a Chinese food store, though there was no further detail about the shop's location. Erin's children had also eaten the beef Wellington, but not the mushrooms, which Erin had scraped off.

After consultation with his supervisor, McDermott said Erin should be transferred to Monash Hospital and started on preventative treatment. At the front of McDermott's mind was the possibility of a public health issue, so he called the doctor back to get more information about the source of the mushrooms. The phone was given to Erin, who said the button mushrooms were pre-sliced and in an unmarked or unbranded package from Leongatha Woolworths. She clarified that she had also used mushrooms from a Chinese food store in the suburb of Oakleigh, the brand unknown. She said she'd bought them in April 2023, and that they were dried. She hadn't kept the packaging for either.

McDermott conducted a Google search for Chinese food stores in Oakleigh, then asked Erin if she could remember the name of the store. She couldn't. When he offered to read out the names of those listed, she declined, saying she wouldn't be able to remember. Erin didn't offer an address, or even a rough location of the store. In investigations, sometimes a little thing like a landmark can trigger a memory. When McDermott pushed further, Erin told him the Chinese food store might have been in Mount Waverley, bringing the doctor's probing questions to an end. Time to get Victoria's health officials onto the case.

Sally Ann Atkinson is a senior public health adviser with Victoria's Department of Health. In July 2023 she managed the enterics team, responsible for gastric-type illnesses, within the department's communicable disease prevention and control team. On the afternoon of 31 July, Doctor McDermott notified Atkinson about a possible amatoxin outbreak – amatoxin is the toxic compound found in death cap mushrooms. When two or more people are possibly affected, this constitutes an outbreak.

Atkinson and her team's first task was to investigate the source of the incident to prevent others getting sick.

McDermott confirmed that five people had been at lunch on 29 July, that beef Wellington, including mushrooms, had been served, and that two children may have been there, though he didn't know if they'd eaten. He told her that four out of the five attendees experienced the onset of gastro-like symptoms between around midnight and 2 am the next day. McDermott then briefed her on what he believed to be the provenance of the mushrooms – fresh from the local Woolworths, and dried from a mysterious Asian grocer in either Mount Waverley or Oakleigh.

McDermott outlined the connections between all those affected and passed on details of the next of kin for those who were ill. He also passed on the contact information for the one person who wasn't presenting as desperately ill – a key person in the ensuing investigation and, most importantly, the person who'd prepared the lunch: Erin Patterson.

Atkinson knew that amatoxin poisoning was rare. This was the first case she'd handled, and there was a potential danger to public health if store-bought mushrooms were the cause. It was imperative to locate them and have them immediately removed from sale. To this end, she contacted the Food Safety Unit, who worked with local councils and environmental health officers and coordinated food sampling and recalls.

Erin wasn't Atkinson's first call. Instead, on 31 July she contacted Simon Patterson. She rang just before 6 pm and noted that he wasn't happy to chat – possibly, Atkinson speculated, because he wasn't sure where she was calling from. His reticence was prudent, given the imminent avalanche of media that was soon to descend upon him.

Atkinson followed up quickly with an email from her health department address, which broke the ice, and they chatted. Simon confirmed that the children were okay, and that they were at the hospital having blood tests. The conversation then moved to Erin's lunch preparations. Atkinson asked if she was the type of person who'd pick mushrooms herself, but Simon said it wasn't something he'd ever known her to do. She also asked if the group had eaten together recently, and Simon said that the last time would have been at a family function years ago. He had either forgotten the lunch his parents had been at a month before or took the question to literally mean a gathering of those exact five people.

Around 8.30 the next morning, Atkinson was on the phone to Erin, who was in hospital but said she was feeling okay. This was the first detailed discussion Erin would have about what happened, and her responses would later inform the police investigation. At this stage, it was a discussion driven by public health concerns, not potential criminality.

Erin told Atkinson that she had started to feel unwell just before midnight on 29 July – an assertion she'd come to contradict in subsequent stories – and in the early hours of the 30th experienced 'explosive diarrhoea' every twenty or thirty minutes, which continued throughout that night and the rest of Sunday, gradually abating slightly to forty-five-minute intervals. By late Sunday afternoon, she said, she'd started to feel a bit better and had eaten a bowl of cereal, which triggered a resurgence of her symptoms. Erin told Atkinson she still wasn't feeling well the next morning but got her children ready for school and onto the bus, then took herself to hospital.

Atkinson then asked for details of the lunch, with Erin confirming the menu of beef Wellington served with mashed potato and beans. She said she'd never made the dish before and had wanted to do something special. She said she'd also bought a packet of gravy that could be reheated, adding that most of the food was purchased from Woolworths in Leongatha. Of the Asian mushrooms, she reiterated what she'd told McDermott, adding that her mother in-law Gail had brought a cake, and Heather had provided a fruit platter.

With the potential public health issue at the forefront of her mind, Atkinson then focused on the source of the Asian mushrooms. Erin told her that on the day of the purchase, she'd driven around a lot, and while she couldn't specifically remember where she'd bought the mushrooms, she thought it might have been in Oakleigh, Mount Waverley or, in a new addition to her story, Clayton, all of which are in Melbourne's south-east and close to Erin's other home. When asked about her driving around, she said it had been during the

April school holidays, explaining that she would take the children to activities in the area then drive around waiting for them to finish.

Erin said the mushrooms were dried, not frozen, and that she'd stored them in a Tupperware container. When asked about the packaging, she said they'd been in a small see-through bag with a white label that didn't have a lot of writing on it and didn't, in her view, look very professional. She claimed to have opened the package not long after buying it because, Atkinson recalled, 'she had purchased it originally for a specific meal she was making, which I think was a pasta dish or something, but when she'd opened it, she thought they smelt funny ... she decided she probably wouldn't use them all, so she put the rest in a container'.

The conversation then moved to making beef Wellington. Atkinson said Erin explained that she had rehydrated the dried mushrooms, 'then chopped them up and added them to the chopped mushrooms from Woolworths'. The fillet steak was bought on the Friday night and cooked the next day. This was yet another story that would change. Contemporaneous recollections carry weight, so when the story changes as the case evolves, this can be blamed on memory or on details being tailored to suit a different version of events.

Erin also told Atkinson that the Wellingtons were individually plated and that everyone ate the same food. With no other guest able to comment, Erin was the only source.

When asked about her children, Erin said they'd gone to the movies while the adults lunched, but the next evening the children had eaten leftovers but with the pastry and mushrooms scraped off, so it was just the meat. The remaining leftovers were put in the garbage bin.

The conversation lasted about fifteen minutes.

Next, the local councils got involved, sending their officers to the local Asian grocery stores to see if there were any dried mushrooms fitting the description Erin gave, and to confirm where the leftover mushrooms from the lunch preparations had ended up. The Oakleigh, Mount Waverley and Clayton areas are home to quite a few Asian food stores that cater to the growing local Asian community.

Another question that needed a fast answer was what type of shallots had been used – spring onions or bulb shallots, or anything that could have been mistaken for shallots.

The plan was to conduct a thorough investigation to identify and eliminate any potentially harmful components of the dish. Atkinson tried to contact Erin again, but she didn't answer her mobile or respond to SMS messages.

Erin finally responded shortly after 4 pm on 1 August, explaining that she'd been in meetings at the hospital. Atkinson inquired about the children – they were okay – and said she'd try to ring again after 5 pm. But when she did, there was no answer, so she left a message. She tried again the next morning just before nine, but again, there was no answer. For someone spearheading a public health investigation, this lack of response from the key witness was frustrating – and potentially dangerous.

Around 9.30 am Atkinson texted Erin, acknowledging that she had a lot on, but saying there were questions that needed answers. She offered to email them, if Erin could provide an address. Atkinson's questions were detailed, and all targeted at isolating the likely causes and ensuring there would not be a repeat of this event.

Her SMS questions were:

1. *Can you please confirm that it was definitely only the one other time you cooked with the dried mushrooms when you first opened them? No-one else reported symptoms or issues when you consumed them?*
2. *Please advise what drinks were served at lunch.*
3. *Please confirm what kind of shallots were used in the beef wellington. Were they spring onions or the small individual shallot-type onions please?*
4. *Did you possibly use your card to purchase the mushrooms, and can you please check your bank statements for the shop? That would be amazingly helpful.*
5. *Could there possibly be any other food leftover still in the fridge? We could get council to meet your children on-site and collect for testing?*
6. *Can you look [at] the maps and think of the streets you parked on, or near, that would be helpful for the shops in Oakleigh, Mt Waverley or Clayton? We are urgently organising sampling to get started today.*
7. *Can you recall the size and type of packaging, including colour. What made you pick that brand over any others? Thanks again for your assistance and please feel free to call me back if you prefer.*

Erin didn't respond.

But Atkinson's phone did ring at 11.18 am. It was Katrina Cripps from the Child Protection Services unit of the Department of Families, Fairness and Housing. She was planning on visiting Erin's home in Gibson Street to inquire about the health and safety of the two children. Atkinson asked her to call when she was there, as Erin hadn't responded to her pressing questions.

At 1.14 pm Cripps rang Atkinson and put Erin on the phone, and they went through the questions. The drinks were water, coffee and tea served with milk from Woolworths at Leongatha, and Erin assured her that the Asian mushrooms hadn't been used in any other dishes.

In this conversation, Atkinson said Erin told her she'd planned on using them in a pasta dish but 'they smelt funny when she'd originally opened them, so decided not to use them. Erin said she thought they might be too overpowering for the meal she'd originally planned them for, and so just put them in a Tupperware container to decide what to do with them. And not use them.' She was a bit perplexed by the answer, as she thought that in their initial conversation Erin had said she'd used them in a dish.

That matter wasn't clarified, and she pressed on, confirming that it was the bulb type of shallots that had been used. Erin had also checked her bank records for April for the Asian mushroom purchase but didn't find anything. She told Atkinson that for small purchases she was likely to have used cash.

On the question of leftovers, Erin told her some fruit from the platter was the only thing left, saying Atkinson was welcome to collect it. The conversation then went back to the elusive Asian grocer, but no further revelations were forthcoming. Atkinson doubled back, asking Erin again if she had foraged the mushrooms – a point that would become very significant in Erin's police record of interview and when the case finally got to court – but Erin reiterated they had all been purchased from stores.

Atkinson's next call was to the Food Safety Unit, who were contacting Woolworths to investigate their supplies in case a food recall was required.

Later that afternoon, Atkinson messaged Erin again to get some more detail about her Woolworths purchases. Erin responded:

'I'm not sure exactly what time of day. I went a few times last week and I know I got some of the ingredients on maybe Wednesday or Thursday. I know I bought some discounted eye fillet steaks one time on one of those two days and then I went back on either Thursday or Friday and bought a couple more but they weren't discounted, just normal price. And I bought the rest of the ingredients at one of those shopping trips. I often go daily or every second day to pick up a bag or two and get what I need as I go so it's hard to pinpoint an exact day I bought this.'

This conversation only added to Atkinson's confusion, as she'd thought Erin had done her shopping on the Friday, the day before the lunch.

Atkinson sent Erin some photos of ziplock bags to try and get an idea of the packaging the Asian mushrooms had been in. Council officers had found that most of the Asian food stores had mushrooms in fairly distinctive packaging, and only one store had bags of mushrooms that may fit the bill. Those photos were forwarded to Erin, who said the mushrooms she'd bought weren't like the shiitakes shown but instead were sliced and half the size, the colour of a button mushroom and similar-looking to porcini. The packaging, however, was the same.

The next morning, 3 August, Erin and Atkinson were again messaging, and this time the kitchen was the focus. Erin had chopped the Woolworths mushrooms in her food processor, and rehydrated the dried mushrooms before slicing them by hand. She'd fried the shallots and garlic in oil, then added the mushrooms and cooked the mixture until it was almost a paste. She said she then coated the individual beef portions in the mushroom paste, using it all up, and then wrapped them in puff pastry. The pastry was Pampas brand, and Erin recalled it may have been a combination of basic and their pricier butter puff – she'd had some already in the deep freeze and bought more on her shopping trip.

The Department of Health investigation ended on 11 August, and a final report on the incident was prepared. The report found: 'Although initial information suggested amatoxin-containing mushrooms may have been purchased from an Asian grocer and used in the meal, the epidemiological and environmental investigation established that it was highly unlikely that the commercial mushrooms supply chain was contaminated with amatoxin-containing mushrooms.'

Atkinson said the report was partly informed by the fact that death cap mushrooms prefer to grow near oak trees and not in commercial mushroom-growing media. The investigators established that mushrooms sold by Woolworths came from large commercial growers and there was no evidence of tampering. The report also zeroed in on the mushrooms at the lunch as the cause. Ultimately, the risk to public health was deemed to be very low, but the resources expended to investigate Erin's fake story were significant.

14

THE POLICE ARRIVE

Any suspicious or sudden death, and particularly one involving previously healthy people, prompts a police investigation. A competent investigation is not unlike a large jigsaw puzzle, with each piece found, assessed and either discarded or retained. The evidence drives the investigation forward, with police ever mindful that their actions will later be scrutinised in court, by families and their advocates, and by the media.

For a police officer, one phone call, email, radio message or visit from a senior officer looking troubled can bring dramatic news that may change their career, and sometimes their life, forever. And almost every time, that news means other people's lives have already changed dramatically – often due to one exceptional, unpredicted and deeply sad incident.

The Victoria Police Homicide Squad entered the investigation on 1 August 2023. Up to that point, local police had been involved, along with specialists from Victoria Health, who were treating the aftermath of the lunch as a possible mass food poisoning event.

Detective Senior Constable Darren Lomax of the Bass Coast Criminal Investigation Unit notified the homicide squad of the mass food poisoning. At that point, no-one had died, so the criteria hadn't been met for homicide to be involved, but it was a judicious decision to bring the case to their attention. The next day, Leading Detective Senior Constable Stephen Eppingstall of the homicide squad was told that the cause of the poisoning was likely to be death cap mushrooms. At that point, alarm bells started to ring.

On 3 August, Eppingstall and his colleagues travelled to Wonthaggi Police Station where they were briefed by Lomax. They were told that at least one of the lunch guests was unlikely to survive, and that the hospital had expressed concerns that Erin Patterson might not have been as unwell as her four lunch guests.

Eppingstall is a big bloke, at 188 centimetres tall, broad-shouldered and with a build that suggests he's not somebody to be messed with. He's a reservist in the Australian Defence Force, and has over fifteen years of policing experience. He was a safe pair of hands for a case set to land squarely in the media spotlight, and one that could easily go pear-shaped if not deftly handled.

For the team, the goal was to gather as much information about the events leading up to the lunch as quickly as possible. They needed to investigate the movements of all those involved – not only where they'd been but what they'd eaten. While police are careful to avoid the cardinal investigative sin of confirmation bias – that is, searching for or giving weight to evidence that confirms a preconception – Erin was quite reasonably the prime suspect.

The next day, the team assembled at 7.30 am and received the grim news that Heather Wilkinson had died. This was now potentially a murder case.

Investigations like this involve long hours and little sleep. One of the first tasks was to get hold of as much documentary evidence as possible – what was once called a paper trail but is now substantially electronic – to give a backbone to the investigation. This painstaking task fell to Senior Constable Meg Crawford, the tactical intelligence officer, who got an early hit as she trawled through Erin's bank records. It's often a small thing that expands into key evidence, and these can take days to find, but in this case, the 'eureka' moment happened on day one.

Crawford discovered a transaction that took place at 11.29 on the morning of 2 August 2023, just hours after Erin's discharge from the Monash Medical Centre, with an organisation called the Dasma Group. Further investigation revealed that Dasma was a waste management organisation that operated the Koonwarra Transfer Station – more colloquially known as the tip – about ten kilometres from Leongatha. Investigators went straight to the tip to see if the operators had any CCTV for the morning of 2 August – and they did.

CCTV, along with a suspect's internet browsing history, is a common and persuasive tool in criminal investigation. The dubious award of most filmed murder in history can be claimed by Roger Rogerson, the former New South Wales police detective who, along with former detective Glen McNamara, murdered drug dealer Jamie Gao in Sydney in 2014. Their exploits, from the rendezvous with Gao to preparations for disposing of his body, were recorded on a slew of CCTV cameras. You'd think they'd have known better – a comment that could also be applied to a true crime afficionado like Erin Patterson. Like with Rogerson and McNamara, CCTV was one of a few things Erin overlooked, along with her internet search history.

The CCTV from the tip showed Erin Patterson pulling up outside a green shed at the transfer station in her distinctive red car. She then opened the boot and removed an item, which she placed in an e-waste bin. The item was removed by workers at the tip and handed to police.

Police found that the item – a Sunbeam Food Lab dehydrator – had been bought by Erin on 28 April 2023 at 12.17 pm from Hartley Wells Betta Home Living in Leongatha for $229.

The dehydrator was inspected not only to identify if it had been used to dehydrate mushrooms, but also to check for fingerprints and DNA on the exterior of the device, to confirm that this was Erin's dehydrator.

While investigators were buoyed by their progress, the day ended on a deeply sad note as they received news of the death of Gail Patterson. This tragedy continued to escalate, and the investigation became shrouded in a shadow of grief and horror.

The police also knew that with people being interviewed, and potentially vital evidence found, they needed to act quickly, just in case the media got a whiff. So, the next morning, 5 August, they were at Erin's home at around 11.40 am armed with a search warrant. The warrant indicated that police would be searching for items including mobile phones and communications devices, electronic storage, food waste, including mushrooms and food packaging.

To reach the house, police had to navigate through the media pack, who'd been camped out beside the house for the previous few days, hoping for a glimpse of Erin, a soundbite or a doorstop interview. At this stage two people had tragically died and two others were perilously ill following a family gathering where beef Wellington was served. The cause was still not known but speculation was growing – a public health issue or something more sinister? The story had spiked the interest of media around the world and they wanted more.

The late morning arrival was quite civilised, and reflected the calm and professional manner in which the investigation was being conducted – as opposed to an aggressive investigation, with police arriving at dawn when the targets are often asleep. But civilised or aggressive, police don't make an appointment to execute a search warrant.

The search team of five knocked on the door. When Erin answered, Detective Sergeant Luke Farrell introduced himself and explained the purpose of their visit. She was also told that at this point Heather and Gail had died. Erin, according to police, looked surprised.

During a search, the primary resident at the place being searched remains with an officer while others go about their task. In this instance, Erin remained with Eppingstall, with a female officer on hand to escort her to the toilet if required. The children, who were also at home, spent most of the time in their rooms. Erin was only permitted to use her mobile phone under police supervision to get legal advice. Eppingstall later commented that one of the prime objectives in searching Erin's home was to seize all electronic devices, including mobile phones, tablets, computers and storage devices such as USBs and SD cards.

In addition to the electronics found and seized, police also found a manual for a Sunbeam dehydrator and a copy of the RecipeTin Eats *Dinner* cookbook. Farrell thumbed through the book and found a recipe for beef Wellington, noting it was 'splattered with cooking liquids'. In the fridge he found the remains of a fruit plate and a jug containing what he thought was gravy. In a drawer, they found a number of plates, including four grey-coloured dinner plates and one smaller plate that wasn't a match for the others.

Police also found Erin's library of over 400 books, a chunk of which were true crime, though these were not individually catalogued.

While the other officers conducted the search, Erin and Eppingstall chatted. Among the topics of conversation was the cookbook they'd found on the kitchen bench. Eppingstall recalled it was 'a general discussion, but beef Wellington came up'. Erin went on to tell him that she'd used the book, and that the recipe for the dish was around page 250. Eppingstall checked, and noted that the recipe was on page 252.

During the search, Erin asked to use her phone to call a lawyer. The police allowed her to do so, but with Eppingstall standing nearby. At 3.29 pm, with her calls complete and the search at an end, Farrell asked Erin to hand over her mobile. She volunteered her PIN when asked.

But the day didn't end there. Erin was taken to the Wonthaggi Police Station to be formally interviewed.

Meanwhile, Luke Farrell and colleagues headed to Erin's other property at Lyons Street, Mount Waverley to execute another search warrant. They arrived just before 5.30 pm and, like at Gibson Street, were hunting for mushrooms, food packaging and electronic devices. There was no-one at the property, and after a look around revealed nothing of interest, the search ended at 5.40 pm.

Back at Wonthaggi, the interview with Erin had been a formal one, conducted in the knowledge that if Patterson was later arrested it would form a crucial piece of evidence. It would also play a vital part in the early stages of the investigation. Quite simply, they were giving Erin the opportunity to tell her story and, importantly, to make comments that could be tested as facts or lies.

Conducting the interview were Eppingstall and his colleague, Detective David Martin-Alcaide. Eppingstall, as the senior officer, would be asking the questions, with his colleague there for corroboration. The interview would be recorded on a DVD, with a copy provided to Erin at the end.

After establishing that Erin was comfortable and had been provided with water, the interview began formally at 4.41 pm. After announcing their names for the record, Eppingstall said, 'Erin, I intend to interview you today in relation to the death of two people, being Gail Patterson and Heather Wilkinson. Before continuing, I must inform you that you do not have to say or do anything, but anything you say or do is being recorded and may be used in evidence in court.'

After Erin said she understood, Eppingstall continued. 'I must also inform you of the following rights. You may communicate with or attempt to communicate with a friend or relative to tell that person of your whereabouts. You may communicate with or attempt to communicate with a legal practitioner. If you're not an Australian citizen or permanent resident here in Australia you may communicate with or attempt to communicate with the consular office of the country of which you are a citizen.' This was the Victorian version of the Miranda warning we see in American crime shows and something occasionally requested by those arrested in Australia – making it clear they've been watching too much television.

Erin declined to call anyone, including a lawyer. With the formalities done, the interview got underway. After establishing some basic details, they quickly moved to the purpose of the interview: to discuss Heather's and Gail's deaths, noting that their livers had failed, and the illness that beset her luncheon guests.

Don, Eppingstall said, had undergone a liver transplant overnight but his condition remained 'extremely critical'. What they didn't know at the time of the interview was Don's condition was deteriorating and he would die at 11.30 pm that night, bringing the death toll from Erin's lunch to three. Eppingstall was investigating a tragedy that was either a dreadful accident or potentially mass murder.

Erin's responses so far had been monosyllabic, extending to 'yeah' and 'okay'. When asked if she understood why she was being interviewed, she engaged further, saying, 'Yes, I do. But I'm sure you understand too that, like, I've never been in a situation like this before, and I've been very, very helpful with the Health Department through the week because I wanted to help that side of things as much as possible because I do want to know what happened. So I've given them as much information as they've asked for and offered up all the food and all the information about where the food came from.'

Eppingstall told her that Ian Wilkinson's health was also deteriorating, and expressed his curiosity that Erin wasn't similarly ill, an observation that yielded an 'mm' in response, and nothing else.

Eppingstall was thorough and measured as he took Erin through the items they'd found in the search at Gibson Street, including the recipe book she'd used to make the beef Wellingtons and the paucity of any foods from either Asian or Indian grocers. In some cases, what you don't find can be as useful as what you do find. Erin responded, 'Did you look in my fridge? I've got a lot of Asian cooking stuff in my fridge.'

When asked if they'd find Asian foods at the Mount Waverley house, she said she'd had a big clean-out there as a prelude to selling the property. She said she'd originally bought the house because of its proximity to her alma mater, Monash University, but her son had decided on a career as a pilot so proximity to the university was 'of no use'. With her children now going to school further away, she'd been thinking of buying something nearby.

At that point, Eppingstall changed tack sharply, shifting his focus to the mushrooms and their origins. Erin denied being a forager, said she had never been a forager and had no interest in preserving or dehydrating food. The first big lie was now on record. Eppingstall then asked about the reasons for the lunch, and Erin explained she had no family other than Simon's, saying they were the only support she had left.

'They've always been really good to me and I want to maintain those relationships with them in spite of what's happened with Simon. I love them a lot. They've always been really good to me, and they always said to me that they would support me with love and emotional support even though Simon and I were separated and I really appreciated that because both my parents are gone. My grandparents are all gone. They're the only family I've got.' She added, 'And they're the only grandparents that my children have and I want them to stay in my kids' lives.'

Erin put the boot into her husband, perhaps in an attempt to distract the police from their obvious suspicions. 'I think Simon hated that I still had a relationship with his parents, but I love them.' For detectives investigating a murder or possible murder, alarm bells ring at the first whiff of discord in family relationships. When it comes to crimes in a family setting, the culprit is usually someone known to the victim(s).

While Erin was elaborating, Eppingstall was doing what all good interviewers do, letting his quarry do the talking. He offered minimal interference, little more than a head nod and the occasional 'yeah'.

He moved on to her brief stay at Leongatha Hospital on the Monday after the lunch. Erin confirmed she was only there for five minutes, and had only gone because she'd felt dehydrated and needed a few bags of saline. Eppingstall did not ask why she thought the hospital did takeaway intravenous drips.

She continued, saying that hospital staff had wanted to admit her and send her to Melbourne. She had resisted, noting that she had animals at home, and 'children who have multiple after-school activities, you can't just be told to drop everything and you're off to Melbourne overnight, so I had to go home and feed the animals and pack my daughter's ballet bag'. All the hallmarks of a responsible parent, but unusual thinking for someone whose lunch guests were, at that time, unwell.

Erin said she then left the hospital and returned later. She told Eppingstall that on her return she needed to go to the toilet and mentioned to a hospital staffer – she wasn't sure if she was a nurse – that she had diarrhoea. On emerging from the toilet, Doctor Chris Webster was waiting. 'Don't worry about me,' she told him, 'I'm just a gastro case, I'm not urgent obviously.'

Webster, according to Erin, asked her name, and when she told him, he allegedly said they'd been expecting her because her lunch guests were all sick. As Erin explained to Eppingstall and his colleague, Webster said, 'We've got a concern they've eaten death cap mushrooms.' She said, 'What?' and Webster confirmed his statement, then began questioning Erin about the menu. She recalled they'd attached her to a drip and a female doctor called Foote told her they wanted to put her on 'protective medicine' for her liver. With this done, Erin said she'd been taken by ambulance to a hospital in Melbourne, where she remained until the following day.

At this point, Eppingstall became talkative, telling Erin for 'full disclosure' that they'd obtained warrants for her medical records, then he quickly changed the subject back to the search of her home, leaving her ruminating about what those records might reveal.

He showed her the tape of the search, starting with the discovery of the dehydrator instruction manual. When asked, she denied owning a dehydrator, adding, 'I've got manuals for lots of stuff I've collected over the years. I've had all sorts of appliances and I just keep them all.' When pressed, she said she might have owned one years ago, then added, 'Like, when I first got the Thermomix I got really excited about, like, making everything from scratch,' and 'I could've had something like that.'

Erin was doing a good job of digging a hole to fall into. Despite her years of true crime enthusiasm, evidently she hadn't worked out that capable investigators mainly ask questions to which they already know the answers.

Eppingstall then talked Erin through the rest of their findings: the gravy in what they called the butler's pantry, the phones, computers and tablets they had located, and so on. In establishing this, they got Erin to agree to what had been found and taken for examination.

As we'd find out later, police would suspect her of having another phone, but in this interview they hadn't asked if there were other devices and Erin hadn't volunteered this information.

With the end of the interview looming, Eppingstall asked about an earlier police visit at Gibson Street, on 31 July, for what he said was a welfare check. Erin had been in hospital at the time, and Eppingstall noted her assistance when they rang her, giving them the PIN code to open the front gate and directing them to a bin, where they found and seized some lunch leftovers.

Without being asked directly, Erin volunteered that 'my kids ate that meal, but there was stuff left over and it went straight in the bin'. She informed Eppingstall that she'd also told hospital staff, when the issue of food poisoning arose, that there were leftovers in the bin, saying 'I'll go and get them if you want'. That invitation was politely declined and instead the police collected them.

The interview concluded at 5.30 pm. Eppingstall had established that Erin wasn't telling the truth, but getting the evidence they needed to establish 'reasonable cause to suspect', which is the entry-level threshold to justify an arrest, would take more work.

When the video of that interview was released to the media in August 2025, criminologist Doctor Xanthé Mallett commented about Erin, 'she was calm, she definitely thought she had the measure of the police. She chose not to have a lawyer. She showed no sympathy, empathy towards two people she'd found out had died. It really spoke to her mindset literally days after the murder.' Criminal psychologist Tim Watson-Munro had a similar view and said, 'what struck me at the time was her complete lack of affect. There was nothing there – two people you knew and professed to love. Zero, deadpan affect, nothing. This was a police interview that she'd probably role-played in her head many times before, in anticipation of being wheeled in. She stuck to her script, thought she was in control, but the police – clever and experienced – got her off balance.'

What Erin thought at that point will forever remain a mystery, but she must have realised she'd found herself in her own true crime show – one where the plot was still unfolding. She'd gone from obsessed spectator and commentator to taking centre stage in the drama she'd created. Was Erin Patterson like the arsonist who joins a fire brigade?

15

THINK OF THE KIDS

Katrina Cripps, the child protection worker who'd helped Atkinson reconnect with Erin, had been drawn into the investigation after her organisation was told, by a report to their after-hours service on 31 July, that Erin and Simon's children were both at Monash Children's Hospital. Cripps spoke to police on the morning of Tuesday, 1 August, and she and colleague Naomi Schroder had spoken to Simon and Erin. Cripps and her colleagues made copious and contemporaneous notes of their observations and conversations.

For the family, this was a time of trauma beyond comprehension. The involvement of child protection, while their work is essential, is one of the greatest nightmares imaginable for responsible and capable parents. However, the imperative was to make sure the children were safe, well cared for and supported emotionally. Their family had been battered, and over the next few days it would go on to be utterly devastated.

Erin gave Cripps a thumbnail sketch of their family life, including the 2015 separation and custody arrangements. She was quick to allege that Simon was having some problems with the children, with Cripps recalling, 'The children had started to talk to her and ask questions about not wanting to go to Simon's for the weekend and wanting to stay home. They talked about Dad yelling at them and him sleeping a lot on the weekend, so they weren't really wanting to go.'

When the conversation moved on to child support, Erin told Cripps that it changed her relationship with Simon. Erin said he'd been 'mean' but never 'nasty'.

Moving on to the family relationship, Erin maintained the position that she'd use in her public-facing comments over the following months, and then years, insisting Don and Gail had been like the parents she hadn't had. Cripps recalled Erin saying 'they'd always treated her like a daughter-in-law, that she cared and loved them very much and felt very supported by them but that relationship had also changed recently as well. She felt isolated from them.' Erin laid the blame for that isolation squarely at Simon's feet.

Erin then upped the ante, telling them that Simon could be controlling and emotionally abusive, and that he would often stir self-doubt by questioning her skills as a parent and a mother. It was a hook to contemporary media stories on coercive control, and one that was echoed during Erin's trial, delivered to the court by one of Erin's online friends, leaving Simon unable to tell his story or speak in his defence.

The conversation then turned to money, with Erin telling Cripps she'd shared half of her inheritance from her grandmother with Simon at the time of their separation because she'd thought it was the done thing. Cripps also inquired about prior social engagements, and Erin mentioned she'd had Don and Gail to lunch at Gibson Street in late June 2023. The children had also been there. Erin said she'd been missing Don and Gail and wanted to spend time with them and reconnect. Cripps then asked her about the lunch on 29 July. Erin told her she'd seen Don and Gail at church the week before and asked them to come around. She said she'd invited Heather and Ian as well because she had a medical issue and wanted their advice.

Erin was then asked about the menu, and again explained that she'd bought fresh mushrooms from Woolworths and dried from an Asian grocer. Their differing responsibilities meant Cripps didn't delve into the detail as Atkinson would later, but in their discussions Erin told Cripps she'd only eaten half of her Wellington and recalled that Gail had also left half of hers, which Don had eaten. She thought Heather and Ian had finished theirs. Cripps noted, 'She said that she had dished up all the plates, that everyone was able to – everyone came and chose their own. She took one that was leftover and put two aside for the children.'

This would make for a small but vital difference to the recollection of the only surviving guest, Ian Wilkinson.

Curiously, Erin told Cripps that she'd begun to have 'loose bowel movements' in the evening a few hours after the lunch guests had left. She said that she'd taken her son's friend home and stopped so her son could go into a supermarket. Later evidence would reveal the 'supermarket' to be a Subway, and the event was caught on CCTV.

Erin stayed in the car, and told Cripps she did so because she feared she might have an accident, and hoped sitting down may help prevent that unpleasant occurrence. Cripps wasn't medically trained or alert to the timelines of food poisoning, so Erin claiming to have experienced symptoms within hours of finishing lunch didn't raise any questions in her mind.

Erin told Cripps she'd still felt unwell the next morning. Discussions then covered what the lunch participants had eaten and how much, whether the children were unwell, and the logistics of getting them to hospital for a check-up.

Cripps decided it was appropriate that the children remain with Erin, but organised a home visit the next day to assess the home environment, which was routine in child protection investigations.

Cripps was at Gibson Street on 2 August during Erin's conversation with Atkinson, which was on speaker phone. When the call was over, Cripps and Erin chatted about family support, with Erin saying she thought she'd lost it all. What wasn't clear was the chronology of the loss – post lunch or in the months leading up to it. The subject of bowel movements also returned, with Erin confirming she had begun experiencing diarrhoea before she dropped her son's friend home on the Saturday evening.

At this point, there was no-one to contradict or disagree with her version of events.

In the background, Doctor Dimitri Gerostamoulos, head of forensic science and chief toxicologist at the Victorian Institute of Forensic Medicine, and his colleagues were analysing samples taken from all the lunch attendees, as well as the two children. Doctor Gerostamoulos is one of the nation's most experienced forensic toxicologists, with over thirty years' experience in the field. In his expert opinion, the lethal dose of amatoxins for a 70-kilogram human is about 50 grams, though that depends on the species of plant and how much of the toxin is in the sample. Death cap mushrooms contain less than ten per cent amatoxin per 100 grams.

Testing, unsurprisingly, hasn't been carried out on humans, but has been conducted on rats, mice and dogs. As the doctor observed, 'They're very toxic compounds.' Survival of amatoxin consumption comes down to a mixture of the person's general health, how much they've eaten and how their body responds to the poison.

Doctor David Lovelock, whose PhD focused on 'fungal-like organisms', and colleagues were investigating two samples in two ziplock bags that they believed was beef Wellington. Lovelock said the contents were 'distorted' and it was hard to visually work out what was mushroom and what wasn't. These samples arrived on 2 August and later, on 8 August, they received a jug of gravy and a fruit platter. But that wasn't all of it, and, on 11 August, they received seven tubes each containing a small amount of debris or material collected from a dehydrator. Police wanted all the samples tested for mushroom species. While the Wellington samples were free of deadly mushrooms, the samples from the dehydrator weren't.

16

ERIN'S FIRST CLOSE-UP

John Ferguson of *The Australian* had a brief chat with Erin just days after the lunch. In a piece published on 8 August 2025, he wrote she was standing on the deck of her Gibson Street home 'in the sharp winter light, her black labrador is wagging its tail, the only sign of peace in her deeply troubled life'. Erin was 'frustrated. Nasty angry'. She told him, 'I've been painted as an evil witch, and the media is making it impossible for me to live in this town.'

But the media moment that would take her face around the world came just two days after the search of the house and interview by police. On 7 August Erin Patterson drove her red SUV into the driveway at Gibson Street, cutting through the media pack camped outside. As soon as the gate opened, the media swarmed inside, seizing the opportunity they'd been waiting days for. Their efforts were rewarded – rather than hasten into the house, Erin decided to speak.

Surrounded by journalists, camera crews, still photographers and people wielding smartphones, all jostling for a clear shot of the deadly lunch cook, Erin spoke. There were tears, there was what appeared to be candour and, to the cynical, an ample amount of calculation. Was Erin poleaxed by the terrible events that had occurred, and thus so rattled she felt compelled to speak? Or was she speaking first in an attempt to set the narrative? At this stage, the police and health authorities remained tight-lipped.

Standing her ground beside her car, Erin said, 'It's a tragedy what has happened. I'm so devastated by the loss of Don and ... Don is still in hospital. The loss of Ian and Heather and Gail, who are some of the best people I've ever met. Gail is like, Gail is like the mum I didn't have because my mum passed away four years ago and Gail has never been anything but good and kind to me. And Ian and Heather were some of the best people I'd ever met, they never did anything wrong to me and I'm so devastated about what's happened. And the loss to the community and to the families and to my own children who've lost a grandmother.'

She went on, 'What I can tell you is that I just can't fathom what has happened, I just can't fathom, that Ian and Heather have lost their lives and Gail has lost her life and Don is still in hospital and I pray, I pray that he pulls through because my children love him.'

It was a speech well balanced with emotion, tears and the occasional pause, but were those tears genuine or manufactured?

Then came the questions, hard and fast, from the pack. One journalist said, 'You must be pretty shaken up by this as well.' Erin responded swiftly, saying, 'I'm devastated. I loved them and I can't believe that this has happened. And I'm so sorry that they have lost their lives … I just can't believe it.'

Her moment in the spotlight came to an abrupt end when a journalist asked about mushrooms, at which point she pulled a Woolworths bag out of the car and said, 'Just leave me alone!'

It isn't uncommon for someone in the media pack to go for the big grab as the subject tries to get away. As Erin headed inside, someone shouted, 'You're a suspect,' to which she agreed and said, 'Yes, I didn't do anything, I love them and I'm devastated they're gone and I hope with every fibre of my being that Don pulls through.'

One notable problem here was that by the time of this tear-soaked proclamation, Don, the man Erin was so close to, who she loved, respected and who had a special relationship with his grandson, had been dead for a couple of days. He was not in hospital fighting for his life as she claimed. Ian, however, was still in hospital, enduring what would be a Herculean battle, both for him and the team of medical experts trying to save him. Devastated she might have been, but the error was perplexing.

Be that as it may, the media had their grabs and Erin had experienced her first public brush with what was soon to become infamy. It was clear they had no intention of getting out of her face, so instead she got out of theirs. With the children in the care of Simon and his family, Erin drove to Healesville, about 60 kilometres north-east of Melbourne, where she stayed with one of her Facebook friends, Alison Rose Prior, who Erin would later grant power of attorney. This was the first time the pair had met in person, and Alison would go on to support Erin throughout the subsequent investigation and trial.

In yet another bizarre moment in this bizarre case, on Friday, 11 August, Erin thrust herself back onto centre stage by sending an unsolicited written statement to Victoria Police. In a typical quirk of the media, a copy also landed with the ABC not long after.

On 14 August 2023 the ABC's Dan Oakes, an investigative reporter, published an article that canvassed Erin's version of events. He wrote that she had said: '*I am now wanting to clear up the record because I have become extremely stressed and overwhelmed by the deaths of my loved ones. I am hoping this statement might help in some way. I believe if people understood the background more, they would not be so quick to rush to judgement.*'

Having cast herself as the unlikely villain yet again, and in counterpoint to police statements saying that while she was a suspect, they were keeping an open mind, she went on: '*I am now devastated to think that these mushrooms may have contributed to the illness suffered by my loved ones. I really want to repeat that I had absolutely no reason to hurt these people whom I loved.*' This statement would form the heart of her trial defence.

In the statement she said she'd found the police interview both 'terrifying' and 'anxiety provoking', and in hindsight regretted the occasional 'no comment' she'd given, saying that was based on advice she'd received. She wrote, '*I now very much regret not answering some questions following this advice given the nightmare this process has become.*' Interestingly, in the edited transcript of the police interview, the words 'no comment' do not appear.

She went on to clarify that her children had been at the movies, not at lunch, that they'd eaten leftovers, with the mushrooms scraped off, the next day, and that the Asian mushrooms had been purchased months before. Then there was the dehydrator, about which she said she'd panicked as the drama swelled and dumped it at the tip.

Erin concluded her statement by writing that Simon had been invited to lunch but had declined the day before, and noting that she'd been close with his parents. She wrote, '*I had been close with Simon's parents for a long period of time. Our relationship had continued in a fairly amicable way after I finished the relationship with their son Simon. Our relationship was affected to some degree by seeing them less after my marriage breakdown with Simon however I have never felt differently toward his parents. I had a deep love and respect for Simon's parents and had encouraged my children to spend time with their grandparents as I believed they were exceptional role models.*'

Erin also spoke of caring for Simon after what the ABC described as a 'severe stomach illness unrelated to the current incident', and 'reluctantly nursed him after his hospital discharge and informed him she did not wish to reconcile'. She also indicated a readiness to cooperate with police as the investigation progressed, 'including the possibility of a re-interview'.

Simon, who'd hired a professional media representative by this stage, declined to comment. Simon later said an anti-public relations adviser was a more accurate description because, with the recent deaths of people he loved and the massive media interest, he wanted to avoid or 'minimise the impact of media on his grieving family and especially his kids'.

Following all this, a police spokesperson said there were no updates on the case. 'Beyond that, we are not commenting on specific details of the case or what actions police will undertake as part of the investigation.'

Erin had the last word in this flurry of interest, giving a quick comment to a journalist from *The Australian* on 16 August: 'I lost my parents-in-law, my children lost their grandparents'. She went on to repeat the line she'd used before, 'I've been painted as an evil witch. And the media is making it impossible for me to live in this town. I can't have friends over.' This was an interesting declaration from someone without many face-to-face friends, and someone not known for their hospitality.

Erin still had control of the narrative, but her statement had given the police more leads to follow, more details to either confirm or refute – things that form the building blocks of a strong circumstantial case.

At this point in their investigation, while they had a compelling suspect, the police were still keeping an open mind.

Meanwhile, Erin had made the sensible decision to instruct one of Australia's most capable criminal lawyers, Bill Doogue, to act for her. By late August, with the media packs finally giving up on what had become a futile vigil in Gibson Street, Erin returned to Leongatha. When she was spotted by a journalist from *The Australian*, she said, 'My lawyer has told me not to talk to you.' Given her earlier outings, both to media and police, this was wise counsel.

But others were commenting, and often. Plenty of Erin's Facebook friends and former colleagues, along with numerous experts and online crime afficionados were feeding the voracious media beast.

And on 16 August, the Australian Mushroom Growers Association also joined the fray, saying it was 'absolutely impossible' for a commercial grower to produce poisonous fungi.

17

FORENSIC SCIENCE

The basics of criminal investigation haven't changed greatly over the decades, but the science that supports them certainly has. And in the case of the Leongatha murders, contemporary science was poised to add some substance to the growing suspicion that Erin Patterson was a killer. One of the keys to an investigation, aside from chronology, is geography, and electronics like mobile phones and computers are the richest of sources. Not only do they contain information like messages, emails and search details, but they also hold times, dates and places. In addition, the mobile phone tower a SIM card engages with reveals its location, thus enabling investigators to track, with a reasonable degree of accuracy, a person's movements.

But it's not just a matter of uncovering some useful evidence. Like any other facet of a criminal case, that evidence needs to be obtained ethically and legally. In addition, the science used must be able to be explained in terms an average person can grasp, and its credibility established.

The first major forensic investigative task in a murder investigation lies in the hands of the forensic pathologist. One of the fundamentals is to establish how the person died and the likelihood of that death being caused by foul play. On 4 August, Doctor Michael Duffy performed the autopsy on Heather Wilkinson. He found extensive death of her liver cells and tissues – liver necrosis – along with damage to her small and large bowel, described as mucosal toxicity necrosis. While he didn't find either alpha or beta amanitin – the highly toxic component of death caps – in blood, hair, urine or liver samples, his autopsy findings were consistent with poisoning by death cap mushrooms. The cause of death was multi-organ failure complicating liver failure, with the pathologist noting that the cause of the liver failure couldn't be identified at autopsy, but it was 'compatible' with 'amatoxin toxicity' from eating death cap mushrooms.

Doctor Brian Beer performed the autopsy on Gail Patterson on 5 August, and his findings were similar to those of Doctor Duffy: acute liver failure and multi-organ failure as a cause of death. Again, no finding of alpha or beta amanitin, but the findings were again compatible with the consequences of eating death cap mushrooms.

The last autopsy was that of Don Patterson, which was conducted by Doctor Beer on 8 August. Don had undergone a liver transplant in an attempt to save his life. Don was the only one of the three who had a chance of being saved through this procedure. Doctor Beer found acute failure of the transplanted liver, and similar damage to the bowel as found in Gail and Heather, all resulting in multi-organ failure. However, urine samples taken while Don was still alive revealed traces of both alpha and beta amanitin.

Don died from primary liver necrosis, transplant liver acute failure, multi-organ failure and amanita phalloides toxicity from the alpha-amanitin and beta-amanitin toxins. In other words, death by death cap.

Meanwhile, the cyber sleuths were hard at work on the various pieces of computer and phone hardware that had been seized during the search of Erin's Gibson Street home.

One new and well-used tool of investigators is a person's internet search history. In pre-internet days, the diligent investigator may have looked at a person's library borrowing history, or searched their diaries and any other documentation they could find in the hope of discovering something relevant. The internet, and specifically search histories, have streamlined that process and delivered a bounty of leads for the detectives. It's where old-fashioned shoe leather meets contemporary technology.

It's rather strange how many technically literate individuals forget that their search history is recoverable. Sef Gonzales, who killed his mother, father and sister in Sydney in 2001, formed his homicidal plans by researching the poison ricin online, then ordering castor oil seeds, which are the raw materials, from an online supplier. When the attempt on his mother made her unwell but didn't kill her, he moved to Plan B, using a baseball bat and kitchen knives. They were callous, brutal killings. Detectives had been sceptical about his story from day one, but when they recovered his deleted internet search history that outlined his search for poisons, they had proof of his premeditation and a key plank in the investigation that led to his arrest, conviction and imprisonment. Sef was bright and had planned his attack, his alibi and the performance he'd give for police and the media. But like any narcissist, he lacked the ability to critically review his plans.

There are similarities with Erin Patterson, who was bright, had an active online presence and a penchant for true crime, as well as some intriguing interests reflected in her search history. But as police would soon discover, while her interest in true crime might have taught her how to thwart online sleuths, she wasn't thorough.

The digital forensics team used a variety of software tools to delve deep into the seized devices, which included a Cooler Master computer and storage devices, a Samsung tablet, and mobile phones. Broadly, the searches used key words 'death cap', 'death cap mushrooms', 'mushrooms' and poisoning.

The team found that a Samsung phone seized by police had nothing of note on it at all, which prompted them to wonder why. Digging deeper, they discovered that the phone had undergone what was described as a factory reset, in which the phone is taken back to its initial settings – basically as it was when it came out of the box – a couple of times in the days following the lunch. The reset effectively wipes the phone's contents, and they can't be recovered.

Investigators found that a factory reset had been done on four separate occasions. The first was on 12 February 2023, and the second on 2 August, the day after Erin had left the hospital. That reset had been performed at 11.09 am, about 20 minutes before she dumped the dehydrator at the tip.

The third reset was on 5 August at around 1.20 pm – this prompted a few raised eyebrows, as the timing coincided with the execution of the search warrant, prompting Eppingstall's recollection of Erin making a call.

The final factory reset was done at 5.16 am the following day, while the phone was in police custody, safely locked in Detective Eppingstall's locker at the homicide squad office in Melbourne. This last reset was done remotely.

On the Samsung tablet they found a series of photographs. One was of a dehydrator, which was the same as the one police had recovered from the Koonwarra Transfer Station. The photo had last been modified on 30 April 2023, and as police had evidence of purchase two days before that, the chronology was clear.

The next photo was of dehydrated mushroom slices laid out on the plastic trays of the dehydrator on the kitchen bench at Gibson Street. Then came a photo of what looked like ordinary field mushrooms on a kitchen scale on the bench, with the scale registering a weight of 490.5 grams. This picture had last been modified on 4 May 2023. The scales were the same as those seized by police during their 5 August search. But the big question was: were these field mushrooms or similar-looking fungi foraged by Erin? By this stage of the inquiry one thing was clear: even experienced foragers can be deceived.

A homicide investigation often necessitates finding experts in subjects outside the usual ambit of an investigation. In this case, that meant fungi expert Doctor Tom May, who provided a detailed report on the death cap mushroom. In that report he said he had a 'high level of confidence' that the mushrooms on the scale were 'consistent with amanita phalloides', noting that there were, however, other mushrooms that could have looked the same.

There was also a photo of the scales and the dehydrator on the bench. The police discovered that Erin had shared this picture with her Facebook friends. She'd told them she'd bought the dehydrator and was using it to dehydrate mushrooms, which reduced their mass by ninety per cent, and then was blitzing them into a powder which she used in her cooking without telling the children. They were quite smitten with her mushroom-laced chocolate brownies, she said. This information further raised eyebrows, given her statement denying ownership of a dehydrator.

On 28 May 2022 one of the seized devices had been used to access the search engine Bing and go to a site called iNaturalist.

The website states that it gives people the opportunity to 'contribute to science', noting that 'every observation can contribute to biodiversity science, from the rarest butterfly to the most common backyard weed'. Contributing to the site is straightforward: you record your observations, which usually include a photo, post them to the site to share with your fellow nature lovers, and discuss. The contents are easily searchable. Just type in what you're looking for – death cap mushrooms, for example – and a world map will load, then you simply click on a location for more detail. In mid-June 2025 there were 8950 observations of the death cap mushroom globally, reported by 4505 observers.

Digging deeper, police found that the searcher had gone to a listing posted on 18 May 2022 by someone called Ivan, who reported that he'd found what he thought were death cap mushrooms at Bricker Reserve in Moorabbin, a suburb in Melbourne's south-east. The webpage was titled, *'Deathcap from Melbourne VIC, Australia on May 18, 2022 at 02:36pm by [iNaturalist user], Bricker Reserve, Moorabbin – iNaturalist.'*

The searcher accessed the page at 7.21 pm, but clearly didn't linger on the entry, because at 7.23 pm they'd moved on to search for the Korumburra Middle Hotel to order dinner. An order was placed for two award-winning chicken parmigianas, a family pack of garlic bread, a kid's burger, a kid's fish, and a 1.25 litre bottle of Coke Zero. Erin's credit card was used to pay for the order. It's a fair bet that the person who did the search and placed the order was Erin.

The sighting of these mushrooms was one of three uncovered by police that were posted on the iNaturalist website.

The next sighting was posted on 18 April 2023 by Christine McKenzie, a retired pharmacist who had been a senior poisons information specialist at the Victorian Poisons Information Centre. She'd been out for a walk in the pretty village of Loch, about a half-hour drive from Leongatha, when she spotted what she thought were death caps growing near trees in the Loch Memorial Reserve.

Aware of the threat they posed to both humans and animals, she popped them into a dog poo bag and disposed of them. Later that day she posted four pictures of the mushrooms on the iNaturalist website, noting their location. The mushrooms in these images were later confirmed by mycologist Doctor Tom May as death caps.

While McKenzie's commitment to public safety was laudable, even after the mushroom has been removed, the fungus remains underground and can regrow, depending on factors including moisture, nutrients and temperature. The Royal Botanic Gardens Victoria notes that death caps appear in autumn and sometimes winter, and are abundant in wetter years. Rainfall in autumn 2023 was, according to the Bureau of Meteorology, close to average across the state, but wetter in some districts, including Gippsland.

Doctor May was the third person to report the location of death caps on the site, posting under the name Funkey Tom. On 21 May 2023, he reported seeing death caps in Neilson Street, Outtrim, a short drive from both Korumburra and Leongatha. However, police didn't find evidence on Erin's devices that she had accessed the iNaturalist website at these times.

Examining the mobile phones seized during the search yielded some tantalising results. Police knew that Erin had bought the dehydrator at 12.17 pm on 28 April, and they soon discovered that two and a half hours before that purchase, one of the phones – or, more accurately the SIM card – had travelled to the Loch area, where it had lingered for a while. While this doesn't necessarily mean Erin was off foraging – Loch has an excellent bakery, and numerous other attractions – it was another intriguing snippet.

The phone revealed that the day after Doctor May posted on the iNaturalist website, Erin's SIM card was on the road again, travelling first from Leongatha to Loch at around 9 am, returning to Leongatha around 10 am, and then heading to Outtrim and back around 11 am. Again, this didn't mean that Erin was foraging, but given that the township of Outtrim lacks the culinary attractions of Loch, other reasons for a visit are in short supply. These were compelling discoveries but not definitive evidence that Erin was foraging for death caps. Still, experienced detectives aren't fans of coincidence.

Another device contained an image of an article in which stage four ovarian cancer was discussed, taken from the UK Cancer Council website.

The cyber sleuths also found the messages between Erin and her in-laws, and with her Facebook friends, which combined to paint a very different picture from the one Erin projected. Contrary to her claims, it was clear all wasn't rosy with the in-laws, and her estranged husband, who she claimed to have an amicable relationship with, was apparently a deadbeat.

A strong case against Erin was forming. While investigators were analysing the seized devices, Eppingstall and his team were also hard at work, using less contemporary but still fundamental investigative tools. There were potentially hundreds of people to interview formally, and avenues to pursue afterward. Nothing could be left to chance. Detectives had to put themselves into the minds of the defence, who would cast as much doubt as possible on their work. If the investigation resulted in an arrest, every action would be scrutinised and ultimately, if there was a trial, twelve people would sit in judgement not only of the accused but of how the investigators reached their conclusions.

They tracked down witnesses, conducted interviews, took statements and obtained phone and banking records. Police would end up taking statements from family members and friends of the Wilkinsons and Pattersons, Erin and Simon's two children, doctors and other medical staff, the Victorian Cancer registry, the people who'd sold the dehydrator, and those who were at the tip at the time of disposal and when the police arrived.

Amid these investigations, police also went to great lengths to check Erin's medical history, to test the veracity of her claimed reason for the lunch. Their investigation was informed by an entry in Gail's diary for 28 June 2023, which noted 'Erin – St Vincent's arm lump'. What they found – or rather, didn't find – was any evidence of that appointment, either from Medicare records or at St Vincent's.

They checked Gail's mobile phone and discovered she'd sent a message to Erin that same day, asking how the appointment had gone. Erin responded the next morning: *'Hi Gail, Sorry I had taken* [her daughter] *to see a movie last night. We saw The Little Mermaid. The appointment went ok. Thanks for asking. I had a needle biopsy taken of the lump and I'm returning for an MRI next week and we'll know more after the results of those two things.'*

Medical matters were again on the agenda on 6 July, when Gail messaged Erin asking about tests she'd supposedly had the day before. She replied twenty-four hours later: *'Thanks for your message, Don and Gail. There's a bit to digest with everything that's come out of it all. I might talk more about it with you both when I see you in person. Love, Erin.'*

But again, detectives found no Medicare record, no appointment at St Vincent's, no MRI, no biopsy and, by that point, not much credit in the story Erin Patterson had been spinning.

18

REST IN PEACE

While detectives were deep in their investigation, the town of Korumburra had the solemn task of grieving the losses of Heather, Gail and Don – family members, friends, colleagues, and mainstays of their close-knit community.

On the bitterly cold afternoon of 31 August 2023, with torrential rain battering Korumburra, a memorial service for Don and Gail Patterson was held at the Korumburra Recreational Centre. Over 350 people are believed to have attended. It was an afternoon that captured how deeply these innocent people were loved, respected and missed.

Tributes from their grandchildren brought the room to tears. One said, 'They were two of the kindest, most loving, caring and influential grandparents you could ever hope to have.' Another, in a recording made earlier and played to a backdrop of photos of Don and Gail with their grandkids, said, 'Nanna used to read with me, and I loved cooking with her. Her orange cake was my favourite.' And, 'I loved having salad sandwiches for lunch with your lovely home-made mayonnaise. Nanna and Poppa you were soooo kind.'

Of Don, the former science and maths teacher, one grandchild said, 'Usually, when you get over the neighbour's fence, it's to get the footy or a ball, but not with poppa. In our case it was to rescue a rocket that had gone astray. It's why I love science.'

Don's brother Colin spoke of the two of them growing up together. He said his brother had been a brilliant maths and science student at school, which led to a science degree at Monash University.

He recalled that Don Patterson had met Gail Young at Sunday school in Hughesdale in Melbourne's south-east and the pair had quickly become inseparable. They shared not only their strong Christian faith but also their involvement in boy scouts and girl guides, and enjoyed piano lessons, tennis and family holidays on the Mornington Peninsula.

They married in November 1973 and died just a few months short of what would have been their fiftieth wedding anniversary.

Simon told mourners that in his early professional life, Don had given up a possible career in scientific research and teaching so that he and Gail could go to Botswana as missionaries. Simon recalled being home-schooled by his mother using lessons sent from Australia. He quipped, 'I always say I reached my academic peak in Grade 4, which is no reflection on the teachers that followed but on Mum's ability as a teacher.'

After years of missionary work, the family returned to Australia, settling in Korumburra, where Don resumed his teaching career. He taught at the town's secondary college for around twenty-five years, retiring in the early 2000s. The couple's missionary work in China formed the basis of the school's exchange program.

Simon said his father was so fit that when he was in his sixties, they'd trekked to the base camp of Mount Everest, reaching an altitude of nearly 5500 metres – for comparison, Australia's Mount Kosciuszko is 2200 metres at its highest point. Simon said, 'In fact, he was so fit at seventy that it allowed him to have an emergency liver transplant, although he ultimately died because of the damage already done to his body.'

Simon told the assembled mourners that his parents tackled life as a team, noting that 'the fact that they died on consecutive days was fitting somehow'.

When a loved one dies, their final words can linger in your mind forever. Simon recounted his mother's, via text from her hospital bed to her family's group chat: 'Lots of love to you all.'

He said his parents had 'a pretty healthy view' on the prospect of death, acknowledging the inevitability, and the prospect of life beyond the grave. 'As Mum and Dad lay in comas in the hospital in their final days and each day ... we were unsure if they would recover or not, it was comforting to know that when we said "See you later," we knew it was true. The only thing we didn't know was when. In the meantime, we'll miss them.'

Richard Collyer, who'd taught with Don, recalled their times at the Korumburra Secondary College. Don had 'inspired generations of students' and was fondly remembered for some of his 'wacky' teaching methods. He was highly respected, both as a teacher and as a 'mentor to staff young and old'.

Gail had also worked at the school, firstly as a volunteer in the Learning Assistance Program, then later in the school office.

The mourners also heard of their work as missionaries in Botswana when they were both in their twenties. It was a life of service that continued beyond retirement, when both went to China to teach English.

Matt, Simon's younger brother, read tributes from around the world. Former students in China described the couple as 'like real parents from another country', remembering their 'generous love', all recognising these kind, generous and capable people and their life of service to others.

Sharon Hirst spoke of her friend Gail's service to the community, working at Korumburra's Milpara Community House, a community meeting place and education centre in Korumburra, working with Don on the *Burra Flyer*, reading to people with impaired vision, hosting overseas visitors and new arrivals, along with her commitment to her faith. Sharon said Gail was loved and respected and 'a very caring and lovely person, a kind and wise lady'.

Local Anglican priest Doctor Fran Grimes summed the pair up simply and aptly as 'pillars of the community'. She also spoke of the impact of the loss on the community, noting, 'It has been a trying and distressing time with the overwhelming media scrutiny making normal grief impossible. But I'd like to thank the community for what I have seen as shielding and protecting the family as much as possible, and refraining from the heartless speculation and gossip that we have seen elsewhere. Long after the news cycle has ended, we will be here to look after each other.'

That media scrutiny was destined to last much longer than Doctor Grimes anticipated. Months later, Erin Patterson would be arrested and charged with multiple charges of murder and attempted murder and then, adding to the town's woes, opt for a trial not in urban Melbourne, but in Gippsland's Morwell, a shade over 70 kilometres away.

*

Heather Wilkinson's memorial service was held about five weeks later, on Wednesday, 4 October, not long after Ian had finally been discharged from hospital. The family released a statement, noting that the development marked significant progress in Ian's long recovery. 'This milestone marks a moment of immense relief and gratitude for Ian and the entire Wilkinson family.'

Again, the venue for the service was the Korumburra Recreation Centre and the weather, though slightly less bitter, was wet and windy. Over 300 people braved the tempest to be there. Ian Wilkinson was at the service, arriving slowly and aided with a walking stick. He lingered afterward, talking with well-wishers.

Heather and Ian's son David gave a tear-filled speech. 'Mum considered motherhood to be a wonderful gift. She understood the real value mothers play in the lives of their children and in society. She loved to laugh and have fun, she was so creative in play and encouraged us to find things to do. She loved being a mum and she loved us. She was uncompromising but full of grace. Thoughtful, faithful and welcoming to visitors.'

He said his uncle and aunt, Don and Gail Patterson, had been instrumental in the path his parents had taken. They 'were key to Mum's coming to faith. The example of the conduct of their relationship, their uncompromising Christian commitment, their intelligent thought and their love towards Mum inspired her faith. Mum never looked back from these important years, she had found her saviour and would spend her days in service to Him.'

David also gave a snapshot of his mother's life. Growing up in the sixties, while very fond of books such as Enid Blyton's, Heather also had a penchant for TV action shows like *Zorro*, *The Lone Ranger* and the cult Japanese hit *Samurai*.

He said, 'She was kind, even tempered and with a quirky sense of humour and varied musical tastes, from Handel's "Messiah" – which she often whistled or sang – to going to concerts by Creedence Clearwater Revival and the Rolling Stones.'

Her grandchildren lovingly shared that she was 'always heaps of fun, good at sewing, good at cooking, so kind, gentle and loving. Creative, fun and always smiling, and with plenty of things for us kids to do. We were never bored when grandma was around.'

Like the Pattersons, Heather had also worked at the Korumburra Secondary College, with former principal Peter Biggins telling the mourners that Heather had loved and enjoyed her students and 'was all about caring, helping people'. She'd also been part of the Learning Assistance Program, with Peter Biggins describing her as being 'instrumental' in getting parents to volunteer, and helping students with 'significant' learning difficulties and supporting their integration into the school.

In her later years, she was at Milpara Community House, where Gail had also worked, teaching new arrivals to Australia and those with English as a second language.

Heather's passion for helping others was reflected in a request that, instead of flowers, donations be made to the Austin Hospital or to SIM Australia for distribution to the Galmi Hospital in Niger, West Africa.

Heather was a person who made a positive change to the lives of all she encountered.

19

A DETECTIVE CALLS

By late October, the police were ready to arrest Erin Patterson. Eppingstall and his team had the reasonable cause they needed, and their superiors and lawyers at the Office of the Director of Public Prosecutions were in agreement.

Various news reports suggested that on 1 November 2023 Erin had a 'knees up' at Gibson Street, for a group of 'friends believed to be her four closest mates', which was interesting, given her friends were primarily online. Neighbours had speculated that the event was because she knew her arrest was imminent.

By the morning of Thursday, 2 November 2023, the party was long over, and the police – both detective and uniform – arrived. They were low-key, with the media kept at bay, and the numerous police vans and cars obscured clear shots of the front of the house. Erin wouldn't be doing a 'perp walk'.

For several hours, police searched Erin's house, garage and car, and were seen carrying out bags and sorting seized items into boxes. Specialist technology detector dogs provided by the Australian Federal Police (AFP) were also on site, looking for things like USBs and SIM cards, presumably including the phone police thought she had, which they still hadn't found.

Erin wasn't helping with their inquiries, but the dogs struck gold. As AFP Commissioner Reece Kershaw later told a Senate estimates hearing, 'In November last year, the AFP provided its technology detector dogs to assist our hard-working colleagues at Victoria Police while executing a search warrant relating to individuals who had ingested death cap mushrooms. Technology Detector Dog Georgia found one USB, a micro secure digital card and a SIM card. Technology Detector Dog Alma found a mobile phone, five iPads, a trail camera and secure digital card and a smart watch. These were not found during initial searches undertaken by officers.'

After the search, which took several hours, Erin was arrested and taken to Wonthaggi Police Station for interview.

She was then charged with three counts of murder (for the deaths of Heather Wilkinson and Gail and Don Patterson) at Heidelberg (the Austin Hospital), one count of the attempted murder of Ian Wilkinson, and one count of the attempted murder of Simon Patterson, both at Leongatha on 29 July 2023.

Then came the twist that the public didn't see coming – she was also charged with three counts of the attempted murder of Simon Patterson in the eighteen months prior to the fatal lunch. These attempts were from the weekends away to Wilsons Promontory in November 2021 and September 2022, and to Howqua in May 2022.

Detective Inspector Dean Thomas of the homicide squad confirmed the arrest at a press conference just after 1 pm.

He said the day's event was the 'next step in what has been a complex and thorough investigation', adding that there was still work to be done. He didn't take questions but did give the media a few quotable moments, saying, 'I cannot think of another investigation that has generated this level of media and public interest, not only here in Victoria but also nationally and internationally.'

He went on to remind people of the tragedy that lay at the heart of the case. 'I think it's particularly important that we keep in mind that at the heart of this, three people have lost their lives. These are people who, by all accounts, were much beloved by their communities and greatly missed by their loved ones.' He observed that in small communities like Leongatha and Korumburra, a tragedy of this magnitude could reverberate for years.

In wrapping up the press conference, he asked the public to remember the impact of these crimes on the grieving families, saying, 'I encourage people to be particularly mindful of unnecessary speculation and the sharing of misinformation.' Unfortunately, by that point the Erin Patterson industry of tabloid coverage, podcasts, chat groups, social media and even the occasional self-confessed influencer was in full flight, their comments sometimes in the poorest of taste.

With bail refused – common in cases as serious as this – Erin spent what would be the first of a possible lifetime of nights behind bars. The next morning, at the Latrobe Valley Magistrates' Court in Morwell, Erin, wearing glasses and a dowdy beige jumper, was in the dock facing Magistrate Tim Walsh. The courtroom was packed with media, delivering Morwell its first taste of the global spotlight.

In the early days of a prosecution, particularly of a crime of this magnitude, a plea of either guilty or not guilty is not usually entered until after the prosecution have served their brief of evidence.

Acting Sergeant Greg Ellis, who was the police prosecutor handling the case that morning, asked the magistrate for an adjournment of twenty weeks to prepare and serve the brief of evidence, a chunk of that time would involve analysis of the computer equipment seized the day before. Erin's lawyer, Bill Doogue, said his client agreed to the extra time, and acknowledged, 'It could well go for a very long time. It seems to be based on a lot of analysis which we haven't received and hasn't even been completed at this point in time.'

Both prosecution and defence tried to have the case moved to Melbourne, but the magistrate declined and set the case down for Morwell on 3 May 2024.

Erin was also remanded in custody, thus consigning her to her first Christmas away from her children. Meanwhile, her kids would spend their first Christmas without their mother or their grandparents.

The devastating consequences of that lunch will ripple on forever.

20

ON THE FAST-TRACK

After arrest and before committal proceedings, little can be formally said. While social media may hum with speculation, rumours and outright lies, mainstream media, alert to sub-judice obligations, has little it can report. But occasionally a snippet comes along that can add a little oxygen to the story.

In January 2024, exotic mushroom grower Epicurean Food Group was reportedly in financial strife, thanks to a slump in mushroom sales after the events of July 2023. Unsurprisingly, people were suddenly approaching mushrooms with caution.

On 8 March 2024, a little publishable sizzle arrived in the guise of Philip Dunn KC, one of the nation's most distinguished criminal barristers. In his very long career, Dunn had represented the good, the bad and the very bad, including Melbourne gangland figure the late Carl Williams. His win rate in complex and challenging trials was exemplary.

A few days later, on Sunday, 10 March, the media got

another little snippet when the Food Safety Information Council put out a press release warning of death caps and their impending autumn arrival. In most years, this is a release that wouldn't generate much, if any, media interest, but nine months after the Leongatha lunch, it prompted a couple of features.

The organisation's CEO, Lydia Buchtmann, said foraging for wild mushrooms was becoming popular, especially through promotion in social media groups – presumably not those with a true crime focus – and warned that 'gathering of wild mushrooms can be life threatening'.

Three days later, and with the fear of foraging suitably stoked, Philip Dunn was back in the news, telling Melbourne tabloid the *Herald Sun*, 'I don't know how she's going to get a fair trial.' Referring to Lindy Chamberlain and the tragedy of her missing baby Azaria, and the prosecution of Carmen Lawrence (former West Australian Premier), he said, 'They were persecuted, I think, because they were women. If Carmen Lawrence had been a bloke, if Lindy Chamberlain had been a bloke, if Erin Patterson was a bloke, they wouldn't be vilified in the way those women were and Erin Patterson is now.'

A seasoned media performer with an eye to a grab, he went on: 'Vilified! I feel very strongly about that and I don't know how on earth she is going to get a fair trial.'

Former Queensland Premier Sir Joh Bjelke-Petersen once described dealing with the media as feeding the chooks. Well, on 22 March, the chooks were again being fed. The *Herald Sun* reported the 'first morsels' of the police case against Erin Patterson had been 'laid bare', almost nine months after the 'most notorious lunch in the world'.

The morsels in question were the fact that the police had served their brief of evidence on Erin's lawyers, just ahead of the 25 March deadline. The article suggested that technology would play a major role in the brief, in part thanks to the work of the tech dogs. 'Examination of CCTV, credit card usage, internet history, tollway movements and phone data is part of almost every modern investigation.' Dramatically, the paper noted, 'Only two people can properly describe the July 29 lunch. One is Ms Patterson.'

On 30 March, the *Daily Mail* published an article under the catchy headline, 'Huge development in police case against alleged mushroom killer'. The article reported, 'Deadly mushroom chef Erin Patterson's internet search history and deleted social media accounts will reportedly form a vital part of the prosecutor's case against the accused killer.' The paper went on, 'Police are also looking at her internet history, with specialist teams able to unearth deleted searches.' An alleged police source observed, 'It's not easy but it's doable on most occasions. She might be involved in conversations or narratives where she has talked about this stuff on online forums … it could be the tiniest thing.'

This alleged police source was leaking some very tasty morsels, and they were on the mark. Details like this shouldn't, in the interests of fairness, ever be leaked, but it's usually only a matter of time, especially when the media are clamouring for even the smallest snippet.

An online acquaintance of Erin's told me she had a talent for chaos, and that became apparent in the lead-up to her May 2024 appearance before the magistrate in Morwell. In late March, the Magistrates' Court announced that the case would resume two weeks earlier than originally planned for what was dubbed a 'special mention'. On 22 April, Erin Patterson appeared before Magistrate Walsh via video link from the Dame Phyllis Frost Centre. She'd been on remand for five months by then, and this was her first time back in court.

Instead of Philip Dunn KC at the bar table, Colin Mandy SC, an experienced criminal lawyer and quiet achiever without a high media profile, announced that he'd been instructed to act for the defendant. Neither Dunn nor his departure were mentioned.

Mandy said his client wanted a potentially lengthy committal hearing and wanted it held at the Latrobe Valley Court in Morwell, rather than transferring the case to Melbourne, where the availability of a courtroom and magistrate meant it would be heard sooner.

Generally, in these most serious cases, there are committal proceedings in the Magistrates' Court, during which the prosecution evidence is disclosed. That evidence might be tested by cross-examination of witnesses, all to help the presiding magistrate decide if there is prima facie evidence to support the charges. At that point, the magistrate will decide whether to commit the person for trial. If committed, the defendant is henceforth known as the accused.

Contemporary committals are usually relatively procedural, with paperwork filed and some discussion between defence and prosecution, without going to the extent of lengthy hearings testing the evidence of witnesses.

Magistrate Walsh pointed out that the number of cases coming up at Morwell meant that a committal would likely not take place until the following year. In response, Mandy told him, 'If it has to be next year, Ms Patterson is happy to wait for that.' It was an unusual stance – most people who are being held in custody want their cases underway as quickly as possible. Spending nine or so months in prison before the case even begins isn't a popular or common move.

Prosecutor Sarah Lenthall wanted the committal to proceed as soon as possible. In cases such as these, the family and friends of the victim, or in this case victims, are in limbo until the case is concluded, so getting things underway sooner eases their pain ever so slightly. The case was adjourned to 7 May for further committal mention.

On 7 May, everyone was back in Morwell before Magistrate Tim Walsh. Once again, Erin Patterson appeared via video link from the Dame Phyllis Frost Centre. In court barrister Colin Mandy SC, on his client's instructions, did a backflip and surprised everyone by asking that the case be fast-tracked to trial, rather than a long committal hearing in front of a Magistrate.

Erin also wanted her case tried before a jury of her peers in the local area. While Morwell wasn't quite local, it was the lead courthouse for the Latrobe Valley and the only venue that could accommodate a large criminal trial. The prosecutors, unsurprisingly, weren't keen on uprooting court staff, prosecutors, police and numerous expert witnesses from the city and having to schedule, transport and accommodate them. Even less appealing was the prospect of having to accommodate a jury securely and comfortably.

There was also the matter of the transport and security of the accused person in custody. Police tend not to relish having long-term guests in their cells. In the city, running a trial is straightforward – the machine is well honed – but in the regions, it's a logistical challenge bordering on a nightmare.

In July 2024, the prosecutors sought to have the trial held in Melbourne, noting that Don, Gail and Heather had died in Heidelberg, where the Austin Hospital was located, and thus the murder charges that arose had that as their place of murder. However, Justice Jane Dixon, who presided over the hearing, didn't agree. Victoria's *Criminal Procedure Act* states that the trial of an accused 'is to be held in the court sitting at the place that is nearest to the place where the offence is alleged to have been committed, unless an order is made under Section 192'. Justice Dixon observed that while the prosecutors could frame the charges as they wanted, holding the trial locally meant the community wouldn't be disenfranchised. She said, 'As a matter of common sense, as argued by Mr Mandy, the Crown will submit to the jury that by the time Erin Patterson had administered the luncheon food to the three deceased, she had, on their case, committed the *actus reus* (the act) for murder. The offending will be alleged in the Crown's opening statements to have been committed in Leongatha notwithstanding that the offence was allegedly completed by the death of the three alleged victims in Heidelberg.'

Though the trial was to be held in Morwell, the fast-track hearings were in the Supreme Court in Melbourne, starting on 21 August 2024. The Supreme Court building in William Street is a labyrinth of courtrooms that could be from central casting – lofty timber benches for the judges, a witness box with a commanding view of the courtroom that also offers the judge, lawyers and jury a commanding view of the witness, a jury box not noted for comfort, and media and public areas with seating that, in my long experience in courtrooms, is usually so uncomfortable it's a punishment without a crime.

The venue for the opening of the Patterson matter was Court 15, and I'd headed down from Sydney for a few days to listen in. Even after decades of watching, reporting or being involved in court cases, the opening moments of a major case are always enthralling. The key players are all assembled for the first time – the lawyers, potential witnesses, the accused and the first glimpse of the court watchers, who prowl the day's lists looking for something to watch. They're usually in court for the duration of the trial, and are a great source of behind-the-scenes intel – they blend into the scenery, watch and listen.

The media box, often sparsely populated, was packed with journalists, TV producers/researchers and a smattering of true crime writers, all keen to get their first real-time taste of the case. For those in the media who couldn't make it, the hearings were also live-streamed, but on the strict proviso that they couldn't be recorded and couldn't be reported. This was to ensure a fair trial and avoid contaminating the thoughts of any potential juror.

At 9.55 am everyone, except the presiding judicial officer, was in court and ready, waiting. At 10.12 am the wait was over, and Judicial Registrar Timothy Freeman, who would be conducting the proceedings, entered – fast-track cases are often before a registrar, rather than a judge. He paused to acknowledge those below, then sat down, followed dutifully by the rest of us. The curtain had risen on the theatre of court.

Once again, Erin attended via video link from the Dame Phyllis Frost Centre. The first task of the day was to make sure she could hear proceedings and respond as required. Screens in the courtroom showed her sitting on her own in a bland video booth. She appeared to be quite subdued, her hair was lank, and there was little in the way of animation.

In these fast-track proceedings, witnesses are called for preliminary examination and cross-examination. Most people expect that a trial is underway before witnesses are called, and the jury are present for their examination and cross-examination, unless there is a legal issue arising which might include something wildly prejudicial, but there is no jury in these types of proceedings.

It was announced that sixteen witnesses may be called over the coming days, with further hearings in the ensuing months. The point of these hearings was to streamline the trial, the start date of which had been confirmed as Monday, 28 April 2025. These were witnesses who could have been called had committal proceedings not been waived.

In fast-track, counsel for the accused selects those they want to have a chat with under oath. These proceedings are open to the public but can't be reported by the media.

The first witness called was Ruth Alison Dubois, Heather and Ian Wilkinson's daughter. The registrar was solicitous, making Ruth feel as comfortable as possible, offering water and breaks if or when she needed. Her evidence wasn't extensive. It began by establishing her knowledge of and relationship with Erin, which was very straightforward – they'd met through Simon, had kept in touch with relative frequency, and while they saw each other at church, they didn't always chat. Ruth noted that her father had been the pastor at church for about twenty-five years and that Erin had a minor role at the church, helping Simon live-stream the services.

She'd heard about Erin's lunch invitation from her mother. She'd dined with her parents the night before, and was aware from their conversations that her aunt Gail was looking forward to it, noting that her parents had had little contact with Erin since she'd moved to the house in Leongatha. It would be her father's first visit to the Gibson Street home; her mother had been there briefly to drop off cookies shortly after Erin had moved in. The evidence then switched to the terrible events of the following days.

The key part of Ruth's evidence was that in the days following the lunch she was 'made aware of Simon's suspicions' about Erin. She recalled that around 2 August 2023, Simon had initiated a family chat, telling them he thought his illnesses had been a deliberate act by Erin and that he had stopped eating anything she'd prepared, fearing she'd been 'messing with it'. But he also told them he'd believed he was the only person being targeted. It was the first Ruth had heard of Simon's suspicions. While she'd been aware of his illnesses, she hadn't really discussed them with him, and had no reason to suspect anything untoward until they met that night.

Her evidence was short, with few revelations and nothing in the way of fireworks. It seemed likely that, while she'd remain on the witness list for the upcoming trial, she may not be called again to give evidence.

In criminal trials, the witness list can be daunting, because it starts by covering every possible witness. The list is then reduced through the lawyers discussing whether they need to be called, accepting the testimony without the need to contest it, as well as through arguments on whether their testimony will be admissible in preliminary hearings, and in hearings like this one.

The next witness was a surprise. We'd followed Ian Wilkinson's perilous journey since the near-fatal poisoning. He's a bloke of average height and build, with grey to white hair and a resonant, light tenor voice that, in the early moments of his evidence, was quavering. His accent reminded me of an older generation of Australian men like my uncles. What we couldn't see from the media gallery was whether the live feed with Erin was still both audio and visual, or if the vision had been cut to spare the witness looking at the person who'd allegedly killed his wife and nearly killed him.

In a theatrical flourish before Ian's evidence began, Mandy SC stood and announced there was one matter to raise, then looked at his colleagues at the bar table, who clearly had no clue where this was going. He then sought an order from the judicial registrar to remove witnesses from the courtroom. In criminal cases where evidence is given, the witness must stay out of the courtroom until their evidence is over, the principle being that if they hear earlier witnesses, they could tailor their answers.

With the consent of the judicial registrar, the judicial registrar's associate – legal speak for executive assistant – asked any potential witnesses to leave the courtroom. Everyone in the public and media area had their eyes on swivel, hoping for that first glimpse of a witness, but no-one left the room. And so the focus returned to Ian Wilkinson, who'd taken his place in the prominent and very old-fashioned witness box.

Ian's testimony started with the tendering of the statement he gave to police while still in hospital. With that done, the prosecutor resumed her seat at the bar table and

Mandy SC rose for cross-examination. He was polite and low-key, taking Mr Wilkinson through the lead-up to the police statement. Ian answered thoughtfully, describing his mental and physical recovery from the ordeal, and made it clear that both he and his family believed he was of sound mind when the statement was taken. He said he'd been sedated for quite a long time, and had suffered some bouts of delirium, something he admitted with a nervous chuckle. Mandy suggested 'paranoid', which Ian politely rebuffed.

Ian recalled that throughout it all he wanted to go home, and that at times his mind would play tricks. He 'thought I was in a medical helicopter and my daughter-in-law, who is a nurse, was in the helicopter with me, going somewhere for treatment'. Mandy pressed him on this recollection, prompting him to describe another helicopter journey, this time with his wife, Heather, but at that point he ran out of recollection. Mandy asked if he'd had any of these thoughts about the fatal lunch, to which he replied, 'I don't recall, but I'd say no'.

Ian noted he'd been concerned about his capacity, but was sufficiently self-aware to know that he was capable, something he said was confirmed by the family, though he couldn't recall who had said this. Mandy didn't push. This was, appropriately, cross-examination with kid gloves.

He then told the court that at the time he gave the statement, in early September 2023, he was feeling well enough, but was not aware of any allegations of deliberate poisoning. He recalled saying to the police, 'I don't know what happened to us,' and the officer telling him they were keeping an open mind.

His evidence then turned to the lunch. He remembered looking forward to the event – it would be his first time at Erin's new home. He also said Erin was a regular at his church, and that Heather would call on Erin 'very occasionally, not very often, more than me'. He thought Heather had visited the new house before, bringing food when Simon was there recuperating. Ian didn't appear to be close to the couple, saying he'd been aware of their separation and some attempts at reconciliation, but wasn't aware of the details.

Ian Wilkinson's evidence in this hearing solved one question that had been troubling a slew of people, including me: how did Erin prepare and serve the beef Wellington? And the answer was, as noted earlier, individual beef Wellingtons plated on the four matching plates and Erin's on the odd plate out. This prompted questions about Erin's housekeeping. For someone who was both houseproud and had two children, having only four matching plates was curious – or was it suspicious? That was something we would have to wait until trial to resolve.

Ian's testimony also provided a glimpse of the twenty-four hours that followed the lunch, recalling that suspicions had initially fallen on the beef, before mushrooms were identified as the possible cause.

With cross-examination thus coming to a close, Ian told the court that while he'd had some specific discussions with his family after making his statement to police, any discussions with Simon were cursory. He said he was being cautious not to say too much, as police had advised him. It was good advice, as in criminal cases these discussions can be used by an aggressive defence lawyer to suggest that the conversation may have coloured recollections. Mandy wasn't aggressive, but he was meticulous, which is an even greater challenge for a witness.

When Mandy was finished his cross-examination, the prosecution clarified a few points. Ian was taken back to his state of mind in the lead-up to giving his statement. He said that during his long recovery he reached a time when he could again differentiate fact from the fiction of his dreams, and then came 'a moment when my mind began to clear, a return to reality, and what was a dream melted away'. Then came some more pertinent questions to make very clear what had happened at the lunch – the arrival, the mechanics of finalising the preparation, who was where in the house, the serving and plating and finally to the table. In crime cases, especially ones that rely on an overwhelming weight of circumstances to deliver proof beyond reasonable doubt, nailing the chronology is critical.

Ian's testimony brought day one of the preliminary hearings to an end.

Over the next few days, and sporadic dates over ensuing months, there was a parade of witnesses. They were called for a few reasons, including to give a taste of what their trial evidence might be and to consider arguments about admissibility or what could be heard by the jury and what might be prejudicial or irrelevant. In deciding what may be overtly prejudicial, the judge needs to weigh the value of the evidence and its impact on the jury. Some evidence, for example, might be dramatic and compelling, but will it cause some jury members to jump to a conclusion?

Among those called who were likely to appear at trial were the family members whose lives had been devastated by the events in question. Ian's son David was the next witness.

Aged in his mid-thirties, solidly built, he was neatly dressed in chinos, a crew neck jumper and boots, sporting a closely shaved head and a neatly trimmed beard.

David is a sound engineer. He said he'd known Erin since she and Simon first met, noting that he walked her down the aisle at their wedding. They'd all been regulars at Bible study, where they shared life experiences and 'reflected on the Bible's wisdom'. Erin, he recalled, wasn't the most vigorous of participants, prompting him to conclude she was introverted and not good in groups. It wasn't an uncommon observation.

David said he'd grown up with Simon and their cousin Tim in Korumburra, but that Simon had a stronger relationship with Tim, noting that they were in frequent contact and spoke 'often, deeply and personally'. That observation led him to add, 'I imagine there had been chats about what had happened' in regard to Simon's health.

The reality hit him after the lunch, when Simon requested a family conference at the Austin Hospital. Ahead of that discussion, Simon had emailed him a copy of his medical records. In re-examination by the lawyers for the prosecution, he said that Tim had told him Simon believed his illnesses had been caused by Erin.

Medical professionals comprised the following tranche of witnesses, the most intriguing of which was Doctor Chris Ford, a slim, boyish man in his thirties, looking slightly uncomfortable in a suit. It seemed possible he'd had some training on how to deal with questions in the witness box – he was brief and concise. He outlined his history with Simon, both personal and professional, and the circumstances of February 2023 when Simon raised his suspicions about possibly being poisoned by Erin: Erin's persistent phone calls to see if he'd eaten the cookies his daughter had given to him, which had prompted Simon's own online research about what poisons you could slip into them, and changing his advanced care directive from Erin to Don.

His evidence canvassed the investigations he'd undertaken, including referrals to specialists to try and find the cause or causes of Simon's illnesses. He agreed with Mandy that the question of poisoning hadn't been raised by the specialists in their reports. He also told Mandy that in the wake of the 29 July lunch, he'd alerted his colleague Doctor Webster that, 'I was suspicious of a deliberate poisoning based on the meal that occurred at the house the day before'. He also told Mandy he'd spoken to Don at the hospital and was told that Don had a jar of his vomit, which Ford advised him to hang on to and take with him when he was transferred. Ford thought Don had the jar 'because it could be used in evidence'.

Ford's evidence ended after he was asked for his opinion – based on his medical expertise as a general practitioner – on Simon's illnesses. He said, 'to me there was no other medical reason, there was no other reasons that could fit all of the different admissions and so it seemed feasible that it could be a possible reason'.

The first tranche of these hearings ended on 28 August 2024 with evidence from Erin's Facebook friends, who spoke of their shared passion for true crime.

The preliminary hearings resumed on 14 October 2024, and the opening witness was a surprise: Simon Patterson. Unlike most other witnesses, Simon had dressed formally in a grey suit and a light blue tie.

His evidence began by adopting his statements to police, followed by a few quick points about his illnesses, Erin's observation that the way they related to each other had become toxic, the paucity of family gatherings at 'our house', Gail's comment from her hospital bed that 'Heather thinks it might have been the mushrooms', and the intriguing conversation he'd had with Erin when he'd been in hospital for his illnesses. He recalled she said she didn't know what to say to them, and he thought she was referring to questions being asked by doctors and said she'd asked Don for advice. This last tantalising point wasn't elaborated on. Then it was over to Mandy SC for cross-examination.

As is usual in the cross-examination of a witness as significant as Simon, Mandy SC began gently, and methodically, going through some details in Simon's statements, establishing the chronology – the slow build. However, it quickly became obvious that Simon wasn't a fan of Mandy SC or, by extension, his client. Simon was brief in his answers, pleasant, reserved, and it was clear he'd rather have been somewhere else. We couldn't see if Erin was on screen during the examination.

Simon gave some insight into how the police handled parts of their investigation, recalling that his computers and devices hadn't been requested, but that Erin's had, as had those of the children. This was likely because police needed to examine any equipment that had been at the Leongatha house in the lead-up to, at the time of and after the lunch. He recalled that some of the children's devices had been returned.

The cross-examination then shifted to the fact that Simon had hired a media consultant. In the aftermath of the lunch he'd been contacted by a slew of media types, all wanting an interview or, at the very least, a comment. He'd had notes dropped in his letterbox, phone calls, Facebook messages, attempted contact through intermediaries in the community, and even the more direct route, with people knocking on his door and banging on his windows. One person had even asked him to read the draft of a book he was hastily writing.

Enduring this onslaught amid the challenge of dealing with a rapacious media, the death of his parents, protecting his children, the suspicions he'd harboured about his estranged wife, and an ongoing and substantial police investigation, Simon had decided to put a buffer in place.

He'd contacted Jessica O'Donnell, who he'd met in 2019 when she'd been a consultant at a place where he'd worked. He said he'd engaged her for media advice 'the day Dad died' because he was 'aware the media would have an interest and were beginning to publish'. He said he had no media experience and needed help.

Aside from handling the media, Jessica's role was to advise Simon on what to do when the case was over. This included looking into options for books and interviews, including approaches by documentary producers from around the planet. While agreeing that this would include discussing the deals offered, Simon was keen to make it clear that money wasn't the prime consideration, emphasising the need for the grieving local community to know what had happened – the truth would help them deal with their grief.

The latter was a curious proposition, given the court case and the massive volume of reporting. From my vantage point, Simon was astute and aware of the commercial possibilities of his 'exclusive' story. No doubt there'd be media with cheque books lining up at his door. At the time of writing, Simon has reportedly been bombarded with massive offers, including an alleged $500,000 from the *Daily Mail* in the United Kingdom. These offers have all been declined, and he and the family maintain a dignified silence.

When being cross-examined, the best tip for a witness is to say as little as possible, thus giving the lawyer less to work with. Until this point, Simon had taken that approach, but the segue into media matters ruffled his feathers. He told Mandy he thought that, as Mandy was paid by Erin, he may have been trying to damage his reputation, noting that Erin 'seeks to harm me', which was surely a contender for understatement of the year. In response, Mandy simply changed the subject, moving on to how Simon and Erin met.

Often in cases when you 'open the door', as Simon had, to a line of questioning, the lawyer will seize upon the opportunity. There may have been a few reasons for Mandy to pass on Simon's comment about Erin's harmful intentions, such as not giving Simon the chance to make potentially incriminatory comments about his client, or – more likely – after seeing that Simon could be provoked, saving a more intensive and fiery cross-examination for trial, denying him the chance to prepare for that onslaught. This is often called 'keeping your powder dry' and is quite common in preliminary hearings and committal proceedings.

When before a jury, if a question is likely to provoke the witness to drop a metaphorical bomb, the judge will ask the jury to leave the courtroom while the evidence is explored for its integrity and admissibility. This gives rise to the stories that emerge after the case – what the jury didn't hear.

Mandy took Simon through the decades he and Erin had known each other, touching on milestones such as travel, moving house and so on. When they discussed Simon's views on Erin, he said he thought they were a loving family all round, with Erin being particularly close to Don. He recalled that the pair could talk for hours about books, that Erin sought Don's counsel on matters and that he was an important part of what Simon called Erin's 'support network'. However, while they'd often gone to Don and Gail's for family dinners – not to Erin's, as noted earlier – and Erin would go to their house for dinners without Simon, in the year or so leading up to the lunch, Simon thought there had been some distancing. He also thought Erin was jealous of Don and Gail's relationship with their other grandchildren, his siblings' children.

Simon thought Erin's relationship with his parents had been comfortable, noting that she didn't, in his view, like large groups that weren't 'family'. He also observed, 'Erin is very good at relating to people, learnt in the way of a person with high-functioning Asperger's,' asserting that she 'knows how to appear to be enjoying herself and often she did appear to be'.

The suggestion that Erin is a person with Asperger's or autism is one that pops up occasionally in conversations about her. What is elusive is any evidence of a diagnosis by a competent professional – not Doctor Google.

As the first day of Simon's evidence drew to an end, there was a tantalising one-liner from him, prompted by questions about their aborted trip to Botswana owing to the Covid-19 pandemic. He said it had been Erin's idea, and that it was the first time since the children had been born that she'd suggested something like this. He agreed with Mandy that 'up until September or November of 2022 there was nothing untoward' as far as he could tell about his relationship with Erin. Simon's response was a showstopper, 'if you mean by untoward anything that would indicate that she'd tried to kill me, then that's correct.'

Cross-examination resumed the next morning, with Mandy inquiring if Simon had discussed his evidence with anyone. This is a well-worn tactic in criminal cases that seeks to wrong-foot the witness – if the answer is yes, the lawyer then suggests that their evidence may have been coloured by discussions with others. Simon stopped that tactic dead in its tracks by giving a firm 'no', accompanied by a look of mild exasperation.

Mandy moved on, touching on some basics of the trips Simon had taken with Erin where he'd fallen ill. Simon observed that he couldn't recall some details, but told the court he'd kept a spreadsheet of what he could remember, suggesting he could refer to that to refresh his memory. It's common for a witness to seek access to a document to stimulate a recollection, especially when that document was developed around the time of the events. Mandy didn't take Simon up on the offer, possibly due to concerns about what that document may have contained.

Instead, Mandy continued asking Simon about the holidays he'd taken with Erin. It was simple, nuts-and-bolts testimony, taking Simon dryly through the details – locations, menus, how food was stored and served, and the ensuing medical treatments and recovery.

When discussing their trip to Wilsons Promontory, Mandy pushed Simon on what he believed may have been the cause of his illness. He wanted to know what the doctors had said.

While this was outwardly an innocuous question, it was one that could have great significance. The problem facing the prosecution in the three attempted murder indictments relating to Simon was a conspicuous lack of evidence. There was no forensic evidence from the locations where Simon ate and later became ill, nor was there any direct medical evidence of the cause of his illness. There were no overt threats or actions by Erin – to the contrary, she'd behaved with care and compassion. All the prosecutors had was the fact that Simon had become ill, and that his parents had subsequently died as the result of a later event. Their evidence to support the three charges came down to chronology, so any suspicions raised by Simon's doctor could have provided another brick in the wall of the prosecutors' case.

Later, in these preliminary hearings, intensive care specialist Professor Andrew Bersten, who was called to give his opinion on both Simon's illnesses and some of Erin's medical issues, agreed with Mandy's proposition that in regard to Simon 'ultimately no infection cause was definitely found'. He also agreed that 'no evidence of a toxic substance was found'.

Simon said he couldn't remember any specific comment being made by the doctor, explaining that he'd assumed he'd been hit by gastro and that no-one had disavowed him of that thought. Simon's answer made it clear that no-one had considered foul play, which would be helpful for Erin's defence. A similar observation came a little later, when Simon talked about his subsequent hospitalisation, during which he'd been in a coma and undergone urgent and major surgery, resulting in a large portion of his bowel being removed. Again, it struck me that the absence of any medical reason for his illness went hand in hand with the absence of any suspicion that poisoning, either deliberate or accidental, could have been the cause.

Simon confirmed that he had told his father and other family members of his growing suspicion that Erin was the cause of his malaise, describing the hard decision to change his next-of-kin arrangements, taking medical decision-making away from Erin.

The testimony then moved to the lead-up to the Leongatha lunch and its aftermath, with Simon recalling that the invitation to lunch was made while he and Erin were working the live-stream at church. He said she'd told him she had some serious medical issues to discuss and wanted advice on how best to share the news with their children.

He confirmed he'd told Erin the day before the lunch that he wouldn't be coming, and then gave a fairly brief outline of what happened subsequently, making the observation that 'Erin has a big clue what the symptoms [of poisoning] were like, so did she fake it or lightly dose it?'

Mandy concluded his cross-examination with one of a barrister's favourite questions, asking Simon if he'd been told about the content of other people's statements. Simon said he wasn't sure what had gone into their statements but conceded that there would have been discussions before statements were made. Not a gotcha, just perfectly reasonable behaviour by a group of people struck down by tragedy.

Re-examination by the prosecutor – commonplace in trials, to clarify any points that arose in cross – was brief, and touched on Simon's decision to hire a media adviser, the change in his relationship with Erin following the tax return issue, and the menu on each of their camping trips and how the food was served.

One thing Simon's appearance had made clear was that he was likely to spend a long time in the witness box at the upcoming trial.

21

BUT WAIT, THERE'S MORE!

The preliminary hearings continued with a mix of child protection professionals and medical experts, including Doctor Dimitri Gerostamoulos from the Victorian Institute of Forensic Medicine, where he was Head of Forensic Sciences and Chief Toxicologist. He'd examined specimens from the lunch, and in addition to his statements he'd produced what he called 'monographs' – on the poisons hemlock, ricin and beta amanitin, with the latter found in death cap mushrooms. He told Mandy that he'd been asked to do so by the police for hemlock and ricin, but had included beta amanitin because it had been detected in the specimens he'd examined. He said the monographs were common accompaniments to a tox report when something had been detected or there was an interest in detection of a particular substance.

Hemlock is a plant that can cause vomiting and respiratory failure, and was allegedly what killed the philosopher Socrates in 399 BC.

Like death cap mushrooms, hemlock grows in the wild in Victoria. It's a pleasant-looking herb with white flowers that gives a hint of its dark side when crushed by emitting an unpleasant smell. Its greenery looks quite similar to that of carrots, parsnips and parsley, so it can be ingested, either accidentally or deliberately. All parts of the plant are toxic, and there is no antidote – those poisoned can only be supported, and luck plays a major role in recovery.

Ricin is a poison made from the shells of castor beans and causes symptoms including diarrhoea, nausea and vomiting. If the dose is sufficient, it can be fatal. Ricin is usually in pellet, mist or powder form, and can be inhaled, dissolved in a liquid and injected, mixed with other chemicals and applied to a wound, and ingested through ricin-contaminated food or liquid. Like hemlock, it has no antidote.

The doctor told Mandy that he'd never detected ricin in his work but had detected hemlock 'in other deaths'. His evidence stimulated the imagination of those listening, and I couldn't help wondering if either poison might have been an addition to some of Erin's recipes she'd served Simon. It wasn't until after the trial that we learned police, when digging deep into Erin's internet search history, had found searches on poisons and, in particular, hemlock.

Doctor Julian Rong, a consultant gastroenterologist who'd worked in Gippsland since 2010, gave evidence that he'd treated Simon and that his notes on the case ran to a mammoth 171 pages. He said that in March 2023, Simon had told him of his suspicions about Erin. His notes say: 'patient feels it might be to do with ex-partner food'. His evidence ended that tranche of hearings.

Further rounds of hearings took place from late October 2024 through to the end of the year. This time, however, it was back to relatively minor witnesses, and the nuts and bolts of electronics experts giving a taste of their findings.

Those experts included mobile phone data expert Doctor Matthew Sorell, who had examined four years of Erin's mobile phone records and, in particular, her travels that were indicated by the location of cell towers that her phone's SIM card connected to. It was incredibly detailed technical evidence with regular reference to the word 'spreadsheet', and evidence that gives great credit to lawyers who had to come to grips with it, and give thought to how best to present it later to a jury.

The cyber-investigator was Shamen Fox-Henry, a digital forensics officer with the Victoria Police. With this witness and Doctor Sorell, Mandy probed how they had conducted their analysis, looking for any potential points that might be used to cast even a minor shadow of doubt, or perhaps give an opportunity for a defence expert to question their findings or offer an alternative scenario. What we didn't hear was the detail of what was found by the cyber sleuths. That may have been in the statements that were tendered to the court but not publicly available.

The prosecutors finished the 2024 hearings by asking for tendency evidence to be admitted, referring to the assertion that someone has a tendency to act in a certain manner or a state of mind that drives them to act in a particular way. In this case, they claimed that Erin had a particular state of mind that drove her to use poison – not only death caps but other poisons she may have used in the alleged earlier attempts on Simon. This tendency evidence can then be used to support or flesh out the facts and, in Erin's case, to negate any defence claim that she'd poisoned her victims by accident rather than intent. The decision on this type of evidence would be one for the trial judge.

The end of the 2024 hearings also marked the departure of Judicial Registrar Freeman from the case. In 2025, the trial judge, Justice Christopher Beale, would be taking over.

*

I went into the Christmas break thinking about how the case might be defended. I'm one of a small number who has worked for both the prosecution, as a police officer, and then for the defence in major cases, using my knowledge of how investigations are conducted to scrutinise them for any errors or omissions. A fundamental error – one made far too often for comfort – is starting with an assumption of who the culprit might be, then letting that position colour your investigation. This is something that also happens in media – the story starts with a premise and everything is shaped to support that premise, often ending up in embarrassment, further hurt caused to victims and their families and friends, and defamation actions.

A recent case of this happening in policing was during the investigation into the 2014 disappearance of three-year-old William Tyrrell. A man named Bill Spedding became the prime suspect in the disappearance, with the investigation wrongly targeting him. Mr Spedding later successfully sued the state of New South Wales for malicious prosecution, abuse of process and misfeasance in public office. He was completely exonerated of any wrongdoing and awarded

$1.5 million damages, a verdict that the state appealed. The appeal was dismissed, with the judgement noting, 'One can only hope that its standing as the worst case is never repeated and is never superseded by conduct that is even worse.'

Though there'd only been glimpses of the workings of the Victoria Police investigation, it was clear they'd done their job well, not making assumptions or rushing, but instead letting the evidence build and guide them to the point where they had reasonable cause to suspect that Erin Patterson had attempted to murder her husband, and that she'd deliberately poisoned her lunch guests.

Having dismissed that possibility, I pondered what other defences might be offered. It was clear Mandy was taking the line that it was all a dreadful accident.

My fertile and devious mind suggested another thought. Would the earlier attempts on Simon, which resulted in dire illness but not death, be explained as trying to hurt him but not with the intention to kill, thus supporting an argument that Erin had intended to hurt her in-laws but not kill them? Retribution instead of infamy.

Hovering in the back of my mind was the recent case of Gregory Lynn, who'd been charged with the murders of Carol Clay and Russell Hill in Victoria's alpine country in 2020. They'd been involved in a dispute with Lynn while camping. Police alleged he'd murdered and subsequently nearly destroyed their bodies, in a crime the trial judge would later call 'brutal' and 'horrific'. This was another case that obsessed Erin.

The jury had found Lynn not guilty of the murder of Russell Hill but guilty of the murder of Carol Clay. It was an outcome few had predicted, and means that if the conviction for Clay's murder is overturned on appeal, Lynn walks free. Erin was facing charges of attempted murder in five incidents and murder in three, so if the jury weren't satisfied that she'd intended the lunch to be fatal, things could get very intriguing. As for the earlier alleged attempts on Simon, forensic evidence was zero, and the strongest evidence the prosecution had was the compelling chronology. To add to the intrigue and complexity of this case, if the charges arising from the lunch failed, that compelling chronology would become far less compelling. However, in the final days of the countdown to the trial, that would all be consigned to history.

In February 2025, the trial judge, Justice Christopher Beale, took over the fast-track proceedings. Beale is a former Crown Prosecutor who was appointed to the bench in 2014. He'd presided over many high-profile cases, including the 2016 killing of Karen Ristevski by her husband. In 2018, during a terrorist trial, he'd banned the niqab-wearing wife of the accused from the public gallery, noting, 'Whilst all are welcome in my court, spectators in the public gallery must have their faces uncovered, chiefly for security reasons.'

After the pleasantries that are a fundamental part of the courtroom ritual, Mandy opened by bringing up the elephant in the room – the question of media coverage of what had become one of the highest profile crime cases in Australia, one that had also attracted global interest and would continue to do so for the duration of the trial. He observed that the media scrutiny had been both 'voracious' and occasionally 'virulent', and that the desperation for any morsel couldn't be expected to abate. He mentioned that there were already more than a dozen podcasts about the case, and said he'd been told things about his client by complete strangers. He claimed, quite correctly in my view, that any potential jurors will have 'family, friends and casual acquaintances who will have an opinion', insisting that 'the spectre of unfair prejudice will hang over this trial'. In his view, the level of interest was 'probably unprecedented' and would linger in the minds of jurors irrespective of any order the judge made.

Mandy pressed on, telling the judge that evidence of Erin's interest in true crime, as displayed in her online life and book collection, was irrelevant. The prosecutor argued the opposite, stating that Erin's online life was highly relevant. Mandy suggested that allowing such evidence, including mention of Erin's large collection of true crime books, was at best 'peripheral' and possibly 'unfairly prejudicial'. He noted that the preliminary testimony of Erin's Facebook friends regarding their interest in true crime podcasts and the like was 'extraordinary' but also possibly 'very infected evidence', meaning that their recollections may have been contaminated by what they'd read, seen and heard.

Justice Beale suggested that the evidence provided by Erin's Facebook friends was more about Erin's relationships and discussions about their personal lives, which included conversations about Erin's unhappiness with Simon, the issue of child support claims and how they were resolved, and Erin allegedly 'railing' online about Simon's parents. If the evidence was found to be admissible, the jury would hear the whole story, including how the Facebook relationships started, developed and what transpired.

After that splash of colour, it was back to arguments about Erin's mobile phone pings, noting that she'd been in the vicinity of Neilson Street, Outtrim and the village of

Loch – both possible death cap mushroom sites, I wondered. It's always intriguing listening to snippets of evidence and wondering which part of the puzzle they play.

That suspicion firmed with a mention of the iNaturalist website, which was listed in Erin's search history in May 2022. The website helpfully provided a map that showed the researcher where death cap mushrooms could be found. At that revelation, the only sound in the courtroom was a sharp intake of breath followed by silence. And with that, the fast-track hearings drew to a close.

The next step was for the judge to return with his decision on the points raised by prosecution and defence, and to find out what evidence would be included or excluded. And that was when a fair-sized spanner was thrown into the works – for both the prosecution lawyers and those of us watching and planning to produce long-form media, like books and documentaries.

On 14 March 2025, Justice Beale returned to the bench and delivered his judgement.

The day began with some housekeeping issues, including the challenges of taking a major criminal trial to a regional courthouse, the pre-recording of some evidence from witnesses under the age of eighteen and a doctor who was likely to be unavailable at the time of the trial. Having children give evidence before the trial in less dramatic surroundings than a packed courtroom can reduce the stress and potential trauma for the child. One likely scenario in this trial was that the children would give their evidence in a remote location with support people at hand.

Then came Justice Beale and his spanner. He had six rulings to deliver. First up, all evidence gleaned from the 'computer records on devices seized from the home of the accused' relating to Erin's searches on poisons was to be excluded.

The second ruling would have been a relief for the prosecutor, allowing into evidence the phone tower allegations that placed Erin in the vicinity of Loch on 23 April 2023 and Outtrim on 22 May 2023. That could be a significant step in the building of a circumstantial case.

But any relief for the prosecution was short-lived, as the next ruling was to exclude the tendency evidence, with the judge noting that it was 'lacking significant probative value' and failed the test in the *Evidence Act*.

Ruling four was to allow into evidence most of Erin's allegedly 'incriminating conduct', which broadly meant witnesses could give evidence, be tested and let the jury decide on the value of the evidence. In his next ruling, the judge also indicated that some hearsay evidence could be included. Hearsay evidence refers to something the witness heard from another person, rather than seeing or hearing it directly.

Justice Beale saved the kicker for last. Ruling number six was to exclude coincidence evidence. This meant the eight charges had to be separated and there would be two trials, with the alleged attempted murder of Simon to be heard in one trial, and the charges arising from the lunch in the other. The shorthand version was the 'Simon' trial and the 'Lunch' trial.

It was soon confirmed that the trial for the charges arising from the lunch – three counts of murder and one count of attempted murder – would be the first, starting in Morwell on 28 April 2025.

The separation of trials may have been because the judge thought the jury could have been swayed by events in the lead-up to the lunch, rather than objectively making their decision based on the evidence presented. Separating the trials would confine them to consider only the evidence about the lunch.

At a practical level, this decision meant that the prosecution needed to rewrite the opening to the trial, and that the vast pile of evidence had to be reviewed and separated. The decision also had far-reaching ramifications regarding what could be reported and what couldn't, in order to avoid sub-judice issues, which are matters yet to be heard and decided by the court. At an extreme level, it meant that reporting of much of the first trial may not be allowed until after the second trial.

Predictably, the prosecutors appealed Justice Beale's decision. On 3 April 2025, the prosecutors, led by Senior Crown Prosecutor Nanette Rogers SC, and the defence, led by Colin Mandy SC, stood before the three-member Court of Criminal Appeal – the highest appeal court in the state. The point of the appeal was that the prosecution believed Justice Beale had erred in his decision.

What followed was a somewhat feisty hearing, with the judges weighing in frequently with questions, often while the prosecutor was mid-point. The prosecution agreed with one of the judges, who suggested they wanted to use the earlier alleged attempts on Simon to prove Erin's intentions at the lunch and, as a judge noted, to prove the lunch wasn't an 'unfortunate culinary incident'. Mandy swiftly said the defence didn't dispute that death caps were in the dish but argued that they were there by accident, not design.

As the legal toing and froing continued, the judges provided one moment of humour. When Erin's preparation of individual Wellingtons was raised, one judge said they thought that was how they were usually prepared, prompting faux outrage from the others, and some tips on how to prepare the perfect beef Wellington – never, ever as individual elements!

On 17 April, the judges returned their decision – the appeal was dismissed. There would be two separate trials. Later that day, in a separate pre-trial hearing, Justice Beale confirmed that the first trial, commencing on 28 April 2025 in Morwell, would be for the murders of Don Patterson, Gail Patterson and Heather Wilkinson, and the attempted murder of Ian Wilkinson. The charge of attempting to murder Simon at the lunch had been dropped. The trials for the earlier attempted murder of Simon would be held at a time in the future.

Mandy was quickly on his feet, canvassing the possibility of suppressing the first trial decision in the interests of fairness to his client and jury selection for the next trial. The judge cut to the chase, observing that was something for discussion on the first day of the trial, when there would be a list of issues to canvass before the jury was selected and empanelled, but he observed that it was likely to be 'futile'. You can suppress publication, but you can't stop people talking.

As it turned out, it was a moot point. Within less than a week, the landscape of the case would change yet again, and this application would be consigned to history.

22

THE SHOW COMES TO TOWN

On 28 April 2025, the Erin Patterson case arrived in the town of Morwell.

I arrived the day before – a Sunday train ride from Melbourne, about 150 kilometres west. It's important to get a feel for the location you're writing about, to ensure you accurately capture the geography, people, the life of the town. Towns, as I've mentioned before, often become characters in the story.

Morwell is an unlikely venue for the trial of an alleged mass murderer. It's in the heart of Gippsland's Latrobe Valley, home to open-cut brown coal mining that until recently fed Victoria's massive power generation industry. Privatisation of these power suppliers back in the late 1990s shook the industry up, and that, combined with changing demands and the environmental impacts of coal mining and power generation, meant employment opportunities waned, and Morwell, once a hard-working yet prosperous town, went into decline. The Princes Highway, which had cut through the town's centre, bringing ample business to the local hospitality industry, now bypasses Morwell, and the impact of Covid-19 lockdowns added to its misery.

These days it's a peaceful, sprawling town, home to a little over 14,000 people, with wide streets and neat and tidy housing. Large trucks no longer thunder along the main street on their way to Sydney or Melbourne, and the town's commercial centres are littered with for lease signs. Many of the pubs that once thrived by slaking the thirst of miners and power workers are closed. Youth crime has become a problem, just as it has in other regional centres, fuelled by easy access to cheap drugs and little else to do. Morwell is a friendly town experiencing tough times, but one that hasn't given up.

The Latrobe Valley Law Courts, housed in a modern building in Commercial Road, is the major courthouse for the region. It runs over three levels, with five courtrooms. Unlike the gloomy interiors of older Australian courthouses, this place has plenty of windows and natural light, with seating for the public that is less punishing than some of the old courtrooms, like the Melbourne Supreme Court where the preliminaries were held.

On the ground floor are the court offices and courts used by magistrates dealing with the sausage machine of justice – minor to middling-weight civil and criminal cases, bail applications for those still lingering in the police cells next door, the early days of the most serious crimes, destined to be sent to higher courts.

On the first floor are courts four and five, which have a jury box. Court four also has a secure box at the rear of the room behind the public seating, where the accused sits during their criminal trial if they're in custody. This box has access from the police station cells via a tunnel to the courthouse basement then a lift, thus making it both secure and private – no parading of the accused before the media pack, all desperate for a photo or a grab.

By Monday, 28 April, the media pack had descended on Morwell and were loitering in the square that separated the courthouse from the police station, hoping for a glimpse of Erin as she was transferred to the courtroom. They soon found themselves out of luck and on the receiving end of an impromptu police briefing on what could and couldn't be filmed. It's a busy courthouse, and care was needed to avoid filming minors, people dealing with domestic violence and other potentially sensitive matters.

Meanwhile, I loitered upstairs outside the courtroom, the perfect vantage point to watch key players in the case arriving.

One of the first people to arrive was the officer in charge of the investigation, Detective Stephen Eppingstall. His head was freshly shaved, and he was wearing a double-breasted winter coat over a plain dark grey suit. He moved quickly to greet a member of the Patterson family, who'd later be watching proceedings in the courtroom.

The first morning of a trial is busy for the lead detective. They're checking to make sure every person, every detail is ready before the judge steps onto the bench. Their eyes are everywhere, checking who is in the foyer – are there family and witnesses you need to get settled? Other faces in the crowd who might be problematic? Like a skilled maitre d', they must make sure everything is in order, every risk minimised.

Eppingstall was also a witness in the case, and didn't engage with the media.

The morning was off to a fairly low-key start for a major trial. There was the usual court traffic on the ground floor waiting for their matters and appointments, and just a few of us on level one, quietly waiting and looking around. The barristers appeared, distinctive in their black gowns but minus the theatre of wigs. And then there was the simple human touch, lawyers scurrying into the poky offices adjacent to the courtroom, carrying milk to dilute the very ordinary instant coffee and tea that is courthouse catering, and a supply of biscuits for a sugar hit during the brief morning and mid-afternoon break – a habit that hasn't changed in generations.

But as the 10.30 am commencement time approached, the media pack deserted their camera people and moved to level one. The relative peace turned to a clamour.

A shade before 10.30 am we piled into the courtroom, with lawyers, police and family first, then media and court-watchers. Trials attract those with clear interest, such as friends or family, as well as court watchers, who spend the trial sitting in the gallery listening intently. While there are long periods of lawyers' submissions and arguments that are necessary but as dry as dust, there are also moments of high drama during a trial, with revelations, comments from out of left field, and the occasional gotcha moment that stops a witness in their tracks.

Inside the courtroom, which was now full with standing room not permitted, the noise level had plummeted to a low murmur. From here on, respect for the court and seriousness of purpose were front of mind. It would be the first of many days of listening and typing frantically on laptops and iPads. The flurry of journalists would prompt Crown Prosecutor Nanette Rogers SC to complain to the judge that their presence was distracting and may also distract the jury. Neither the judge nor defence counsel Colin Mandy SC shared her concerns. In fact, on day one the public gallery of just under fifty seats was substantially full of media, but during the trial, only six seats were allocated to media – the rest were for the public – so it seemed likely the laptop serenade would be short-lived.

At the bar table, the barristers were facing the bench, their solicitors sitting opposite, facing them but with their backs to the judge's bench – a practical use of the limited space. In front of the bar table, immediately below the judge's bench, is where the associates sit, along with the recordist of the proceedings and the tipstaff, who announce the arrival and departure of the judge. The witness box is to the judge's right and, opposite it, on the other wall, is the jury box.

At exactly 10.30 am there were three sharp knocks on the door to the judge's bench, the tipstaff called for all assembled to stand, and in walked Justice Beale KC, wearing black robes trimmed on the sleeves with scarlet. The judge took his seat, and we followed suit. The trial was finally underway.

It was possibly the most impressive array of legal might to grace a regional courtroom. Colin Mandy SC and his junior Sophie Stafford sat to the judge's right, and facing them, with their backs to the judge, were instructing solicitor Bill Doogue and his team.

Mandy is a highly regarded advocate specialising in criminal law who has appeared in major cases around the country. He's also the former vice president of the Victorian Bar. The criminal bar can attract some theatrical, colourful practitioners. Mandy's style is the opposite – detailed, methodical and unwaveringly polite which, if you're before a jury, can be persuasive. He was admitted to practise as a lawyer back in 1992, and began working as a barrister in 2000. In 2018 he was appointed as senior counsel. He comes across as a safe pair of hands if you find yourself in terrible strife.

Mandy's instructing solicitor, Bill Doogue, is cut from a slightly different cloth. He's a big, noticeable bloke with a ready smile and an affable demeanour. Like Mandy, he's been around. He was admitted to practise in 1989, and early in his career he spent two and a half years working for Aboriginal Legal Aid in the Northern Territory, which can be a tough gig and a steep learning curve. He's one of Australia's top criminal solicitors, with a long list of clients from the clerical to the political to the very colourful.

On the other side of the central lectern was the prosecution team of Nanette Rogers SC, her juniors Jane Warren and Sarah Lenthall, and their solicitors. Rogers was admitted to practise as a solicitor in 1979 and spent her first ten years working at the Redfern Legal Centre in inner Sydney, which back then was home to sprawling housing estates and a large Aboriginal community. Her career then took her to the Northern Territory, where she worked as an advocate for the Central Australian Aboriginal Legal Aid Service and later became a Crown Prosecutor. In 1999 she was awarded a PhD from the University of Sydney. Rogers is one of Victoria's most experienced prosecutors.

The key players were in position, but where was Erin? That question was answered as the court rose for the morning adjournment. The judge's tipstaff called us to stand, and the judge stood and headed to the door on his left. I did a half turn to head for the door and saw that Erin, accompanied by a male and female uniformed security officer, had slipped quietly into court and was in the dock maybe two metres behind me.

She wore an oversized grey-green jumper over pants, her hair was long and lank and curiously, given the chilly weather, was wearing a pair of sandals – 'typical Erin', quipped one of her Facebook friends when I later chatted with her.

Trials place a demand on the wardrobe of the accused, especially if they're in custody and, in Erin's case, short on family and friends. Erin's main support came from her friend Alison Rose Prior, who had allegedly visited Erin at the Dame Phyllis Frost Centre. She was now staying occasionally at Gibson Street, and would become a trial regular. She also kept Erin in fresh clothing throughout.

Prison life can wear you down, and Erin was looking time-worn and pale, but hadn't notably lost weight. She was, however, engaged with the happenings and the faces in the courtroom.

Erin had been transported to Morwell from the Dame Phyllis Frost Centre, either early that morning or the night before. Her comfort in the Morwell police cells was an early issue in the trial. Mandy told the judge that Erin had a good knowledge of the massive brief of evidence but needed access to it so she could give instructions to her lawyer. That required access to a laptop – but without internet access – writing materials and notebooks. At Dame Phyllis Frost, the authorities had provided these things, but at the police station, they weren't available. The pen had been deemed a suicide risk and removed, and there was nowhere in her cell to charge the laptop.

Mandy also told the judge they'd arranged for Erin to have a doona and pillow so she could get proper rest during what would be a long and arduous trial, but those things were also missing. While police may have considered this special treatment, Mandy insisted they were the basics Erin required so that she and the defence team could do their job properly. The judge concurred, and it seemed likely that a polite but firm conversation with the police would be forthcoming.

Day one is invariably housekeeping to streamline the trial. The contents of the opening statements were discussed – this precludes the judge having to stop the barristers in mid-flight and send the jury out for a cup of tea. The focus then shifted to the media, and a complaint from Mandy about the reporting from an earlier hearing, which showed that Erin was in custody – prison vans, handcuffs, burly corrections officers – arguing that repeated exposure to such images may prejudice a fair trial.

Mandy noted that in the trial of Gregory Lynn, Justice Croucher had directed the media to make sure all photos were cropped to remove any suggestion of Lynn being in custody. Rogers agreed with Mandy and, later that morning, lawyers for the publications who'd published the pictures that prompted Mandy's complaint joined the courtroom via video link and received a polite judicial dressing down about the inappropriate pictures. Suitably chastised, they agreed to ensure their media colleagues were better behaved, and then it was back to the trial preliminaries.

The judge's proposed script for the jury selection, which included questions about podcasting, was discussed. Mandy suggested that any potential juror who'd listened to a podcast about the case should be excused, noting that some of the investigations by media, and podcasts in particular, may have been 'inappropriate'. Rogers wasn't hugely enthusiastic about the blanket exemption, suggesting that it could reduce a panel of 120 potential jurors very quickly. The judge agreed with Mandy, taking the view that an uncontaminated mind was essential for a juror.

Rogers then raised a curious point, suggesting they canvass jurors about the detail of the dreadful symptoms of poisoning and if that would impact on their reasoning. Beale replied, 'This is a murder trial so there is going to be disturbing evidence. If they don't think they can be objective, then they should be excused.'

The highlight of the day was the belated discovery that on 22 April 2025, the charges for the attempted murder of Simon had been dropped. The reasons weren't canvassed, but on 12 August 2025, the ABC reported the Office of Public Prosecutions told them, 'In the absence of evidence in relation to the lunch, it was determined that there were no reasonable prospects of conviction for those charges.' The comment followed the release of a Court of Criminal Appeal judgement in 2024, which said of the charges alleging Simon had been poisoned that 'there is no direct evidence that Simon was poisoned on any of the three charged occasions. There is no direct medical or toxicological evidence that on any of these occasions he was in fact poisoned, and, without descending into detail, there is only the slimmest medical opinion that his symptoms on the first two occasions could more likely be explained by toxins than by infection.' Contrary to the assertion of that great Victorian lawyer Dennis Denuto in *The Castle*, who claimed 'it's the constitution, it's Mabo, it's justice, it's the law, it's the vibe', the vibe doesn't work in a criminal case.

23

ENTER THE JURY

To put together a jury in Victoria, Juries Victoria ask the state's electoral commission to randomly prepare a list of names taken from the electoral roll. In February 2025, a roll of 15,000 names from the Latrobe Valley was requested to cover Supreme and County Court sittings in the area from 28 April to 1 August 2025.

Next, those people were asked to complete a questionnaire to confirm they were eligible to serve on a jury. Those who are eligible and don't have a reason that excuses them from taking part get a summons to attend court, usually two or three weeks later. Jurors are selected with proximity to the court in mind – easy for city dwellers, where the courts aren't a great distance and usually easy to get to by public transport, but a little more challenging for those living in regional areas. That left around 8000 potential jurors from the Latrobe Valley. In late March, 1400 of those potential jurors were sent a summons to attend court either on 28 or

30 April. By mid-April, 597 of those people remained on the roll, the others having been eliminated for a variety of reasons. Of those, 234 said they'd be available for an eight-week trial.

The pay certainly isn't a drawcard – jurors receive just $40 per day for cases up to six days long and $80 per day thereafter. Your employer, if you have one, is required to make up the difference between this and your daily pay. Being self-employed is a valid reason to be excused from service. Lunch, indifferent coffee and tea and, if you're lucky, a biscuit or two are provided. Jurors usually go home at night but are sometimes sequestered – isolated from the public in accommodation such as a motel – when considering their verdict.

On Tuesday, 29 April 2025, around 112 people arrived at the Latrobe Valley court complex to participate in jury selection for the Erin Patterson trial. The group was then whittled down to 85 for various reasons, such as knowing someone involved in the trial or for medical reasons. Then out came the ballot box and in went the names. As the names were called, the defence and prosecution both had the right to challenge each juror. The defence challenged three, the prosecution none.

The jury selection, thanks in large measure to the agreed upon script, was swift and efficient, starting late morning and finishing just before 2 pm. Fifteen people – ten men and five women – were selected. In Australian courts there are usually twelve jurors in a criminal trial. If the trial is likely to be a long one, fifteen jurors hear all the evidence, and if there are still more than twelve at the end – sometimes a juror might leave due to illness, family issues, or because they allegedly did something inappropriate – a ballot is held to reduce the number to twelve. Those remaining jurors will then begin their deliberations, and their decision must be unanimous. The decision to include extra jurors on the panel would prove to be a prudent one.

At 3.10 pm Justice Beale was back on the bench, Erin was back in her spot behind the public gallery, and it was time for the jury to enter the jury box for the judge to deliver his instructions to them. These covered some basic housekeeping matters and a clear and precise rundown of what to do and what not to do in the coming weeks.

Justice Beale is a judge with a sense of humour – handy in the pressure cooker of a criminal trial, where the occasional light moment can be a relief – but he's also a judge who cuts to the chase, and does so in plain English. When he speaks, it's both concise and precise – words aren't wasted.

He told the jury that over the next few days they'd need to elect a foreperson, whose role was to be their spokesperson, passing notes to the tipstaff on issues that may arise or questions the jury may have. The foreperson would also be responsible for delivering the outcome of their deliberations to the judge.

The judge then raised the lingering spectre of Covid-19. He outlined the symptoms so many of us had tried to forget, and explained that each juror would be given two rapid antigen (RAT) tests. If they experienced any Covid-19 symptoms, they were to advise the court and stay at home. Justice Beale was not going to risk a mistrial courtesy of this virus.

He also let the jurors know they'd be returning to their homes each night until it was time to consider their verdict, at which point they'd be sequestered, though he didn't reveal where they would be housed. Their accommodation was likely to be more functional than luxurious, and isolated from the many others who were also in the region for the trial – although as we later discovered that didn't quite go to plan.

Beale moved on, explaining the roles of each of the key players – the judge, the lawyers and the jury. He also said they'd be given iPads, which would be loaded with things like exhibits that were tendered and various documents, such as the daily transcripts, statements and so on. Their jury's decision should be made on the evidence presented to the court, and on that evidence alone. 'You must dismiss all prejudices or sympathies you may have. Your duty is to consider the evidence using your head, not your heart. You must completely ignore anything you have seen or heard in the media, including social media, about this case, and the people involved in it.' Beale said that if they saw something about the case reported in a newspaper, online or on television, they should not read or watch it – just turn the page, scroll on or change the channel. They were only to discuss the case with their fellow jurors.

He then explained some details about evidence, noting in particular the difference between circumstantial and direct evidence. As Beale explained it, direct evidence was someone saying they'd seen or heard the rain, while circumstantial evidence was seeing someone carrying a wet umbrella or wet raincoat and thus believing it was raining. He said that it made no difference at law whether the evidence was direct or circumstantial.

Then it was to the reality of their task. The onus was on the prosecution, through the work of the Crown Prosecutor and her colleagues, to present evidence to prove the charges against Erin beyond all reasonable doubt. Beale said that it was almost impossible to prove anything with absolute certainty, but beyond reasonable doubt is realistic. He said, 'Ms Patterson does not have to prove anything. That never changes from start to finish. It's not for her to demonstrate her innocence, but for the prosecution to prove the charges they have brought against her. It's not enough for the prosecution to prove the accused is probably guilty, or very likely to be guilty.'

Beale then switched gears to finish on a lighter note, saying that some members of the public might consider that the jurors starting their work at 10.30 am and finishing at 4.15 pm might be 'pretty slack'. This got smiles not only in the jury box but also around the courtroom. 'But as the trial goes on I think you'll find it pretty demanding.'

I've never been on a jury, but having spent quite a bit of my career both involved in trials and covering them, I can confirm that a day in court is intense and tiring, even if you're merely a spectator. With the weight of a person's future and the hopes and expectations of the victim(s) and the families on your shoulders, that fatigue is no doubt enormous.

Beale ended his directions with a final warning: 'Shut down any conversations with anybody, family, friends, who want to know more.' Then the jurors departed for home, to return the next morning for opening addresses.

The last instruction given before the court rose for the day was that the first prosecution witness, Simon Patterson, should be ready to commence his evidence after opening addresses, noting the possibility of subsequent witnesses starting Thursday afternoon.

Wishful thinking, I thought to myself. And I was half-right – the first witness did start on the Thursday but the anticipated trial duration of four to six weeks was definitely classified as 'wishful thinking'. The trial would run almost double that length.

24

THE CASE AGAINST ERIN PATTERSON BEGINS

The trial proper began on Wednesday, 30 April at 10.30 am with the arrival of Justice Beale. After some discussions between the judge and the lawyers regarding corrections to the transcript, IT issues and what they hoped would be quieter typing by the media pack, the jury were brought in, looking fresh, rested and ready. Erin was in her usual spot at the rear of the court, flanked by two officers. She was wearing a blue-and-white striped shirt.

While the hearing was live-streamed to the media at the Latrobe Court and the Supreme Court in Melbourne, that feed was via a court-operated camera – media cameras are not allowed in. For media elsewhere, there was a live audio feed. In the courtroom was the sketch artist Paul Tyquin, hired by a pool of media outlets. He's no stranger to a courtroom, having sketched his way through several major cases in Victoria, including the Gregory Lynn murder trial and preliminary hearings for the case of Patrick Orren Stephenson, charged with the murder of Ballarat mother Samantha Murphy.

The judge began by again taking the jury through the four elements the prosecution had to prove for each of the three murder charges and what had to be proven in the case of the attempted murder charge. The judge offered a checklist of what the jury had to consider on the murder charges:

1. *The accused caused the death of the deceased by serving the deceased a poisoned meal (the alleged conduct); and*

2. *The accused's alleged conduct was conscious, voluntary and deliberate; and*

3. *At the time of the alleged conduct, the accused intended to kill or cause really serious injury to the deceased; and*

4. *The accused killed the deceased without lawful justification or excuse.*

In relation to the murder charges, Beale explained that 'the prosecution have to prove all of those elements beyond reasonable doubt. It's cumulative. That word "and" at the end of each element is critical.' His knack for delivering simple and concise instructions to the jury was clear in his next comment: 'If the answer to that question [the first question] is "yes", you go on to Question 2. If the answer is "no", the accused is not guilty in relation to that particular count of murder, all right?'

The judge also offered an analogy on what conscious and voluntary meant. 'Someone is sleep-walking and they engage in some conduct that would be otherwise criminal, but it's not conscious and voluntary. Or, let's say you're ... walking down a corridor, you get to the top of some stairs and someone is standing near the top of the stairs, and you stumble and you knock them over and they end up falling down the stairs and dying. It's not conscious, voluntary and deliberate conduct.'

On the question of intention – not motive, as television dramas love to focus on – Beale said, 'Has the prosecution proved that at the time of the alleged conduct, the accused intended to kill or cause really serious injury to the deceased?'

He went on. 'Now, many people may think for a murder charge, only an intention to kill would suffice but that's not the case. An intention to kill or an intention to cause really serious injury is sufficient. If the prosecution prove that state of mind – either of those states of mind in relation to a murder charge and prove that beyond reasonable doubt, that's sufficient proof of intention for the alleged crime of murder.'

On the charge of attempted murder, the requirement was similar: the prosecution must prove she'd served Ian Wilkinson a poisoned meal, that this act was more than 'merely preparatory' to killing him, that she intended to kill him, and finally that she had no lawful justification or excuse.

Then it was over to Crown Prosecutor Nanette Rogers SC to outline the Crown's case. All eyes were on her as she began her address, methodically and concisely outlining the key elements of the case the prosecution would be presenting to the jury. Her style was low-key – no flourishes or dramatic pauses. The courtroom was silent bar Rogers' voice and the soft tapping of the six journalists on their keyboards.

She started by telling the jury that the cases arose from a lunch at Erin's Leongatha home on Saturday, 29 July 2023, attended by Simon's parents, Don and Gail Patterson, Gail's sister Heather Wilkinson and Heather's husband, Ian. Eleven or twelve hours later the four became ill with what appeared to be severe gastroenteritis. Within days, three of the four were dead. Ian Wilkinson survived but endured a long recovery in hospital.

With the jury leaning forward on occasion, listening intently to every word, Rogers said 'all four were each clinically diagnosed by treating doctors with amanita mushroom poisoning, caused by consuming poisonous mushrooms. Another guest was invited to the lunch but declined the invitation and that person was Simon Patterson, Erin Patterson's separated husband. What was initially thought to be a mass food poisoning event was investigated by police.' She gave the jury a thumbnail sketch of Simon and Erin's relationship, from their first meeting at Monash Council, their marriage in 2007 and the birth of their son in 2009 and daughter in 2014. She said there were periods of estrangement in the marriage that were reconciled, but in 2015, the year after their daughter's birth, they separated permanently. Their relationship was 'amicable', she said, with shared custody of the children and joint family holidays, both interstate and overseas.

Those travels included trips to Darwin, Adelaide and New Zealand, as well as more adventurous destinations, including Zimbabwe, Botswana and Namibia.

After talking about their various houses, Rogers touched on Erin's online life, which started in 2019 with the Keep

Keli Lane Behind Bars Facebook group, and then other groups, with Erin using the names Erin Patterson, Erin Erin and Erin Erin Erin.

With that spicy tidbit, she moved on to outline the story of the Pattersons and the Wilkinsons. Lawyers of this calibre need to be storytellers, and the best storytellers put a face on the story – the victims' lives, their families. Then she deftly moved back to Erin and Simon, telling the jury that 'amicable' went into decline in 2022, when Simon noticed a 'sustained' change, particularly after he noted on his tax return that they were separated. Then came disagreement over child support payments, and a change of schools for the children in term 3 of 2022, something Erin had done without consulting Simon.

Rogers then took everyone to the events of July 2023. She began with Erin's alleged medical travails, the subsequent lunch invitation and the reason given for the gathering – to get some advice about an issue. The day before the lunch, Rogers said there had been a flurry of text messages between the estranged couple, with Simon telling Erin he wouldn't be coming because he felt 'too uncomfortable'.

She then detailed the lunch – the mismatched plates, the seating arrangements and so on – and recounted a comment Heather Wilkinson made from her hospital bed: 'Yeah, I noticed Erin put her food on a different plate to us. Her plate had different colours on it. I wondered why it was.' It was a natural segue to a snapshot of the time the victims spent in hospital, noting that Erin said she was also feeling sick the day after the lunch, but had taken her children to Tyabb, around ninety kilometres away, for her son's flying lessons, and while she was captured on

CCTV entering a service station toilet, it was only for nine seconds.

That night, the children's dinner was leftovers from the lunch the day before – beans, mashed potatoes and beef. Rogers said, 'The prosecution asserts that the children's meal was not contaminated with death cap mushrooms'. At Leongatha Hospital two days later, with Erin reluctant to stay despite claiming she was ill, medical staff asked Erin about the leftovers, and 'the accused said the mushrooms had been scraped off as the children did not like mushrooms'.

Rogers moved to Erin's story about where the mushrooms came from – a combination of Woolworths and an Asian grocer in Mount Waverley, Oakleigh or Clayton – noting that she denied foraging for mushrooms. It was a subtle lead-up to evidence later to be given by witnesses, which would cast massive doubts on Erin's story.

At 1 pm the court took a break for lunch and resumed around 2.15 pm. Rogers' early estimates that her opening address would take about an hour to an hour and a half had been – unsurprisingly – optimistic.

On resumption, Rogers spoke about the urgent investigation conducted by Victoria's Department of Health and the work of an officer hunting down the source of the mushrooms. She said, 'He was not able to find any product fitting the description of the dried mushrooms that the accused had provided,' then moved on to death cap mushrooms and their dire effects on humans.

Having laid the groundwork of her story, it was time for a strong finish, one rich in tantalising snippets. She told the jury about Erin's use of the iNaturalist website, her trips to Outtrim and Loch, where the website reported death caps growing, and then told them that a mobile phone expert would give evidence that placed Erin at these locations, adding that only hours after the Loch trip, Erin had bought a dehydrator, which was later found at the local tip and contained residue of death cap mushrooms.

Rogers ended her opening address by saying she hoped the jury wouldn't be 'over-awed' by the volume and content of the evidence. On the notion of motive, something the judge had canvassed earlier, she said, 'Motive is not something that has to be proven by the prosecution. The prosecution will not be suggesting that there was a particular motive to do what she did.' It was a useful point, and a clear attempt to dispel the vexed question that was on everyone's minds: why? Although this was not something that should form part of the jury's deliberations, it was a question that would go on to dominate pubs, lounge rooms and Facebook groups.

Rogers' address was detailed, and delivered with a subtlety that belied its power. Clearly, she had not been thrown off her game by the keyboard tapping of the six journalists in court.

After a short break, the opening addresses resumed. Colin Mandy SC stood, telling the jury that the opening wasn't a time to argue the merits of what Rogers had said. That would come later. He said there was no dispute that people had died from eating death cap mushrooms, but 'did she intend to kill these four people? That's an issue. Erin Patterson did not deliberately serve poisoned food to her guests. The defence case is that what happened was a tragedy and a terrible accident. She's innocent.'

He went on. 'The defence case is that Erin Patterson did not deliberately serve poisoned food to her guests at that lunch on 29 July 2023. She didn't do it deliberately, she didn't do it intentionally. The defence case is that she didn't intend to cause anyone any harm on that day. The defence case is that what happened was a tragedy and a terrible accident.'

Mandy painted a picture of his client, telling the jury she was a 'devoted mother, caring, kind and attentive to her children'. Erin was also financially comfortable and 'generous and kind to the wider Patterson family, including being generous with her money'.

Building on the theme of his client's relationship with her in-laws and their families, Mandy said that despite the separation, a good friendship continued, with the children having a close relationship with their grandparents and Don tutoring his grandson in mathematics.

While that might have been a high note on which to end the day, there were other matters that needed to be canvassed and conceded, including the fact that his client hadn't been diagnosed with cancer, and that she was a forager for mushrooms, though she had not been deliberately looking for death caps. Erin Patterson was in tears during Mandy's address.

Then he came to the prosecution's allegation that Erin's behaviour after the lunch 'might make her look guilty'. It's a point that arises frequently in criminal cases – people judge others' actions or inactions, but do so based on what they think they'd do or what they expect of others. Like I said at the start of this book, crimes like murder change so many lives forever, and unless you've had that terrible experience, it's not fair or reasonable to judge people by your own expectations.

On this point, Mandy told the jury, 'So you'll need to think about this issue: how Erin Patterson felt about that in the days that follow. That is an issue in this trial. You will need to consider how she behaved and what she did in that important context. How did she feel in those days after the lunch, about serving up a meal that had such tragic consequences? And how might that have impacted on the way she behaved?'

Having planted that seed in the minds of the jurors, he built on it. 'Might someone panic in a situation like that? Is it possible that people might do and say things that are not well thought out and might, in the end, make them look bad? Is it possible that a person might lie when they find out that people are seriously ill because of the food that they've served up? Those are important issues in this case.' He suggested the jury use their experience, common sense and knowledge of human nature to consider the situation, and then he cautioned them 'not to jump to conclusions'. It was a well-crafted slice of his address, prompting the members of the jury to pause and consider, and not rush to judgement.

Mandy told the jury they should consider that perhaps Erin had eaten less and thus avoided the dire consequences of the lunch. Then he turned to the dehydrator, the fact that she'd lied to police about owning it and the tricky issue of disposing of it when her guests were fighting for their lives. He made the point that several of her Facebook friends knew she had one, noting that she'd posted pictures on Facebook. The implication was that as a lie, it wasn't a convincing one and might have been an error in judgement.

He also acknowledged that Erin had lied to police about not foraging for mushrooms, but he denied that she'd foraged for death caps. These were the points that would, like the circumstantial case of the prosecution, form the defence case that Mandy hoped would establish reasonable doubt.

Mandy ended his address by reiterating one simple point: 'The intention to kill or cause anyone any harm at all is very much in dispute. On the evidence that you hear, can the prosecution satisfy you of an intention to kill these four people beyond reasonable doubt?'

That decision was entirely up to the jury.

Both addresses had been delivered with none of the histrionics we see in television dramas. Australian courts, in spite of the dramatic and often tragic circumstances that lead us there, are places that value civility, courtesy and respect, and where raised voices are rare.

Though the addresses had been notably civil, we later learned that at the morning adjournment, Erin hadn't been happy. When the jury had left the court and she had sat down again in the dock, her head tilted up and her eyes closed. She was overheard asking her lawyers, 'Do I have to keep suffering through this?'

*

First up the next morning, Ms Lenthall, Rogers' colleague, took the jury into the essential but unexciting world of how to use their court-supplied iPads – a perfect illustration of how a trial combines the mundane and the riveting.

Then Rogers was back on her feet to announce the trial's first witness – Simon Patterson. It's a common practice in trials to present the civilian witnesses first, with the police following later. A witness like Simon would put a human face on this sad and terrible story.

Rogers also asked that the 'informant' Detective Eppingstall be allowed to remain in court, to which Mandy agreed. In most cases, if you're on the list to give evidence then you can't remain in the courtroom while other witnesses are examined. It's likely that Eppingstall was allowed to remain because, though he'd be giving evidence toward the end of the trial, his depth of knowledge of the case could aid the smooth running of the trial.

Simon Patterson, who was waiting outside, was formally called into the courtroom. He was dressed in a sombre grey/blue suit, a white shirt and a silver-grey tie with a subtle geometric pattern. The tipstaff showed him to the witness box, where he gave an affirmation to tell the truth.

Eye contact with Erin wasn't noticeable, probably because he was aware or had been alerted to the vigilant jury likely – and probably most in the courtroom – who would be looking for interplay between the two. Erin's lawyers may have given her similar advice.

Rogers opined that they had other witnesses on standby for that afternoon and Friday should Simon's evidence be short, a statement that rose eyebrows among the media pack. To borrow from *The Castle* again, she was dreaming. Simon's evidence about his relationship with Erin and that of his family was at the heart of the case – his testimony would take some time.

With Simon standing in the witness box, Rogers started with the basics, getting him to state his full name – Simon Peter Patterson – and to confirm Erin's maiden name of Scutter. Simon then paused, turned to the judge and asked if he could sit down, suggesting Simon had been given a few pointers on courtroom demeanour. When giving evidence, you wait until the judge suggests you sit down or you ask. The judge agreed, and the questions then moved to cover how Simon and Erin met at Monash Council, where he worked as a civil engineer and Erin in animal control for the RSPCA, starting as friendship amid what he described as a 'fairly eclectic' group of people, then developing into a romance, and finally marriage on 2 June 2007.

Rogers then took him through their years together – their shared hopes, holidays, and passion for travel and the bush. She produced a document outlining the Wilkinson/Patterson family tree, which the judge, jury, lawyers, Simon in the witness box and Erin in the dock all had access to via iPad and computer screens.

After setting up the family entanglements, Rogers moved to the decline of their relationship, disagreements, and the notable point that during their marriage it was 'very rare', as Simon said, to have guests at their home. It was observed that the extended families were close but seldom at Simon and Erin's home in Korumburra and later Erin's home in Leongatha, thus the lunch invitation was conspicuous.

It was shaping up to be a long day of brick-by-brick storytelling, but there were some moments that prompted the audience to lean forward with interest. In a poignant moment, when questioned about their early separations, he said, 'When we lived together, it was always her leaving me'.

Simon said that after their final separation in 2015 they remained friendly and ensured their children were well cared for. He paused here, obviously emotional, and asked for tissues. Then he said, 'It's good to be friends with the person you're married to.' He was obviously distressed by talking about this time in his life. When the judge asked if he needed a break, Simon declined, saying, 'I'm just struggling to answer the question, but I'll get there. I'm okay.'

When he'd recovered, Rogers continued, asking what markers he'd use to describe an ongoing friendship. Simon replied, 'To manage the kids well together', explaining that the children were living 'half and half with their mum and their dad.' He told the jury that, until recently, they'd gone on family holidays together, travelling overseas, interstate and to Erin's mother's house in Eden. The weekend trips he took with Erin that ended with him in hospital didn't get a mention.

Rogers moved on to the decline of their relationship after Erin discovered that Simon had said they were separated on his tax return. When asked how she found out, Simon said he was 'unsure' and didn't recall asking. However, he said the change might have been the result of a 'miscommunication' with his accountant, noting that Erin had rejected his offer to amend the return. He told the jury that was 'probably the first thing that made me feel that there was a substantial change in our relationship'. After this incident, he said their relationship became 'functional' and focused on the management and care of their children.

The prosecution was establishing the timeline of a relationship that was in decline. After canvassing child support matters and other domestic housekeeping, Justice Beale paused for the morning tea break.

Fifteen minutes later they were back, with Rogers asking Simon about Erin's relationship with his parents. He said they were occasional visitors to Gibson Street, noting that Erin also attended family gatherings at other places. Simon's parents were 'very active in supporting the kids and having them over and being great grandparents'.

He recalled being invited, along with his parents, to a lunch at Erin's home with the children in June 2023, but didn't recall the reason. What he did recall was declining the invitation in advance, rather than just not showing up or declining at the last minute. Rogers didn't ask the reason for his decision not to attend and he didn't offer it. Another moment of frustration for those listening, who no doubt wondered if Simon had been having misgivings about Erin's cooking.

Simon's evidence then moved to the lunch of 29 July 2023, explaining that his parents did not initially know the reason for the invitation and were intrigued by it, and also by why Erin had also invited Ian and Heather. His father had surmised it might be something to do with recent medical tests Erin had told him about.

They moved on to Simon's change of plan and his messages to Erin the night before the lunch, telling her he wasn't coming because he was 'uncomfortable', and adding that he was happy to discuss 'your health and implications' at another time. In response, Erin had complained that she'd already spent 'a small fortune' on the beef fillet, telling him she wanted him there. Her entreaties failed.

Again, Rogers did not dig deeper into why Simon had decided not to attend. It was something I suspect the jury would like to have heard, but possibly could lead into the murky waters of Simon's suspicions about his illnesses.

The details of his parents' hospitalisation were outlined until the lunch break at 1 pm. In court, and criminal trials in particular, where vast amounts of information are delivered, daily timetables and their breaks are strictly adhered to.

The afternoon started without the jury. Justice Beale asked Simon if he was aware that, as the spouse of the accused, he had the right to object to giving evidence. The judge soon found out that Simon was not aware of this fact, but nor was he reticent – he was both willing and happy to proceed.

But the chat didn't end there. In an uncommon move, Simon told the judge that the legal process had been very difficult, saying, 'I have a lot to grieve and am grieving a lot about all this stuff here.' It was, he said, challenging for him in not being able to follow the trial so far. He said, 'I'm sitting here, half thinking about the things I'm not allowed to talk about and I understand – I don't actually understand why, it seems bizarre to me, but it is what it is.'

Involvement in a criminal trial is often the result of a traumatic, potentially life-changing moment. Then come the criminal proceedings, where that moment is relived, analysed and probed. A judge needs to be formal, professional and compassionate, but paramount in their mind is making sure the trial is fair, even if some of the participants, and especially those who've never had any experience in the criminal justice system, are a bit baffled as to how it all works. It is a system best avoided if possible.

Justice Beale explained to Simon that after his evidence was over he could remain in court.

The jury returned, and Simon's evidence in chief continued. It quickly became apparent that Rogers was saving some hooks in the story for last. She took him to the events of Tuesday, 1 August when the children and Erin were still in Monash Hospital. Simon had stayed overnight in a room with the children, and he told the court that he, the kids and Erin had spent quite a bit of time together at the hospital. He said their daughter had brought up the subject of mushrooms and the fact that she disliked them, a fact that was well known in the family. Erin told Simon she 'had dehydrated some mushrooms and then put different amounts of mushrooms in the muffins – you know, one gram, two grams, three grams – and did sort of a blind taste test with [their daughter], and zero grams – you know, a control with no mushrooms in it – and they all found it interesting that [their daughter] actually preferred the muffin that did have some mushrooms in it'.

Simon said it was the first time he'd heard the story and that he didn't know when or where the taste test had occurred. He went on to tell the court, 'It felt like news to me that she dehydrated food.' He also didn't know she owned a dehydrator. Why the child brought that topic up wasn't pursued. Was Erin directing the conversation so she could introduce her use of a dehydrator, establishing a key plank in her defence that it was an innocent error?

What was notable for those watching who'd heard the pre-trial evidence was the absence of any mention of Simon's medical problems in the eighteen months or so leading up to the lunch – the issues that had led to Erin being charged with three counts of attempted murder on Simon. These charges had been publicly announced and were part of the committal proceedings, which, like the arrest, had received extensive media coverage.

These now-departed charges may have hinted at tendency, even though there was no forensic evidence to support them. With tendency evidence ruled out, and the charges gone, the lawyers and the judge were on high alert to make sure no mention was dropped into either evidence in chief or in cross-examination. Even a hint would have seen the trial come to a halt and the jury sent out while legal discussions ensued. It was an area that could place the trial in peril.

With Rogers' questioning complete, Colin Mandy stood and began his cross-examination. Mandy's style isn't theatrical, nor is it the wily approach of a barrister hoping to lure the witness into a trap. Instead, he's polite, methodical and relentless. In a case that would come to easily surpass its estimated six-week duration and that contained a chunk of technical evidence – medical, biological and electronic – Mandy explained evidence to the jury rather than attempting to dazzle or bamboozle them.

Simon was obviously prepared – not guarded, but careful, keeping his answers as short as possible. Mandy's start was almost as brief as Simon's answers. When he put a question to Simon about the nature of his 'relationship', he then quickly apologised and changed to 'friendship' with Erin until late 2022. Simon responded that he felt it was strong. This prompted Mandy to mention responses Simon had given in the preliminary hearings the year before, the judge called a halt and sent both Simon and the jury out of court.

The judge then summed up the thrust of Mandy's questioning so far, saying that Simon 'felt he had a strong friendship' that lasted until late 2022, and that if Mandy felt there were answers inconsistent with Simon's evidence in the preliminary hearing 'by all means go to it'. It's likely this refers to an exchange between Simon and Mandy on 14 October 2024, where there had been a few sparks over Simon and Erin's relationship post separation. Simon had corrected his use of 'amicable' as a description but told Mandy he'd found out that had two meanings. They finally agreed on 'strong friendship'. Four minutes after they had been sent out, the jury and Simon returned. Juries tend to get a fair bit of exercise with the frequent departures and returns to the courtroom.

Mandy resumed, questioning Simon about his friendship with Erin and their post-separation travels with the children, with Simon delivering his concise answers. On the friendship he agreed with Mandy that it was strong, until late 2022, and 'yeah, look, it depends – it's not wrong. Our relationship went up and down over the time.' Mandy then moved to the early days of the relationship, with Simon confirming Erin's inheritance and the purchase of their first home in Western Australia. Simon agreed that the money arrived by instalments to their joint account and that Erin was generous. He also agreed that the inheritance had helped his siblings, with loans to Matthew and Tanya to buy their home in Officer, though he thought the loan wasn't $400,000, a figure mentioned by his brother Matthew in the preliminary hearings, but closer to $250–$300,000; a loan to brother Nathan and his partner, Merryn, of a few hundred thousand dollars to buy their family home; and finally a loan to Anna and Josh of 'several hundred thousand' dollars to buy their family home in Blackburn South. He agreed the loans incurred no interest other than inflation and indexation.

Mandy's path through Simon and Erin's marriage continued without any notable disagreement until afternoon tea break at 3.10 pm. On resumption, and after more of the same, Mandy changed tack, asking if Erin was originally an atheist. With religion being a strong feature in Simon's and his parents' life, the question was not unexpected. Simon told him, 'I'm a Christian as well, it's really God's leading that makes us Christians, or not, if that's what you're asking, but she did become a regular church attender.' He added she also participated in Bible study. Mandy then changed tack again, asking about Erin's relationship with Simon's parents. His technique was one commonly used by both lawyers and police – to present propositions to be either agreed or disagreed with. The rhythm of the questions can be lulling, so it's imperative to remain alert under this style of questioning, and to carefully consider each answer. Mandy asked:

'Do you agree that, from your observation, they loved Erin?' – 'Yes'.

'And Erin loved them?' – 'She seemed to, yeah.'

'And you only observed them to have loving and respectful relationships with each other?' – 'Yeah, that seemed to be the case, yep.'

'That is, Don and Gail with Erin and Erin with Don and Gail?' – 'That's how it appeared to me.'

Mandy went on, delving into Simon's earlier evidence that Erin and Don were particularly close through their shared love of facts, books and science and, as Simon agreed, their 'inquiring curious minds'. He agreed that his parents were an important part of Erin's support network, and Mandy led him through their regular catch-ups, their support during the pandemic, Don and their son building a rocket two weeks before the lunch, Simon's cousin David walking Erin down the aisle and so on. This line of questioning established over a decade of a caring family into which Erin was accepted, loved and supported.

Mandy, brick by brick, was building a picture in the minds of the jury of how utterly bizarre and out of character it would be for Erin to wilfully plan to harm his parents –

the doting grandparents of their children – and then to put that plan to deadly effect. And while establishing motive or answering the question of why isn't a requirement of a murder prosecution, it's still something that lingers in everyone's mind and, so far, the answer to that question was missing. Mandy and, by extension, Simon were showing the caring side of Erin, while the other face or faces remained hidden. But that would soon change.

As the afternoon wore on, Mandy moved on to the question of Erin's crockery, to try and negate the thought she may have chosen to serve individual Wellingtons on specific plates to avoid a poisoned meal. By bringing some clarity to how the individual beef Wellingtons were served, Mandy was again suggesting to the jury that the dire outcome of the lunch was just a dreadful accident rather than a cunning plan.

Mandy deftly led Simon to the topic, starting with the logistics of family gatherings – often and usually at Don and Gail's home, the homes of his siblings or at Coleman Park in Korumburra. Simon doubted any had been held at his marital home before the separation or jointly post-separation, recalling that he may have hosted 'seldomly' but 'just not with Erin'. Mandy then focused on Erin moving to Gibson Street, taking all her belongings from the Shellcot Road house, and Simon agreed he was familiar with Erin's crockery. With that established, Mandy moved to his aunt Heather's question, 'Is Erin short of crockery?' and Simon's response, 'Yes, Erin doesn't have that many plates and that may be the reason for the different coloured plates.'

Erin's crockery and how it was used on the day of the lunch was a question burning in many minds. In a household with two kids and someone not short on either funds or pride in her new home, there was the expectation of a matching set or two. Simon confirmed Mandy's proposition that there was no 'formal or uniform set of plates at Gibson Street' and said, 'She had a mixture of plates and it's not that they were all different to each other but she had a bunch of ceramic plates generally that weren't all the same but there were a few the same as each other and then a couple more that were sort of the same as each other but different to the first lot.' Simon agreed there were only about eight to ten plates in the house.

With the thought now planted that there may be a perfectly reasonable excuse for Erin's own food to have been served on a notably different plate, Mandy switched topics again, saying, 'Erin's self-image wasn't great?' Simon agreed, and also agreed that she'd put on a lot of weight over the years. When asked if she was embarrassed, Simon said she hadn't said too much about it but he thought, given society's perception of body image, that she probably was, observing that she didn't have high self-esteem.

Another change in tack, quite timely given the lateness of the day, to the tax return that was the catalyst for the change in their relationship. Mandy asked Simon to read out a sample of the ensuing messages between him and Erin regarding child support, confirming that the support, after all the unhappiness caused, ended up being around $40 per month – 'hardly anything', as Simon observed.

At 4.09 pm the court rose.

The first piece of news the next morning was that Juror 25 – the anonymity of the jury is closely protected – had been elected as foreperson. Then Simon was back in the box and back on familiar territory, discussing the nuts and bolts of family relationships and custody of the children. The court was shown vision of Don Patterson and his grandson just two weeks before the lunch, with a matchbox-sized red car, modified with what the family called a rocket. The rocket lit up but the car didn't move. Gail was in the background and could be heard to say, 'Oh, it's working but why isn't it going?' With a sad smile and a tear in his eye, Simon said he recalled the moment.

Mandy then brought up Simon's invitation to lunch on 29 July, and this is where a few sparks started to fly. The first came when Mandy asserted that Erin hadn't, as Simon recalled, used the words 'serious' and 'important' in relation to what she wanted to discuss at the lunch. Simon said that while he couldn't remember the exact words she'd used, they were 'probably reasonable descriptions of what she communicated'. In response, Mandy brought up Simon's statement to police, which he'd finalised in August 2023. Simon agreed that events had been fresher in his mind back then, and Mandy pressed harder, asking if he thought it was important that he included everything he could recall in that police statement.

Simon said it had been a hard time for him back then, explaining that it was 'really difficult to know what level of detail to provide'. In a conciliatory move, Mandy noted that Simon knew the importance of being as thorough as he could. Simon agreed, and took the opportunity to vent his frustration, saying, 'It's been really difficult, including talking to you people today and yesterday, to balance the need to be succinct with the need to be accurate and sometimes they – to me, there is a tension about that and I've found that difficult.' They continued to debate the semantics of 'serious' and 'important' for a little while longer – a relentless lawyer and his quarry, an intelligent, frustrated witness devastated by an alleged terrible crime.

Mandy then moved to Simon's recollection of the motivation for the lunch and comments made by his parents, uncle and aunt. The somewhat prickly day got a little more so when Mandy asked if Simon, already aware that Erin had some medical issue to discuss, had contacted either his parents or Erin post-lunch to ask what that issue might have been. Simon said, 'No, I didn't.'

The tension level rose further when Mandy asked Simon about his conversation with Don at the hospital the day after the lunch, with Mandy suggesting Simon could have misheard his father when he said Erin had told them of her cancer diagnosis.

In asking about this, Mandy made a point of mentioning Don's illness and the brevity of the conversation, but that didn't cut it with Simon, who was certain of what he'd heard. 'Her diagnosis wasn't in doubt.'

Mandy asked again if Simon could have misheard, and he fired back, 'I reckon we're starting to get in the realm of flying teapots territory'.

Mandy, perplexed by the reference, said, 'I'm sorry, I missed that?' so Simon elaborated. 'It's possible that there's a flying teapot going around Mars, but it's pretty unlikely … Miscommunications happen. It's possible I've misunderstood everything you've said so far and you've misunderstood me. But I don't think we probably have.'

Mandy asked about Erin's medical history, thus setting up the possibility of a serious issue to be discussed and the apparent oddity of Simon not following this up. Simon said that in the past Erin had told him she struggled with heart arrhythmia (an abnormal heartbeat). He said he had no reason to doubt her, her hospitalisations, or her mention of other chronic illnesses that might have been things like lupus or multiple sclerosis. He said she'd talked about these alleged chronic illnesses, had blood tests but no diagnosis. But he was adamant she'd never mentioned ovarian cancer.

There was one notable mention in his evidence that grabbed attention. Simon said, 'She struggled a lot with mental illness, both post-natal depression, especially after X [her son] was born, and I believe that was real'. The spectre of mental illness, which had long been hovering in many minds, had entered the courtroom. Was Erin, as Australia's leading criminal psychologist Tim Watson-Munro later asked, mad or bad? It's worth noting here that at no time during this case was Erin's fitness to plead and instruct her lawyers ever in question.

The questioning then focused on the day-to-day lives of the Patterson family in the lead-up to 29 July 2023. Their lives, which were notable for their routine and ordinariness, revolved around the needs of their children – transporting them to school events, sport, movies, weekend entertainments and so on. The picture Mandy was painting was of a very average life – a stark juxtaposition to what their future held. As the cynical observer may note, it's a great way to make a person wonder how anyone as outwardly ordinary as Erin Patterson could do something so extraordinary.

The questioning moved to conversations on 31 July, with the court hearing of a message Erin sent Simon while in Leongatha Hospital, complaining that she may have to go to hospital in Dandenong. She said medical staff were arguing with her and that the doctor wasn't listening and was 'being a bit mean about it'. As a result of that exchange, Simon drove from Korumburra to the children's school and picked them up. He recalled staff at Dandenong Hospital telling him to take the kids straight to Monash Hospital.

Erin and Simon then messaged about a 'squeaky wheel', which Simon explained was a term Erin used when she tried to stir bureaucrats to act. In this case, he'd been told to take the kids to Monash and not Dandenong. The matter resolved when Erin messaged him that she was going to Clayton – where Monash Hospital was.

Simon complimented Erin on her efforts and assured her that 'the kids [were] in good spirits'. The next message was also from Simon, telling her the kids were waiting to be seen and hadn't shown any symptoms. Erin responded by saying that she felt nauseous and had a 'sore tummy' and had been given Ondansetron (a drug to combat nausea and vomiting). She also reminded him that their daughter hated blood tests.

Mandy took Simon through more messages, all practical and amicable considering the bizarre circumstances in which the whole family was by then embroiled, and showing no concerns on Simon's part regarding Erin's hospitality.

Mandy then took Simon to further message exchanges, this time in early to mid-August, which again were practical and dealing with the day-to-day needs of their children. The first week of the trial ended at lunchtime on Friday with Mandy taking Simon back to the disagreements of December 2022, which Simon agreed had descended into pettiness.

Cross-examination would be continued the following Monday. Simon no doubt endured an uncomfortable weekend – giving evidence can be brutal, particularly given the events he was being forced to revisit. Meanwhile, for the rest of Australia, the Erin Patterson trial took a brief step back from the limelight as the nation went to the polls to vote in the Federal election.

25

THE TRIAL RESUMES

As criminal trials begin to drag on, public interest usually dissipates. In the case of the Erin Patterson trial it was the reverse. The horde of journalists, cameras and sound crew remained constant, reflecting the nation's passion for the story, as well as a serious amount of money allocated to cover it. The media weren't having any luck getting more than their six balloted seats in the courtroom because the court watchers were out in force, no doubt keen to get a look at the jury, members of the Patterson and Wilkinson families and, of course, Erin. This trial had become a spectator sport.

Legal discussions meant the jury were cooling their heels in the jury room until just before 11 am on Monday, 5 May. When they were finally seated and with pleasantries out of the way, Simon Patterson returned to the witness box. Mandy got off to a soft start, saying gently, 'The process of being examined in this courtroom in minute detail is a confronting one?' Simon replied, 'Minute detail doesn't bother me; I remember what I remember. But yeah, it's not an easy thing, being here.'

Then it was back to Simon's vigil at Monash Hospital and the continuing decline of the people he loved. Mandy's questions focused in particular on an answer Simon had given earlier in his evidence, stating that Erin had not asked about his parents' condition. Mandy's implication was that in fact, it wasn't that Erin hadn't asked, but rather that Simon had forgotten. Simon's response was concise: 'I'd say possible but unlikely because it stood out to me. It's a feeling I remember, which is, "that's odd".'

As Mandy neared the end of his cross-examination he returned to the events of November/December 2022, including the messages from Erin to his parents, some of which were 'inflammatory' and 'extremely aggressive'. In one, she said, 'I foolishly trusted him to do right by me and the kids when it came to the crunch'.

And then, just before noon, Mandy was done, and it was over to Nanette Rogers to re-examine her witness. Unsurprisingly, the allegedly feisty messages were at the top of her list. Simon told the court that his parents had read the late 2022 messages and decided Gail wouldn't read any more. His mother had 'really struggled with anxiety' after a bout of encephalitis, and that anxiety had 'coloured their whole lives'. Simon was relieved that the message that caused him the most concern had arrived after Gail had stopped reading the messages.

The message in question had been sent to a group chat with Erin, Simon and his parents, in response to a message from Simon, some of which Simon said was about their son, saying he was 'exhausted tired not just normal' when

Simon had him on weekends and asking if Erin could make sure he got to bed earlier during the week. While Simon's message was sent only to Erin, her response was sent to the group chat, and was 'extremely inflammatory and, I tell you what, if Mum had of read that, I don't know what that would have done to her'. While the content of the message wasn't canvassed word by word, Simon explained that it was 'having a crack at me accusing me of some things'. While he wasn't fazed by the content, he was by the fact she'd sent it to the group chat.

Simon then clarified that the Mount Waverley home had been purchased after their separation but still in joint names, and though this was perhaps an act of goodwill and they had discussed reconciliation, the gesture still puzzled him. On Erin and religion, he said she'd become a regular church-goer after their separation in 2015, noting that in the years prior they'd travelled extensively and only went to church occasionally. When Simon later resumed regular attendance and usually had the kids on the weekend, Erin came along regularly too.

Moving to why he hadn't followed up after the lunch to ask what Erin's medical issue was, the reason was quite straightforward. Given that the lunch took place a few weeks after the invitation, he figured the issue wasn't pressing, and felt that 'it was her news to tell'. After a few more questions, Simon's ordeal in the witness box finally came to an end, and the jury left for lunch.

But before the judge and lawyers could take a break, Erin's need for a fully charged laptop in her police cell had to be attended to. While you'd think this would be a relatively straightforward requirement, it wasn't. Mandy addressed the judge, then a prison officer was brought in to give evidence. The arguments came down to Erin's need to review the brief and legal notes to help her defence. The judge would then consider what was a quite complex series of points including prisoner safety, their needs, and the expectations of the prisoner, lawyer and those with responsibility for her custody. It should have been something quite practical, but in law, that's often elusive. Mandy withdrew his objection to the custody conditions a few days later noting 'things have improved for our client in the cells'.

Ian Wilkinson was expected to be the next witness, but that didn't happen. Mr Wilkinson was apparently still at home in Korumburra, an hour's drive away, waiting for the call to attend. With his evidence likely to run for a few hours, Rogers suggested it would be best given the following day. Instead, that afternoon they would hear from Erin's Facebook friends, Christine Hunt, Daniela Barkley and Jenny Hay, who'd give evidence via video link – two were from interstate and the other had family commitments. No doubt the three were thankful not to have to sit in the witness box with all eyes upon them.

The first witness via the video link was Christine Hunt, with Ms Lenthall asking the questions. Hunt introduced herself as the manager of a large not-for-profit organisation, and said she'd got to know Erin about six years ago in a Facebook group of around 2000 people focusing on the Keli Lane case. She said the group had some issues, with 'a lot of disagreement and disharmony', so some members formed a smaller group of around twenty to thirty. Christine used her own name for her profile in this smaller group, as did Erin initially, though she later changed this to Erin Erin. Hunt said the group discussed current affairs, royalty, politics, crime and personal stories, observing that 'it was a small enough group where we did lean into each other's lives and we were a support for each other'.

She recalled Erin talking about her kids, Lego, and buying her property in Leongatha. 'General life type stuff. Information about herself, her husband. Just the challenges she was facing, the difficulties of being a single mum.' The latter didn't prompt Ms Lenthall to clarify the mention of husband and single mum. Hunt said Erin was well regarded in the group, a 'really good researcher', stating that earlier, when the group was focused on true crime, Erin had a reputation as a 'bit of a super sleuth' for her online research abilities.

Hunt said the group closed down in 2019, but she and Erin remained in contact. Apparently another group started up, which Hunt didn't join until about ten months later, at Erin's behest. Membership numbers varied from about seven or eight to fifteen, and Hunt noted they were people who'd bonded. She said her relationship with Erin was good. They'd had four or five phone conversations over the years, but the two had never met in person.

Lenthall then asked about Hunt's understanding of Erin's relationship with Simon, and that's where the trial took an intriguing turn. She said they'd 'sort of grown apart, going in different directions', adding that she understood that Erin was self-sufficient and thought she had concerns about Simon paying his share.

Then came the bombshell – one that hadn't been aired in her evidence to the preliminary hearing. Hunt said Erin 'used the word "coercive" at times and also that his family were very demanding and that she was really challenged by their demands and particularly around the kids attending a faith-based education'. Erin also said she was 'unsettled' when the kids weren't around.

Given the recent political, media and public attention on the issues of domestic violence and coercive control, Hunt's use of the word 'coercive' ratcheted up tension in the courtroom dramatically. Suddenly, there was a new theme in this murder trial, and one guaranteed to get attention far and wide. Was there something dark about the benign, devastated man we'd just seen in the witness box?

Hunt went on to say that Erin and Simon disagreed often over the kid's medical issues and 'she never seemed happy with his follow-up and his commitment to what was happening'. Erin had also told Hunt that being an atheist while Simon had a strong Baptist background was challenging, especially when it came to issues like separation, divorce and the kids' education. What was missing from these offerings was the timeline. And what we didn't hear, and probably will never know, is if the notion of coercion was canvassed in any of the pre-trial conversations. All evidence concerning Simon, however, emanated solely from Erin. In light of her other fabrications, it is very clear that the suggestions that he was either coercive or controlling had no basis in fact.

Hunt's evidence in chief ended and Mandy rose to cross-examine. He questioned the chronology of events, with Hunt telling him the small, more intimate Facebook group started in 2020. Hunt agreed that they talked about each other's lives, current affairs, cooking, books and podcasts, films, their children and, especially, offered support to group members as needed. Erin, she said, often talked about her children and shared photos and videos of them, noting that her life seemed to 'revolve around them'. When Mandy put it to her that Erin appeared to be an 'attentive and devoted' mother, Hunt concurred.

With that endorsement ringing in the jury's ears, it was back to Simon. 'You don't remember any specific words she used when describing her husband?' Hunt said she strongly recalled the regular use of the words 'controlling' and 'coercive'. After a polite nudge from Mandy suggesting the word 'abusive', she said that may have been Hunt's term 'for the fact that coercion is abuse, sir'. Hunt agreed that she hadn't used that word in her statement to the police, and reiterated her assertion that coercion is abuse. Mandy closed that part of his cross-examination by asking, 'What you're saying there is that it's accepted that coercive behaviour is and can be abusive behaviour in the dynamic of a relationship?' She replied, 'Yes, sir.'

Again, the only evidence for any coercive or controlling behaviour on the part of Simon came from Erin, an admitted liar, pushing for some sort of sympathy from her friends and, by extension, the jury.

Cross-examination concluded with questions about Erin's relationship with religion. Under questioning, Hunt said that Erin had shared, on a few occasions, that she was an atheist. Mandy tested her recollection, putting it to her that Erin had been an atheist in the past, but when talking in the group chats, she said she believed in God and went to church. Hunt thought that, when it came to religion, Erin was two-faced, clarifying that family situations took her to church but online 'she didn't necessarily believe in God'. She also added that Erin wasn't happy about the children being at a faith-based school. The conclusion seemed to be that Erin was frustrated with some of Simon's beliefs. With that, the cross-examination ended. Ms Lenthall had nothing to clarify and the video link ended. But the words 'coercion' and 'control' were digging deep into Simon, and he had no right of reply.

Daniela Barkley was next up. She gave her occupation as a stay-at-home mum who ran a couple of businesses from home. She didn't mention that she was also a first-time author, poised to self-publish a novel loosely based on Erin's case, which was something that was mentioned in her evidence to the preliminary hearing.

She said she'd met Erin in one of her true crime groups in early 2019. The two had never met in person. It was a group of around 35–50 members.

She said Erin was active in this group for the first few years, but in the year leading up to the lunch, she'd barely posted. Erin spoke to Daniela and a few others, probably around five in total, in a private chat, telling them that Simon was 'so religious' it was causing problems, and that he was favouring their daughter over their son. She recalled Erin saying Simon wanted to be more involved with the children, which was okay, but she thought Erin felt that Simon put church before family. This last comment prompted the judge to suggest she focus on what was said rather than on 'what you feel she felt'.

Lenthall then cut to the chase, bringing up the crimes and asking if Erin had talked about the dehydrator in their online chats. Barkley said it did get a mention in their private discussions, along with shared photos of dehydrated mushrooms, and comments about using the mushrooms in brownies. Erin, apparently, was excited about dehydrating mushrooms.

Barkley recalled that about two weeks before the lethal lunch, Erin had asked for some pointers on making beef Wellington. The conversation stuck in Barkley's mind because she didn't know what the dish was. 'I'm mostly vegetarian, so I made a joke about no, but if I could, I'd make a tofu Wellington and everyone just thought that was awful, so we had a good laugh about that and then Jenny [Hay] – I believe Jenny replied, giving her some advice, because she had previously cooked a beef Wellington.' She recalled that a few days before the lunch, Erin had told the group she was out buying beef fillet. Apparently she was struggling to find a piece of meat that was big enough, and was complaining about how expensive it was. Barkley assumed the dish was for Erin and her children.

Barkley noted, 'It was probably the last time we really heard about the beef Wellington.' The last time she'd heard about it from Erin, at least.

Post-lunch, Barkley said she'd heard Erin's voice in a group video call but didn't really engage with her. That ended her evidence in chief. Mandy started his cross-examination straight away, with Barkley confirming she'd been in four chat groups including the private group of five or so that chatted via Messenger. She confirmed that Erin's life revolved around her children, stating that she thought she was 'a wonderful mother'.

Jenny Hay was next up, informing the court she was a semi-retired social worker. Like the others, she'd met Erin on the Keli Lane Facebook group, and confirmed a similar background to the others in the groups as earlier witnesses had told the court. Like those witnesses, Hay had never physically met Erin. She said the private group that started in early 2020 had involved lots of chat about the challenges of Covid-19, with Hay locked down in Tasmania and Erin in Victoria. They'd also discussed current affairs, family matters and 'were quite open with one another'. Hay used her own name in her profile. She confirmed that Erin had bought a dehydrator and had been 'blitzing' mushrooms so the kids would eat them, noting that Erin's daughter didn't like mushrooms. Hay was asked if Erin had ever discussed foraging for mushrooms, to which she responded, 'No'.

Moving to beef Wellington, Hay recalled that toward the end of July 2023, Erin had messaged the group with 'something about the beef'. Ms Lenthall then jumped to early August, with Hay confirming she'd heard of the deaths at Leongatha on the news on Sunday, 6 August. She said that Erin had contacted Hay via her work email on the Monday, and that the pair eventually spoke by phone. Erin told her the mushrooms had come from an Asian grocery store and that she was sick and had been in hospital. She also said the children had been 'checked out' and were okay. The call lasted about ten minutes, with Erin ending it because a call from her lawyer was coming in.

Mandy, in his cross-examination, took Hay back to the beef and she told the court that beef Wellington was one of her favourite dishes, and that Erin had asked how to make sure the pastry didn't end up soggy. Hay's tip was to wrap the pastry around the dish at the last possible moment before putting it in the oven.

With the afternoon's witnesses dealt with expeditiously, the jury got an early mark at around 3.15 pm. Simon Patterson was visibly unhappy as he left court, and no wonder. His reputation had taken a pounding in a public arena thanks to Hunt's evidence, and he had no right of reply or opportunity to challenge. When he left court that afternoon he walked resolutely through the very excited media throng without offering any comment.

*

The next morning the media were on high alert – rumour had it that Simon was intending to give a statement. While the content was yet to be disclosed, it seemed likely he wanted to address the allegations of being coercive and controlling. A press conference, though sometimes useful to vent and correct, was a lousy idea during a live trial and brought with it a number of problems, ranging from the slim but dreadful possibility of a mistrial through to him being recalled for further cross-examination. The prosecution got wind of the plan and had a word to Simon, and perhaps to his media counsel, pointing out the potential dangers. The press conference didn't go ahead.

After legal discussions, the jury came in at 10.50 am for the first witness, Darren Fox, the proprietor of the store where Erin had bought the dehydrator. The point of the purchase was made, there was nothing contentious raised or revealed, and he was soon out the courtroom door.

Next up, it was Ian Wilkinson's turn, with prosecutor Warren handling his evidence. He was wearing a black vest and grey shirt – formally casual for a country pastor perhaps, and carrying a water bottle. He gave his occupation as pastor of the Korumburra Baptist Church in a clear yet softly spoken voice, and delivered calm and considered evidence with the occasional smile. As usual, Erin looked noncommittal but, as she had through all the evidence so far, she listened closely and took notes.

When asked about his reaction to the lunch invitation, Ian recalled with a smile that Heather had been fairly excited, although both were wondering what had prompted the invitation, which was somewhat out of the blue. Ian said he'd hoped it meant their relationship with Erin would improve. Days later, Ian and Heather learned they weren't the only ones on the guest list.

Ian's evidence in chief canvassed his menu in the days leading up to the lunch, and included a description of Erin's house and her reluctance to let her guests into the pantry. He confirmed the seating plan shown to him by Ms Warren, with himself at the head. He said, 'It was a casual arrangement, we seemed to just sit down naturally in a place.' He then described the plates used – four large grey dinner plates and one smaller orangey tan one. Gail, he recalled, picked up two of the grey plates and Heather the other two, which they took to the table. Erin took the odd plate.

He told the court there was some light-hearted banter about husbands who finish their wives' serves, adding that with the generous serves of beef Wellington, mash and beans, no-one had much room for the cake and fruit the guests had brought for dessert.

Then came Erin's news. Ian said 'she announced she had cancer' and 'believed it was very serious, life threatening'. She wanted their counsel on what to tell the children. He didn't 'quite catch' the type but thought it was cervical or ovarian. He said she claimed to have had a test that revealed a tumour, but didn't recall any conversation about a treatment regime.

Ms Warren then took him to what happened next, with Ian recalling Don advising Erin to be honest with the children, advice with which everyone concurred. It was a short conversation, Ian recalled, 'maybe 10 minutes. But in a moment of tension like that, maybe more time passes than you think.' The conversation was curtailed by the return of Erin's son and his friend, and at that point Ian Wilkinson's evidence was almost curtailed, as his chair had a minor malfunction. The poor witness was seen sinking into the witness box, prompting some welcome light relief from Justice Beale, who quipped, 'We do this to all our witnesses.' With a smile, the sinking Wilkinson responded, 'I thought I was being lowered to the basement.' Erin remained impassive throughout the exchange.

On resumption, the evidence moved to Ian's recollections of his illness, his hospitalisation, from Leongatha to Dandenong and then to the Austin, where he was a patient in intensive care until 21 August 2023, and then to his discharge on 11 September to the Heidelberg Repatriation Hospital. He agreed he was finally discharged and allowed home on 22 September 2023.

Mandy then rose to cross-examine. He was gentle and respectful, noting that the witness had known his client for a long time and commonly saw her and the children at his church. When Mandy suggested Erin was a regular attendee, Ian demurred, saying she was there, on average, once a month. Mandy then recapped details of Ian and Erin's interactions over the years. When he took Ian back to some of his answers in the 2024 preliminary hearings,

Ian said that some of his answers 'on reflection, were not satisfactory', admitting that he'd thought about them since. He said he was now sure that on the day of the lunch, Erin was proud of her house, but he couldn't recall if they'd had a tour.

They moved on to recap Ian's observations of the meal preparation and service, and Ian reiterated that four of the plates were the same. Mandy prodded him on this recollection, but he didn't budge. On the service of dessert, it was do it yourself, he said, but he couldn't recall definitively if there were fresh plates.

The questions then went back to his police statement of 13 September 2023, taken just days after he'd arrived in rehabilitation. Mandy took him to his recent testimony about Erin's alleged cancer, and the semantics of whether Erin had said this was a confirmed diagnosis or a possible diagnosis. After some polite argy-bargy, Wilkinson was respectful but firm in his disagreement with Mandy's suggestion that it was a suspected diagnosis.

Mandy finished by asking, 'When the lunch was finished and you were leaving, there'd been nothing out of the ordinary, apart from that discussion, that had happened on that day; is that fair?' Ian agreed that it was. Re-examination by Ms Warren involved only a few questions, and Ian Wilkinson's tenure in the witness box was over just after lunch. He was now free to sit in court and watch the remainder of the trial. The two most anticipated witnesses in the prosecution had now been heard, and neither had been dramatic or pivotal. All they could do was to set the scene for the lethal lunch, with evidence that was not quite a whimper, but definitely not a bang, either.

The two other highly anticipated witnesses were Stephen Eppingstall, the lead detective on the case, and Erin. Ultimately, the only person who knew the real story and was still around to tell it was the accused, and at this stage of proceedings, we didn't know if she'd tell her story under oath or exercise her right to remain silent.

With Simon Patterson and Ian Wilkinson finished, the prosecution moved to other witnesses – people like the medical staff, from the paramedics and ambulance officers who helped Don, Gail, Heather and Ian to the various doctors describing their involvement in the case. Other family members were also called, giving snapshots of their lives before the lunch and the sad, challenging days that followed. Not always the most exciting or anticipated evidence, and sometimes utterly heartbreaking, but all essential in the massive jigsaw puzzle that is a criminal investigation and prosecution.

Some of the evidence would be uncontested. In those cases, rather than have the witness attend, their statement was read into the record. One such witness was Jennifer McPhee, the Baptist church secretary and a friend of Don and Gail's for over thirty years. She was one of the people Ian Wilkinson had met with after the lunch. The meeting took place around the Wilkinsons' kitchen table. Jennifer recalled Heather talking happily about the delicious meal they'd had at Erin's. Jennifer referred to the beef Wellington as beef stroganoff – a detail that was clarified by the prosecutor – noting that Heather had been impressed by the work involved in its preparation. Angela McPhee, the church treasurer was also at the meeting, and she said Heather 'raved' about the meal.

One intriguing statement was from Danielle Romane of the health department. Under Victorian law, reporting of a cancer diagnosis is mandatory. She'd checked the registry and found no report of Erin Patterson receiving a diagnosis.

On 7 May, the court heard from Simon Patterson's brother Matthew, who confirmed that Erin had loaned $400,000 to him and his wife, Tanya, to buy their family home. Matthew also described a call he'd made to Erin from his father's hospital bedside on Monday, 31 July 2023, wanting to know the source of the mushrooms. The call had been short, at just seventy-three seconds, polite and to the point. Erin had told him the mushrooms came from two sources, but Matthew got the impression she was trying to recall those sources as she spoke.

*

Doctor Chris Webster was also in the witness box on 7 May. He's a big bloke, with a voice of authority, and one that carries. Webster is also someone who doesn't mince words – something that would become apparent once the trial was over. He was treating Ian and Heather at Leongatha on the evening of 30 July and thought they were responding well to initial treatment. However, after a phone call around 7 am the next day from Doctor Beth Morgan at Dandenong Hospital, he reviewed that thought. Doctor Morgan had been treating Don and Gail, and both had 'grossly abnormal' liver function tests. Webster was on duty when Erin arrived at 8 am, complaining of gastro. Webster told the court he recognised her as the 'chef' and asked her where she'd sourced the mushrooms, to which Erin simply responded,

'Woolworths'. As we'd later discover, that response set off alarm bells in his head – but observations like that aren't for the courtroom.

He was surprised to later learn that Erin had left the hospital, and that she wasn't responding to his calls, given that he'd just told her she may have been exposed to death cap mushroom poisoning.

His riveting evidence had all eyes on him, including Erin, who he later said was glaring at him. Because she hadn't responded to his attempts to contact her, which included a voicemail message in which he said he'd contact the police, he called 000. This took us to the dramatic recording of Webster's 000 call.

'I have a concern regarding a patient that presented here earlier, that has left the building and is potentially exposed to a fatal toxin from mushroom poisoning, and I've tried several times to get hold of her on her mobile phone.' He told the operator that of the five people who had eaten lunch together on the previous Saturday, two were in intensive care at Dandenong and the other two were en route. Meanwhile, Erin had discharged herself against medical advice.

When Erin finally returned to the hospital, a discussion ensued about the children, Webster told the court, describing her reluctance to bring them in for examination, and his chilling, forthright comment, 'They can be scared and alive or dead.' The court would hear from the children the next day.

26

THE CHILDREN SPEAK

One of the witnesses called on 8 May, prior to the children's evidence, was their aunt Tanya, who was married to Don and Gail's son Matthew. She'd been involved in the children's care since the lunch and was one of the few family members to give evidence.

Tanya said she'd observed the relationship between Erin and Simon deteriorate in the lead-up to the lunch, saying, they 'did not really interact that much at family events. Simon did not go to their Christmas holiday that they normally had and also, Erin had taken the kids out of school and [enrolled them] into a different school without telling Simon.'

Tanya had asked Erin if she would like her to visit while she was in Monash Hospital, and Erin had told her that would be 'lovely' but wasn't sure if she'd still be there, though she was still feeling nauseous and dizzy. Tanya arrived around 9.30 am on Tuesday, 1 August and Erin asked her how everyone was – 'going downhill fast' was Tanya's sad response. Erin told her she'd heard Don and Gail were in a coma, and they discussed some other snippets until medical staff arrived and the visit ended.

In cross-examination, Tanya told Mandy her family had always had a good relationship with Erin and believed her to be an attentive and doting mother. Again, Mandy was subtly suggesting the probability of a terrible accident rather than an appalling crime.

In all the reporting and the preliminary hearings in the lead-up to the trial, two voices hadn't been heard – those of the Patterson children, one aged around sixteen years old at the time of writing and the other eleven. The trauma the two had endured is unimaginable, robbing them of the magic of youth and casting a shadow over their lives forever.

While the lawyers at the bar table were skilled advocates, the question of how best to question young people and children is always a delicate one, particularly in cases in which their lives have been devastated. In Victoria, the VARE (Visual and Audio Recording of Evidence) system is used, which involves video and/or audio recording of their evidence. Early on in the criminal investigation, those interviews are conducted by a child protection practitioner and a police officer who has specialised training in the area. When a criminal prosecution is probable, a formal statement is recorded in this manner. The welfare of the child or young person is paramount. The child or young person must be available for cross-examination and re-examination – just like an adult witness – if required.

While the evidence given by the Patterson children has been made public, their names have not, and they're subject to a suppression order until the last of them reaches twenty-one years of age. Both sides had agreed on this suppression, and on the method of giving evidence.

The children's recorded interviews were finally heard on the afternoon of 8 May, as the end of the trial's second week loomed. Some technical problems with the recordings and transcripts caused a few issues, so the daughter's evidence resumed the next morning, with the transcripts to be provided later, after a few more technical bugs were resolved. The recordings took close to two hours to play. There was no cross-examination.

The interviews had been conducted on 16 August 2023 by a police officer who introduced himself as Jason. He was calm, open and reassuring. It had been barely three weeks since the event that had torn the children's lives apart. Three people they'd loved were dead and one was fighting for his life, and their mother was being splashed across front pages around the planet. Their home was being treated as though it was a crime scene.

Erin and Simon's daughter was sitting at a table in a green chair, her legs dangling, as her feet didn't reach the floor. There was a box of tissues on the table, and some coloured pencils in case she needed to respond in writing or draw a picture to illustrate what she was describing.

The interview began with the basics, making sure she understood what the truth was. She told Jason that the truth was 'what has happened'. Satisfied with her response, he then asked if she knew why she was being interviewed. She said, 'I don't know why I'm here,' then after some gentle prompting, she replied, 'The lunch at my mum's house'. It's important to note here that a key feature of interviewing, especially when interviewing the young, is not to ask closed questions – those with a predetermined answer like yes or no, which can result in putting words in the person's mouth – and to encourage them to remember what they'd seen, heard or felt, but not push them into embellishing to please the interviewer.

When asked about the lunch, the girl said she didn't know too much as she wasn't there, adding that 'my mum told me that she wanted to have a lunch with my grandparents and Heather and Ian. I can't remember what she said but I just remember she said she was having a lunch with them. She said she was going to have lunch at the dining table.' On the reason for the lunch, she said Erin told her she 'just wanted to talk to them', and on the topic, her mother said it was 'adult stuff'. When asked if her parents were separated, she replied 'they're man and wife'.

But she did agree they lived separately. Returning to the day of the lunch, she recalled seeing the beef in the oven and said Erin had told her that she'd drop the children and a friend of theirs at McDonald's in Leongatha for an early lunch, then they'd go to see a movie, which started at 12.30 pm.

Simon picked the children up after the movie and dropped the boys at Gibson Street, then father and daughter went to Simon's home in Korumburra, where they 'hung out for the rest of the day'. Simon dropped her back to Gibson Street about 9 pm where she spent a quiet Saturday night, with her brother on the computer and Erin on her tablet. When asked by the officer when she became aware of her mother being unwell, she said, 'I don't remember when she felt sick but I remember she started to feel sick the next day. She just needed to go to the toilet a lot and she felt sick in the gut.'

Erin told her she was 'not feeling well' and 'had diarrhoea and her tummy was sore'. Erin, she recalled, had used the toilet about ten times. On the Sunday evening they ate leftovers from the lunch, but she said the steak didn't have anything on it. As to her mother, she said she was still unwell and not hungry. Her brother, on the other hand, was hungry and ate the rest of his mother's serving.

She said that her mother was a good cook and that sometimes she and her brother would help. When asked about how she knew the food they ate was leftovers, she said 'Mum told me'. This makes an interesting point, given that the children, who were examined for symptoms of poisoning but found to be fine, were relying on their mother's assertion that they were lunch leftovers, but hadn't seen the leftovers in the refrigerator, nor her mother removing them, then reheating and serving them. She also told Jason she hadn't seen her mother doing any food preparation on the day of the lunch.

Jason lightened the moment by asking what her favourite food was. The answer, unsurprisingly, was ice cream. It was a good interview technique, and it set up the different angle of his next questions – about the family that cooks together. She couldn't recall using mushrooms when cooking with her mother, nor had they gone foraging for mushrooms, but she did recall buying them at the supermarket and, yes, she did eat them. When questioned about Asian grocery stores she said she'd never been to one with her mother, but added that they had been at the Mount Waverley house during the recent school holidays, though they didn't go to any supermarkets.

Jason had done a professional job of getting factual evidence from someone so young, and evidence that in part could be used to dispel some of Erin's stories about the origin of the mushrooms. It wasn't breakthrough stuff but was useful in establishing a verdict beyond reasonable doubt. He wrapped the interview up by asking the girl if she had been told anything since the lunch or told not to say anything. It was a question with a lot of weight, but she answered readily, saying that her father had told her she didn't need to speak to the police if she didn't want to, but she'd decided it was fine to do so.

Erin was in tears at the end of the interview, rocking back and forth in her chair in the dock.

Next came her son's interview, conducted in the same room on the same day as his sister's.

The start was the same as the interview with his sister. He was asked to state his full name, followed by a question to make sure he knew what the truth was. 'Something that's right,' he said, and confirmed that he'd tell the interviewing officer what really happened. He gave an overview of the lunch – when, where, who was coming and his relationship to them, noting that his father had been invited but didn't come, saying he didn't know why.

It was quickly apparent that he was a mature and observant teen. When talking about his parents' relationship, he said they'd 'had a few arguments', and though his mother had moved house, they had never divorced nor, he said candidly, was he aware of any other relationships. He said that when he was eight or nine he'd spend the weekends at his father's home and that Erin would be there for dinner on the Friday night. Weekend visits more recently sounded somewhat fraught, with him telling the interviewer that while Simon was keen to have his children each weekend, they weren't so keen because 'they never did anything'. On the occasions they stayed, Simon would drop them at school on Monday morning.

Of his parents' recent relationship he said it was 'very negative' and there had been disputes over the children's schooling.

The questioning then moved to the lunch. The boy said he didn't know the reason for the lunch and he didn't know his father had been on the guest list. On the guests, he said his mother had invited Don and Gail over before, but for Heather and Ian, the lunch would be a first. He also said they went to their grandparents' home for 'events', but when asked about the family relationship with Ian and Heather, he didn't know much other than 'it's not a negative one, but it's not strong'.

On the day of the lunch, he and his friend returned from the movies and he spent about half an hour with the guests before they left. Everyone, he recalled, seemed happy. When the guests had departed he helped his mother clear the table, but couldn't remember if there was any food left on the plates. He thought the plates were white and about fifteen centimetres in diameter. When asked whether he liked mushrooms, he said he didn't like how 'squishy and mushy' they were. The interviewer then moved on to more general fungi questions, with the son saying he hadn't been mushroom foraging with his parents, but did recall Erin taking a photograph of some while on a walk because they 'looked nice'. It was, he said, 'a very fond memory'.

After helping his mother clear up, the boy said he'd spent a bit of time with his mate, before Erin and her son took the boy home around 5.30 pm. They got home about 6 pm, and Simon dropped his sister home about 9 pm. The boy couldn't recall if his father came into the house.

However, the next morning he recalled his mother drinking a coffee and telling him she was 'feeling a bit sick' and also had diarrhoea. She was also, in his view, a bit quieter than usual. They skipped church, with his mother telling him she 'didn't want to spread it to people', and he was somewhat perplexed when his unwell mother decided she could drive him to his flying lesson in Tyabb, as there wouldn't be many people there. They left about midday, with his sister joining them, and before departing Erin commented that she hoped she'd make it to Tyabb without needing to go to the toilet.

The boy told the interviewer he didn't know why she'd decided to drive him.

When they were about ten minutes from Tyabb, the boy's instructor called and cancelled the lesson, so it was back to Leongatha with a quick stop on the way – not for the toilet, but for dim sims and hot dogs. The children ate the food while Erin had coffee. When they got home, he recalled that his mother raced to the front door then headed straight to the toilet.

He confirmed his sister's recollection of having leftovers for dinner that night, noting that it was fillet steak, 'some of the best meat' he'd eaten. He said there was nothing on the steak. He thought it had been cooked earlier and reheated for dinner, rather than cooked fresh that night, and said it was 'a block, I cut it into cubes and ate it'. Erin had told him it was leftovers and there wasn't any gravy. When asked about the preparation of the meal he said he didn't see it being prepared, but did recall seeing meat in a frying pan.

That night he said his mother made dinner for herself but didn't eat any, telling him she was feeling unwell and still had diarrhoea. She also told him Gail and Don were unwell. The next morning, his mother woke him at 6.30 am and he saw her drinking coffee before driving him to the bus stop to go to school. She'd told him she'd been to the toilet a few times during the night. Around lunchtime that day, both children were taken from their school to Monash Hospital to see Erin. She told her son she was feeling 'clammy and dizzy' and tired, but the conversation soon swapped to their day at school.

That brought the interview to a close.

The interviews, though conducted professionally and compassionately, were tough on the children, but also on their parents. Simon had to endure this snapshot of the reasons for the distance between him and his children – bad enough in private, but this was with the world listening in. During her son's interview Erin, who looked as if she was going through a cavalcade of emotions, nodded along as he gave details of events and at times dissolved into anguished sobs and tears.

27

THE WORLD OF THE EXPERT

Professor Rhonda Stuart, medical director of infection protection and epidemiology at Monash Health, gave her evidence on 13 May. In response to questions by Nanette Rogers, she said she'd spoken to Erin at the hospital, who had said she was there because her children needed to be checked out after eating the leftovers from the lunch, with the mushroom paste scraped off. Erin told her the mushrooms for the dish had come from two sources: the supermarket and an Asian grocery store in either Oakleigh or Mount Waverley. Erin told the professor she couldn't recall the grocery, but might recognise it if she drove past. The mushrooms, Erin said, had a strong smell.

Her story was similar to what she told the next witness, Monash emergency doctor and toxicology registrar Doctor Laura Muldoon, who'd assessed Erin and thought she had food poisoning from the beef Wellington she'd eaten two days before. Erin denied using foraged mushrooms.

Muldoon's evidence was simple and startling. She said that aside from chapped lips, Erin looked 'clinically well', and her blood tests and vitals were all normal. A later witness, Doctor Varuna Ruggoo, a consultant emergency physician at Monash, also gave evidence that Erin's liver function test was normal, with no sign of toxicity at the time of her discharge, and that she 'appeared clinically well, in a normal mood'.

The contrast between Erin and her four guests was stark – they were in hospital, battling for their lives. Meanwhile, Erin had chapped lips.

Muldoon also provided a key link in the chain of evidence. She told the court that the remains of the beef Wellington had arrived in a plastic bag around 3 pm, carried in the ambulance that conveyed Erin. Muldoon arranged for them to be taken by taxi urgently to the experts at the Royal Botanic Gardens. Mandy's cross-examination was brief, and didn't touch on Muldoon's professional observations.

This was a trial rich in expert evidence taking the jury, and probably almost everyone else in the courtroom, into areas they'd never dreamt of exploring.

Fungi expert Doctor Tom May told the court about the iNaturalist website, which he said was the 'largest citizen platform' for fungi. Other evidence confirmed that the seized Patterson devices had been used to visit the site. May said that by February 2024, over 440,000 images of fungi in Australia had been uploaded to the site. He told the jury that death caps could be found in eastern Melbourne through to the Dandenong Ranges and in regional centres. In Gippsland, he said there had been three reports in the last twenty years, noting that other mushrooms, such as the stubble rosegill and marbled death cap, look similar.

The death cap flourishes in autumn, usually after rain. May agreed with Rogers' proposition that fatalities have resulted from people mistaking a death cap for an edible mushroom.

Doctor May confirmed he had been a contributor to the site in May 2023, after he found death caps on a walk in the village of Outtrim. His post included photos and GPS coordinates of the find.

Rogers showed him photographs of mushrooms on scales that had been found on Erin's devices, and he said he thought one showed commercial mushrooms, but noted that another was highly consistent with a death cap. When cross-examined by Sophie Stafford for the defence, he agreed that distinguishing between toxic and edible fungi could be a challenge, even for experts. The court was read part of an article Doctor May had authored for the Victorian Poisons Information Centre, which said, 'accurate identification of fungi is challenging, often requiring microscopic examination in the laboratory, as well as DNA barcoding and phylogenetic analysis'.

Interestingly, Doctor May also observed that foraging for mushrooms had become increasingly popular, a trend that was perhaps in part attributable to the Covid-19 pandemic.

May was followed by another mushroom expert, Doctor Camille Truong, a research scientist at the Royal Botanic Gardens. Laura Muldoon had called her and said they had a case with three people who were hospitalised who had consumed a meal that had contained mushrooms, and could she help identify them. Truong then clarified it had been four patients.

Doctor Truong had told Muldoon it was 'probably impossible' to buy death caps, as they only grew wild and couldn't be cultivated. She also said, 'I told her there were absolutely no sightings of death cap mushrooms during the last months. Based on the information I received, it was highly unlikely to be a case of death cap mushroom poisoning.' Doctor Truong was the recipient of the sealed bag of leftovers for analysis. After putting on gloves, she used sterilised tweezers to pick out the mushroom component.

The path of the leftovers from Erin's home to Truong's tweezers had been in part covered earlier in the trial, in the evidence of Senior Constable Adrian Martinez-Villalobos from Leongatha, who'd stated that he'd gone to Erin's house after Doctor Webster at the local hospital had asked him to recover any leftovers. It was quick and decisive thinking by Webster. At Gibson Street, guided by Erin via phone from the hospital and double-gloved to prevent evidence contamination, he'd found them in a red-lidded garbage bin outside the house. The leftovers comprised steak in what appeared to be a paste and pastry, partially crushed and seeping inside a Woolworths paper bag. He put the leftovers into plastic evidence bags, then he and his colleague drove to the hospital and handed the bags to nurse Mairim Cespon. The bags then travelled via ambulance with Erin to Monash, then by taxi to Truong.

Truong's examinations found that there were no death caps in the leftovers, just field mushrooms.

Her evidence raised the question of whether the food found and delivered to Truong was actually left over from what had been served to the guests, or a second dish that would see the mushrooms scraped off, as per Erin's story. The only person who knew the truth was Erin.

Court on 15 May began dramatically with a rare occurrence, and one initially played out in the jury's absence. Juror 84 was discharged because Justice Beale had become concerned he had been discussing the case with family and friends. In the absence of the jury, the judge said the Supreme Court had received an email sent to the court's general email address making the allegations. The person gave their name and, later, their mobile phone number. Anonymised copies were provided to defence and prosecution, both of whom said the juror should be dismissed, agreeing there was prima facie evidence that the email was genuine. In a criminal trial you don't take chances, so the judge's tipstaff collected the juror and his belongings and brought him to the jury box. After the judge made some points, the juror was escorted out of the courthouse. Investigations into any alleged conduct were for the court officials to pursue. There were fourteen jurors remaining.

Both defence and prosecution were keen for the juror's departure to be the subject of a media suppression order. The judge granted an interim order, noting the point made by Rogers that reporting the event might compromise any proceedings against the departing juror. However, late that afternoon, following submissions from a lawyer acting for a slew of media organisations, that order was lifted.

The morning of 15 May was taken up with the evidence of child protection worker Katrina Cripps. Cripps recounted her discussions with Erin about the lunch, including the source of the mushrooms, how much Erin had eaten – 'half', Erin told her – and the relationship with Simon, which Erin had said was 'strained', noting 'there was tension in it'.

Erin also told Cripps that Don and Gail were 'the parents she hadn't had'.

One of her responses got an intake of breath from those in the court. When asked what Erin had told her was the inspiration for the menu, she said she'd found it in a cookbook by Nagi Maehashi, saying she 'wanted to do something new and special'. The popularity of the cookbook, *Dinner*, guaranteed huge media attention – and Nagi has a massive social media presence.

Like other witnesses, Cripps' evidence provided a contemporaneous account of the story Erin had told to independent witnesses, not family, meaning the evidence was not potentially coloured by tragedy. This is the circumstantial evidence that builds the case when you don't have a literal smoking gun.

After the court's lunch break, Doctor Dimitri Gerostamoulos, head of forensic science at the Victorian Institute of Forensic Medicine, was in the witness box, with Ms Lenthall taking him through his evidence. He told the jury 'death cap mushrooms, depending on the species but primarily the most common toxins are the Alpha-amanitin, the Beta-amanitin and, to a lesser extent, there is another product called Gamma-amanitin'. He went on to explain, 'They are quite toxic in terms of their potency. They can lead to someone experiencing symptoms of diarrhoea, vomiting, feeling really unwell. And they progressively get worse if the toxins are not removed. They progress to tissue necrosis, organ failure and can obviously lead to death if not treated appropriately or supportively in hospital.'

When asked what the estimated lethal dose of amatoxins for humans was, he said, 'That will depend on the amount but it is estimated to be point one milligram of a kilogram, which is a very small amount. It's estimated for a seventy-kilogram adult it's about fifty grams or three tablespoons, if we can put it in common terms. But it will depend on how much of the toxins are there, the species of the particular plant.' He also noted the studies weren't conducted on humans, 'for obvious reasons'.

On the specimens he examined for traces of the various amanitin, he found that Erin and her two children had no traces, and there was nothing in the samples from Heather and Gail, but it was present in samples taken from Ian and Don. The doctor gave a litany of reasons for the variation in results. He also told the jury that samples from the dehydrator tested positive for both alpha and beta amanitin.

Before the next tranche of scientific experts, who'd take the jury deep into the world of computer forensics and mobile phone data, prosecutors called Christine McKenzie, a retired pharmacist who'd worked for the Victorian Poisons Information Centre as a senior poisons information specialist. While not an expert on mushrooms, McKenzie said she was 'fascinated by the world of fungi', which got some smiles around the courtroom. She was also an avid contributor to the iNaturalist website, which she said was for 'citizen scientists'. Under her profile name ChrisMcK she had posted around seventy times. She got more smiles when she said that on a guided walk around the 'beautiful old oak trees in the gardens of Parliament House [Melbourne]', she'd spotted what she thought were death cap mushrooms growing under those trees, and made the first of two posts on what she suspected were the deadly mushrooms.

Her second post was on 18 April 2023, after she'd spotted what she thought were death caps under a single oak tree at the oval at Loch on the Loch Poowong Road. She took photos with her phone, then, knowing they were toxic to both humans and dogs, removed them, putting them in a dog poo bag they had with them. Examining nearby oaks, she found more. McKenzie said, 'I also know that the Loch kindergarten sometimes have bush kinder where they take the kids to that sort of general area, so I was very keen to remove all of the samples that I could find of them.'

Prosecutor Warren then asked an intriguing question: did McKenzie know if there was a risk that more would grow? McKenzie said she wasn't sure, but thought there was a risk that more would emerge in the following days or weeks. She also told the court that she posted her photos and observations that night, noting that the find was 'about 2 metres from large oak trees on Loch recreation reserve' and 'under tree canopy'. One reason for posting was the hope that others with more expertise could comment on whether they were death caps or something similar.

Warren showed the jurors a screenshot of the post, showing a dropped pin at the location where McKenzie found the mushrooms. Under cross-examination by Stafford, McKenzie agreed that she hadn't gone back to check for regrowth.

With McKenzie's evidence, the prosecution had confirmed the ease of finding mushrooms highly likely to be death caps not far from Korumburra and Leongatha. The discovery sat comfortably in the chronology of Erin's actions, both in buying the dehydrator and also in evidence they were about to hear.

Doctor Matthew Sorell is the principal of Digital Forensic Sciences Australia. He's the go-to expert in criminal cases involving mobile phone network data. Sorell could comfortably pass as the expert from central casting, in a tweedy-looking jacket and wavy hair just shy of a bouffant. While at home explaining complex information likely to baffle both jurors and lawyers, Sorell has a knack for pithy, simple summaries. The doctor is also media friendly. When lawyers and witnesses arrived at court in the mornings or back from lunch, most ran the media gauntlet, keeping their reactions and interactions as close to zero as possible. Doctor Sorell took a more amiable approach, smiling for the cameras, and even repeating his walk to the courthouse door at the request of a cameraman who wanted a better shot for the evening news.

Sorell said he'd been given a number of reports by police in January 2024, mainly from Telstra phone towers which connect to a base station. These reports spanned a four-year period ending in August 2023 for a phone number ending in 783 – one of Erin's phones. Sorell had also been given the Telstra call charge records for that phone.

The jury was shown a diagram of the base stations near Korumburra. Sorell illustrated the complexity of his analysis, telling the court, 'The base station with the best service at the front of your house may be a different base station at the back of your house.' Sorell's evidence in chief was complex, technical and, in essence, could be distilled to two points.

He said he'd been asked to see if the phone had been in the Outtrim area and, if so, whether it had been passing through or had lingered. He told the court the phone could have been in the area between 11.24 am and 11.49 am on 22 May 2023 – the day after Doctor Tom May had posted about a possible death cap sighting in Outtrim.

The doctor's analysis also suggested the phone had connected in the Loch area on 28 April 2023, also following posts on iNaturalist. The implication was clear, but was the evidence definitive? If the phone was in the area where death cap sightings had been reported, were the mushrooms still there, and was Erin picking them? There was no evidence in the prosecution case to answer that. I can't help wondering if Erin could have searched iNaturalist on the mysterious missing mobile phone – yet another instance of only Erin knowing the truth.

As the ABC reporting of the case observed, 'It's been a very dry morning.'

The next day, 21 May, Shamen Fox-Henry, the Victoria Police cyber-crime expert, was called to give evidence about the investigation of the electronic devices. Fox-Henry's testimony provided another steep learning curve for the jury on the intricacies of contemporary detective work, and came complete with a PowerPoint presentation to explain data extraction and analysis techniques. The lunch adjournment came as a relief.

Around 3 pm, there was a glimmer of hope that the technical education was nearing an end when Fox-Henry was asked about the computer with the three drives that was seized, and his keyword searches for 'death cap', 'death cap mushroom', 'death cap mushrooms', 'mushrooms' and 'poison'. He told the court he'd found a Bing search that took the user to the iNaturalist website on 28 May 2022, followed by a takeaway food order at the Korumburra Middle Hotel. The search led to a posting: *'Deathcap from Melbourne VIC, Australia on May 18, 2022 at 02:36pm by [iNaturalist user], Bricker Reserve, Moorabbin – iNaturalist.'*

Fox-Henry's evidence flowed into the next day, where the focus shifted to phone messages, but the jury had a brief respite with a segue to a nurse from Leongatha Hospital. Nurse Mairim Cespon said she cared for Ian and Heather, and saw Erin on 31 July 2023, when she first arrived at Leongatha Hospital. Cespon was also there when Erin returned, and she reported that when Erin was told the children needed to be tested, she became emotional and cried.

Cespon kept a record of Erin's bowel movements and told the court that when she went to collect a specimen Erin assured her, 'It does look like wee but it's a bowel motion'. Mandy cross-examined, with the nurse agreeing that Erin had told her she was in pain, around a seven out of ten in magnitude, and had high blood pressure of 130 over 100. She said Erin appeared to be distressed and emotional.

Some of the most poignant and heartbreaking evidence came on Friday, 23 May – the eighteenth day of the trial. Professor Stephen Warrillow, the director of intensive care at Austin Health, appeared via video link. He'd had direct involvement in the care of Don, Gail, Heather and Ian. The professor said Don had been treated at Korumburra before being transferred to Dandenong Hospital, where he was diagnosed with acute liver failure likely caused by amanita mushrooms. With his condition deteriorating rapidly, he was transferred to the Austin, home to the Victorian Liver Transplant Unit. The hospital, and Professor Warrillow himself, had also treated other patients with amanita poisoning.

Don's 'clinical course was pretty typical'. The professor said of this evil poison, 'Unfortunately the body tends to recycle it internally, and that can actually cause persisting injury to the liver.'

The professor also said that activated charcoal is used to attempt to remove the poison from the bowel and break that recycling process, along with other drugs in what was a 'lot of very intense treatments in ICU [intensive care unit]'. Despite this, Don's condition continued to deteriorate over 3 and 4 August, and his bowel essentially stopped working.

The professor said, 'The only possibility of saving his life was through a liver transplant'. The transplant went ahead, but Don's condition didn't improve. The professor recalled, 'We had no other treatments to offer. There were no other therapies. He was dying.' Don passed away on 5 August.

The courtroom was silent and the profound sadness of the professor's evidence weighed heavily on all who were listening.

Moving then to Gail, the professor recounted a similar story, explaining that by 2 August she was extremely unwell, still suffering from watery diarrhoea and her liver was 'essentially not working at all'. He said, 'She was on everything we had,' but was too sick for a liver transplant. Over 3 and 4 August her condition remained in decline, and an abdominal X-ray showed what was likely gut ischaemia, which, the professor explained, 'essentially means the blood supply to the bowel, or the gut, has stopped flowing and the bowel – or that section of the bowel has died'. It was, he said, an extremely grave prognosis. Gail died on the afternoon of 4 August.

The professor said Heather's issues were similar to those he'd already described. With her condition deteriorating, the possibility of a liver transplant was discussed but, like Gail, she was too unwell. Heather's condition, the professor said, was not survivable. Heather died in the early hours of 4 August.

The professor's evidence then turned to Ian Wilkinson, who arrived at the Austin like the others, intubated, on mechanical breathing, critically ill and with liver failure. He said that, as with the other three, they'd investigated other possible causes but concluded he was suffering from amanita mushroom poisoning. His condition was deteriorating and he developed an abnormal heart rhythm.

On 4 August, worried Ian may have an 'evolving abdominal catastrophe' such as an ischaemic bowel, the doctors performed a laparoscopy – a minimally invasive procedure which found no significant bowel abnormalities. Over the following days, the professor observed, there had been 'slow but important improvement', and that improvement continued. On 14 August Ian's intubation was removed – he was no longer on life support and was able to breathe on his own. On 21 August he was moved from ICU to a ward.

When asked how close Ian had been to dying, the professor said sombrely, 'We thought he was going to die. He was very close.'

Ms Lenthall asked Professor Warrillow if there was a specific test for amanita mushroom poisoning. He said there wasn't a test to specifically identify the toxin, but observations of the patients led to what he said was the 'clinical cause highly consistent with amanita mushroom poisoning'. He went on to say there were a number of treatments that could keep the patient alive long enough to survive. He finished his evidence by noting that those treatments are 'clearly not 100 per cent effective' and 'there's a high mortality recognised even with what would be considered optimal care'.

Then it was over to Mandy, who may have spoken for everyone when he said, 'We need a break, Your Honour'.

I've been attending court cases for nearly five decades, and the evidence we'd heard that morning – the mechanics of slow and horrible death – was the saddest I can recall.

Fifteen minutes later they were back. Ms Lenthall asked if the high mortality rate from amanita mushroom poisoning was referring to the patients he saw in ICU. 'Correct,' he replied. Mandy didn't cross-examine – the professor had left an indelible impression, and there was little to be gained by extending his time in the witness box.

Week four of the trial ended that day with the prospect of the original four- to six-week trial now definitely confirmed as wishful thinking. There was still a long way to go. Stephen Eppingstall had yet to give evidence, and we still had no idea what the defence would involve, or if Erin would be stepping into the witness box.

28

ERIN SPEAKS

The prosecution saved a chunk of their investigator's evidence until last. Health official Sally Ann Atkinson took the court through the work she had coordinated, including the search for stores selling Asian mushrooms, and her conversations with Erin and Simon. In one of those conversations, she'd asked Simon if Erin foraged for mushrooms, and he'd told her he wasn't aware she had.

Atkinson finished her evidence on 27 May, the twentieth day of the trial, and was followed by Detective Sergeant Luke Farrell, who'd been the senior officer at Gibson Street on 5 August 2023 when the search warrant had been executed, and later that day when the warrant was executed at Erin's Lyons Street home in Mount Waverley. Farrell took the court through the chronology of the search, including finding the *Dinner* cookbook on the kitchen counter. He said the book was closed but had a slip of tissue paper used as a bookmark, and while the bookmark didn't take him to the beef Wellington recipe, he soon found it, noting it was stained with cooking liquids. He showed the court a photograph of the kitchen, which showed the book, and the book was tendered as an exhibit. Farrell's evidence was straightforward, and there was no cross-examination.

Late that afternoon, the prosecution called its final witness, the officer in charge of the case, Leading Detective Senior Constable Stephen Eppingstall.

From an observer's perspective, Eppingstall's evidence would recap the case, leaving the jury with the clear view that this wasn't the terrible accident pitched by the defence, but that Erin had planned and executed the poisoning, committing terrible crimes against four innocent people.

Eppingstall, sombrely dressed in a grey suit, entered the witness box. In response to Ms Warren's questions, he introduced himself as a member of the Homicide Squad and the lead investigator on the case. He was responsible for directing the investigation and producing the brief of evidence that formed the cornerstone of the prosecution case and the basis for the defence case.

As a witness, Eppingstall was thoughtful, direct and concise. Detectives are trained in the art of giving evidence, and taught to say as little as possible in response to a question. 'Yes' or 'no' are the best answers, followed by 'I don't recall', though that's one to use sparingly. The more you say, the more potential questions you face on cross-examination. Eppingstall had the habit of referring to Rogers respectfully as 'ma'am', prompting Justice Beale to tell him, 'You don't have to say ma'am – we'll save time.'

Eppingstall's evidence took in the sweep of the case, starting with homicide taking charge of the investigation on 3 August. The early questions included key points like the discovery of the dehydrator, the execution of the search warrant at Gibson Street, the seizing of electronic devices at the house, and the RecipeTin Eats cookbook. Warren then led him through the details of the search video, noting that Erin had spent 20–30 minutes using her mobile phone while he waited nearby. It was detailed, meticulous evidence. He also touched on the work of the mobile phone expert, Doctor Sorell, and Erin's computer and records.

Eppingstall's first day in the witness box ended with the tendering of his record of interview with Erin as an exhibit. For the first time since her plea on day one of the trial, Erin's voice was heard in the courtroom, albeit on video.

All the video and photographic evidence tendered as exhibits was made available on the jurors' iPads.

The next morning covered more investigative finds, including Erin's Woolworths shopping history in the lead-up to the lunch, which included the purchase of two 500-gram packs of sliced mushrooms on 23 July. Eppingstall also described text messages Erin had exchanged with Gail about a needle biopsy on 28 June, confirming that investigations had revealed there was no such appointment. He also confirmed there was no record of Erin receiving a cancer diagnosis on the government registry.

The jury also again heard that police believed Erin had another mobile phone, referred to as 'Phone A', that had never been found. Ms Warren put to him that police were looking for it. What we found out after the trial was that on the day of the first search of Gibson Street, Erin gave police a phone and her PIN code, quipping to police 'make your job easy'. As previously mentioned, this is the phone that she'd reset on a few occasions and would do so remotely while it was in police custody. The phone was named 'Phone B' but 'Phone A', which she'd likely been using in the lead up to the lunch, wasn't found. Erin's story was police had just missed the phone during their search.

The mystery of that missing phone, its contents and search history remains exactly that – a mystery.

Eppingstall's evidence in chief finished early in the afternoon of 28 May. Then it was Mandy's turn.

Some cross-examiners go hard at the police, trying to cast doubt on the integrity of their evidence and how that evidence was gained. Mandy was in a different position. The defence had already agreed about Erin's involvement. Where they differed was on whether the events in question reflected a terrible accident or intent to kill.

Mandy would test the evidence, encourage alternative interpretations, but it was unlikely that sparks would fly. There are occasions when experienced detectives and barristers go hard in cross-examination, but that didn't happen here. These were two quiet achievers doing their professional best. The theatre of cross-examination, as we later discovered, would be saved for the defence case.

Mandy took the Senior Constable through Erin's medical records, with Eppingstall agreeing she'd had a self-administered test for cervical cancer in March 2023 at Leongatha Health but there was no mention of ovarian cancer in her records, aside from a 2021 reference noting her concerns. After going through a series of text messages, the detective agreed that Erin was worried about her health. He also agreed Erin had a history of discharging herself from hospital contrary to medical advice. Mandy was diligently building the notion that Erin's behaviour, while perhaps different to what the jurors thought they'd have done, was, for Erin, not that unusual. He was trying to take them for a walk in her shoes.

The next day, Mandy took Eppingstall through messages between Erin and her online friends. This was evidence the court hadn't yet heard, and which may have shone a different light on her relationship with Simon and his family. In one message she wrote that she should forget about them all and live her life. '*Simon is probably loving how upset I am about all this.*'

The next message, posted in response, said, '*You are human and you have every right to be upset and angry. Hopefully he will have to pay up soon.*'

Another unidentified user offered, '*I'm so sorry Erin, it's so fucking hard when you're not believed or listened to, or understood. I went through similar with my ex in-laws. She was wonderful until we split up.*'

The detective agreed these were people venting. Mandy then drew his attention to later in the same conversation, where they'd segued to the death of Hollywood actor Kirstie Alley. Eppingstall agreed the exchanges represented 'random conversations about pets and children and other issues in their lives'.

The civility of the cross was on show when Mandy suggested that the CCTV taken at Subway didn't show Erin's son but someone else. Mandy used stills taken from the CCTV and compared them to stills from the son's interview and the video of the boy with Don and their home-made rocket. Mandy put to Eppingstall that he was 'not suggesting there's not a visit to Subway', but merely that the person in the picture wasn't the son. Eppingstall replied, 'I believe it to be, but that's a matter for the jury'. When Mandy persisted, he said, 'I've got the wrong one, is what you're saying. I don't think so, but that's a matter for you, sir.'

Cross-examination then moved to Signal messages exchanged between Erin, Don, Gail and Simon and the humdrum of many of them, which discussed things like statistics on Covid-19 cases in Korumburra, the children's homework, wishing each other well and declaring that Gail was '*the best mum-in-law anyone could ever ask for*'. That last message was sent on Mother's Day, fourteen months before Erin murdered her.

Eppingstall's last day of evidence was on 2 June, day twenty-four of the trial. It started with some innocuous questions, then moved again to phone evidence and factory resets, with the detective agreeing there were three mobile phones – two Samsung and one Nokia – and that one of the Samsungs, known as Phone A, was the missing phone. It was the sort of evidence that prompted dozing off, and a reminder that a fair trial involves long and detailed work, punctuated by the rare moment of drama. In this trial, those moments were very rare.

Mandy finished his cross-examination, and when the jury had departed, he told the judge that after Ms Warren had re-examined her witness and concluded the prosecution case, he'd announce what the defence would do. The question on everyone's mind was: would Erin give evidence? After legal discussions and a lunch break, the court resumed at 2.16 pm. Warren's re-examination was brief, covering Erin's discharges against medical advice, and a few questions again about messages, mobile phones and Subway CCTV.

The prosecution case closed and the jury went off for a break, as did the judge and lawyers after some legal housekeeping.

At 3.30 pm on 2 June 2023, with the jury back and weeks of speculation poised to end, the defence case opened. Colin Mandy stood, saying, 'I call Erin Patterson'.

Ian Wilkinson was in the courtroom, along with members of the Patterson and Wilkinson families. Simon wasn't among them.

Erin, flanked by security staff, was escorted through the courtroom to the witness box. She was wearing a paisley-patterned long-sleeve shirt and dark pants. I was listening by audio link and hoping someone inside the court would comment on whether she was in shoes or sandals, but they didn't.

It used to be quite an unusual move to put your client in the witness box in a criminal trial. Old courtroom cynics thought it was an act of desperation, or the demands of a client who wanted their moment in the limelight. Recently, my criminal defence mates tell me the stigma of desperation has diminished. Juries want to see the accused and hear their story.

The downside of this hasn't changed, however. The potential problems include the risk of the witness opening doors to lines of questioning previously averted, behaving in a manner that may annoy or anger the jury, or spinning a story that can be successfully attacked in cross-examination.

Erin Patterson would prove herself to be a capable witness. No dramas, no histrionics, calm and assertive.

Mandy began by aiming to tell the jury the Erin Patterson story from before the lunch. It was a story we'd only had glimpses of so far, gleaned primarily through media reports, social media speculation and research. After stating her full name – Erin Trudi Patterson – she said she was fifty years old. Mandy then asked Erin to tell the court about her children. It was a comfortable, unchallenging start to get a first-time witness over the discomfort of the process, and also a handy way to establish her doting mother credentials. She talked about their new school, where they'd started in July 2023. She said they were coping 'a lot better than I expected. They seemed to settle in quite well, make some friends and connections quite quickly.' The new school, she said, would help with her son's 'individual learning needs' more effectively than the former.

The children were living full-time with her and seeing their father when they wanted. For her son, that was generally at church or youth group. Erin also had plans of her own, and in early 2023 had been accepted into a Bachelor of Nursing and Midwifery at Federation University, which she planned to begin in 2024. According to the university this is a three-year full-time course available at their Gippsland campus near Morwell.

Of Gibson Street, Erin said they'd moved into the house in June 2022, saying, 'I saw it as the final house, meaning I wanted it to be a house where the children would grow up, where once they moved away for uni or work, they could come back and stay whenever they liked, bring their children, and I'd grow old there.' She said she was financially stable and could go to university full-time without the need to work.

Mandy then took her to a less rosy side of her life. She said she felt some distance between her and Don and Gail, in part because she was now living in another town, and expressed concerns that Simon was 'not wanting me to be involved too much in the family. Perhaps I wasn't being invited to so many things.' Her relationship with Simon was 'functional'. 'We didn't relate on friend things, banter, like we used to. That changed at the start of the year.'

Then Mandy moved to how Erin felt about herself in July 2023. She said, 'I'd been fighting a never-ending battle of low self-esteem most of my adult life, and the further inroads I made into being middle-aged, the less – less I felt good about myself, I suppose. Put on more weight. Could handle exercise less.'

Unsurprisingly, Erin's mother may have been at the root of these issues, and she told the court that 'when I was a kid, Mum would weigh us every week to make sure we weren't putting on too much weight, so I went to the extreme of barely eating, then to, throughout my adulthood, going the other way and bingeing.' It was a comment that would also tie in with her allegedly eating three quarters of the cake that had been brought as dessert on 29 July. But, like all Erin's stories of her parents, they were dead and not around to contradict her.

To deal with weight issues, she said she'd been planning 'gastric bypass' surgery.

The questions then moved to when Erin met Simon. Curiously, this was the point where we got to know Erin – but we were not offered anything about her childhood, education, family, including her older sister, or prior jobs. Instead, it was straight to Monash Council, and what was largely a rehash of what Simon had already outlined.

Of Simon's beliefs, Erin said he was a Christian while she was a 'fundamentalist atheist, like I was really very atheist'.

Her interest in religion came at a sermon in Korumburra given by Ian Wilkinson. She said he was talking about 'faith, hope and love' and it was 'like a spiritual experience. I'd been – I'd been approaching religion as an intellectual exercise up until that point. Does that make sense? Is it rational? But I had what I would call a religious experience there and it quite overwhelmed me.'

Following that epiphany, the story moved through a thumbnail sketch of their early relationship, their marriage, then their move to Perth. She said the birth of their son was 'very traumatic', and when asked about her decision to leave both husband and son in Townsville and fly back to Perth, she said she'd 'had a gutful'. Her evidence then moved to the turbulence of their marriage, which led to separation in 2015. She said, 'We just couldn't communicate well when we disagreed about something. We could never communicate in a way that made each of us feel heard and understood. We would just feel hurt.' Again, it was a once-over, gently and frustratingly short on detail. Erin had drawn the outline, but hadn't coloured it in. Just like Erin's appearance in court, it was fairly bland.

On day two of her testimony, we went back to Western Australia and to money. Erin said she'd opened a second-hand bookshop in Pemberton. It lasted for about a year.

Then we jumped back to Victoria, when Erin and Simon lived with Don and Gail temporarily in one cramped room. 'Don and Gail were so welcoming to us and just loved having X [her son] there. I think they loved having all three of us there, but it was a really good experience.'

The passing of her two parents was discussed, including one of the rare mentions of her sister, Ceinwen, as a beneficiary, then the discussion segued into real estate. Mandy said that at one point she and Simon had three properties in joint names, and Erin said, 'I always thought we would bring the family back together. That is what I wanted ... It was something tangible, to say to Simon, I see a future for us.'

She displayed a rare moment of emotion when talking about her weight. She'd tried 'every diet under the sun' and would eat 'everything you could get your hands on' and then be sick, but her gorging was done when no-one else was around. It was an intriguing comment, given her later claim that after the July lunch she'd eaten three quarters of the dessert cake, then been sick.

One of the most captivating pieces of evidence in the entire trial arose before lunch – Erin the forager. She said she liked mushrooms because they were tasty and healthy. She often bought dried mushrooms from stores, including Asian grocers, to use in curries, pasta and soups, but she felt wild mushrooms were 'more interesting'. That interest began during Covid-19 when on a walk with the children in the Korumburra Botanic Park. 'I picked all the mushrooms that I could see because I wanted to try to figure out what they were.' To work out what was edible and what wasn't, she took the bizarre step of cutting a few slivers off a mushroom, frying it in butter and eating it – a dangerous way to build expertise. As her confidence as a forager grew, she began including wild mushrooms in their family dinners.

Erin then conceded that accidentally foraged death cap mushrooms may have been in the deadly lunch. Given this was the first time Erin had admitted to foraging, and it was uncorroborated by the children or Simon, as well as being in conflict with what she told her online friends and what she said in her police interview, you could be forgiven for being sceptical. It was also a very convenient admission targeted to support the core of her defence – it was just a terrible accident, but she needed to explain how death caps got into the mushroom mix. While convenient, it wasn't convincing.

The following morning they were back at it, with Erin denying she'd seen the 2023 posts on iNaturalist by May and McKenzie, and denying she'd foraged for mushrooms in Outtrim and Loch. In contrast, she then admitted she'd lied to Don and Gail about the need for a biopsy on her arm, but said their care had 'felt really nice', explaining that 'the issue started to resolve and I felt a bit embarrassed I had made such a big deal about it. I didn't want their care of me to stop so I just kept it going. I shouldn't have done it.'

The next stop in this whirlwind tour of the world of Erin was the lunch. Erin said she'd followed the RecipeTin Eats *Dinner* recipe 'roughly', but as she couldn't get whole beef fillets, she had opted to make individual portions. Again, a neat snippet that explained a highly suspicious detail. She also admitted to skipping the crepe the recipe suggested be wrapped around the fillet – Ramsay uses prosciutto, but Don didn't eat pork – and said she used filo pastry she'd bought. Some preparation for the dish was done on the Friday, with the hard work done on the Saturday morning.

The evidence also covered the lunch service. Erin recalled saying, 'Grab a plate guys. I'm just going to finish off the gravy.' She said she'd probably used two gravy sachets she'd bought, then put it into a pitcher and 'grabbed the last plate off the bench'. What she didn't recall was which plate she grabbed.

Her answers to Mandy suggested, before that fateful day, it was highly unlikely she would be offered a cooking show.

Erin was shown the CCTV from Subway and, while agreeing she'd taken her son there after the lunch, she denied it was him in the film, thus explaining Mandy's questions to Eppingstall. She then told the court she became unwell around 11 pm that night. The events of the following days were then covered, including when she heard about the illnesses and her meeting Doctor Webster. Her evidence offered little variance to what the court had already heard from earlier witnesses.

Erin did, however, show emotion, voice quavering, when asked about an alleged conversation with Simon in which he asked, 'Is that how you poisoned my parents, using that dehydrator?' and her response, 'Of course not.'

Mandy, in his cross-examination of Simon earlier in the trial, had put to him, 'You said to Erin, "Is that [the dehydrator] what you used to poison them?"' And Simon responded, 'I did not say that to Erin.'

According to Erin's evidence, the alleged conversation, she said, 'Got me thinking about all the times I had used it [the dehydrator] and how I had dried foraging mushrooms in it weeks earlier, and I was starting to think what if they had gone in the container with the Chinese mushrooms. What if that happened?'

With this thought weighing on her mind, and the looming arrival of the Child Protection worker, Erin decided to dump the dehydrator at the tip. The reasonable excuses for her lies were mounting up. As the day came to an end, Mandy took her back to the positives of her relationships with Don and Gail. With a trembling voice and tears welling, she said,

'They were very close. Especially [my son] and Don. They were like two minds separated by fifty years.' The jury left for the day with that picture in their minds.

Erin's story came to an end the next morning, 5 June, with Mandy asking about the dehydrator. He asked, 'Did you lie?' and she said, 'It was'. When asked why, she said, 'Well, I had disposed of it a few days earlier, in the context of thinking that maybe mushrooms I'd foraged or the meal I'd prepared was responsible for making people sick. Then on Saturday, Detective Eppingstall told me that Gail and Heather had passed away and it was this stupid kneejerk reaction to dig deeper and keep lying. I was just scared, but I shouldn't have done it.' She had a similar reason for her foraging lie.

She then told him all six Wellingtons she made were the same, confirming that, yes, the children had also eaten the leftovers, and, yes, her meal had made her sick.

Rogers' cross-examination started late morning, and it wouldn't be conducted in Mandy's low-key style, or that of the wily barrister, ducking and weaving and looking for vulnerability. Instead, Rogers was aggressive and straight to the point. In many of her questions she'd put a proposition to Erin, then demand, 'Correct?' or, for variety, 'Agree or disagree?'

She opened fire with, 'It was a lie when you told police on that occasion that you didn't own a dehydrator. Correct?' Erin replied, 'Correct'. Rogers put it to Erin that in many minds, she had disposed of the dehydrator to hide the fact that it contained death cap mushrooms, which Erin denied.

It was this early questioning that showed Erin wasn't a witness who'd shrink in her seat but, rather, someone who'd stand her ground. She was firm, considered and not swift to anger or annoyance – a capable witness, but one who offered the occasional pedantic or perhaps smart-arsed moment, depending on your view. One example was an interchange regarding the dehydrator. Rogers showed her a photo of the device at the tip, and asked if it had been hers. Erin replied, 'I presume so,' prompting Rogers to ask, 'And why do you presume so?' to which Erin responded, 'Unless somebody else put in a dehydrator as well as me I presume this is the one I put in.' The jury was given a glimmer of Erin the smart-alec and it didn't do her any favours.

Erin agreed that she may not have told her online friends about her foraging. She denied she'd foraged at Loch and Outtrim after the iNaturalist postings, but told Rogers she had foraged for wild mushrooms after 28 April 2023 and prior to the July lunch. Rogers showed her the photo of the mushrooms on a tray that Doctor May believed were consistent with death caps. She said, 'I suggest to you that these were death caps that you foraged on or after 28 April 2023. Correct?' Erin replied, 'No, that's not correct.'

The to and fro continued throughout the day, covering messages, ovarian cancer, reasons for the lunch and so on. As the day came to an end, Rogers said, 'I suggest you never thought you would have to account for this lie about having cancer because you thought your lunch guests would die.' Erin replied, 'That's not true.'

The court took a break the next day, which was the prelude to the King's Birthday long weekend. It was time not only for a break from a trial that was running significantly longer than anticipated, but also to prepare for the addresses that would come at the end of the defence case.

On day twenty-nine of the trial, 10 June, everyone again assembled, quietly hoping that the end was in sight. The short week got off to a fast start with Rogers asking about Erin's alleged gastric bypass surgery. It was a story that had already taken some knocks. Diligent detectives had found the Enrich Clinic in Melbourne where Erin had allegedly booked the weight loss surgery for September 2023, and found that the clinic didn't offer the procedure. When asked if Erin agreed or disagreed with the fact that the surgery wasn't performed there, she said she didn't know, then after some mental gymnastics suggested she might have instead booked in for liposuction. When challenged that she was lying, Erin offered a lame, 'It wasn't a lie, that's what my memory was.'

While Erin remained composed, it was clear Rogers was getting under her skin. Later that morning she moved to the lunch, with Erin denying her allegation that the children hadn't, in fact, been fed leftovers – a question that had been on my mind. 'Incorrect,' Erin said, sounding rather testy. Rogers then asked about the slab of cake Erin said she'd eaten when the guests had gone, and what was in the subsequent vomit, to which Erin said she had 'no idea'.

Rogers' cross-examination continued, picking through every element of Erin's evidence, often in almost grisly detail – bowel movements were a lowlight. Of Erin's hospital departure, Rogers said Erin had headed home to 'cover her tracks', which Erin tersely denied. What followed was more to and fro, with neither Erin nor Rogers relenting. By the end of the day they'd covered Ian's recollection of a smaller plate for Erin's Wellington, which Erin disagreed with. She also denied making a sixth poisoned dish for Simon in case he turned up.

Proposition and denial wore on until day thirty-one – 12 June – another day of denials ending with Erin denying she'd foraged for death caps to kill her lunch guests. Rogers said, 'You did so intending to kill them. Agree or disagree.' Erin replied, 'Disagree.'

Rogers finished just before noon. Mandy re-examined briefly, then closed the defence case. The end of the trial was finally in sight.

29

THE JURY DECIDES

The evidence phase of the trial is followed by addresses to the jury by the prosecution and then the defence, and then finally, the instructions by the judge. Given the volume of evidence in this case, it was clear none would be short.

Addresses to the jury by the prosecution and defence were summaries of the key issues in the cases they'd presented. Rogers began on 16 June and concluded late the next day, taking the jury through the strengths of the prosecution's evidence and Erin's numerous lies, making the point that Erin as a witness was untrustworthy and that, combined with the weight and integrity of all the evidence they'd heard, proved beyond reasonable doubt that Erin had intentionally searched for death cap mushrooms, found them and deliberately served them to her guests.

Mandy countered in his address, saying the prosecution was 'flawed'. He put the case that Erin had 'very good reasons' not to harm her guests, saying that for Erin they were 'the only people in the world who are any support to you and your children, you will lose your children and you will lose everything that's important to you'. He said that by giving evidence and not choosing to remain silent, as was her right, Erin had exposed herself not only to an experienced barrister but also to global scrutiny. Erin, he contended, was 'not on trial for being a liar' and the jury wasn't there to make a 'moral judgement'. He suggested that the proposition that Erin had planned to murder Simon at the lunch was 'absurd'. It was a proposition made safe in the knowledge that the jury had been isolated from details of Simon's illnesses.

By 19 June – day thirty-five – Mandy's address was nearing its end. As is usual in defence submissions, a key point is casting doubt on whether the high bar of proof 'beyond reasonable doubt' has been met by the prosecution. He said the prosecution's four key points were 'convoluted' and 'absurd'.

Those four key points were: that Erin would murder without motive (while not necessary in a murder case, it's the question on everyone's mind); that she used her alleged cancer to lure the guests; that she knew her guests would take the cancer story to their grave (there would be no witnesses); and the 'illogical' proposition that she believed she could pass off the death of three guests and the grave illness of one other as a 'strange case of gastro'.

Mandy wrapped up with the jigsaw puzzle analogy, saying you can't force the pieces together. The jury, he said, couldn't find that she was 'probably guilty', noting that if there was a reasonable possibility it was all an accident, they must acquit. He went on to say, 'If you think maybe she deliberately poisoned the meal, you must find her not guilty. If you think that it's likely that she deliberately poisoned the meal, you must find her not guilty.'

With those words ringing in their ears, the jury retired for the weekend, with Justice Beale's charge to them scheduled to begin on Tuesday, 24 June. It would run for four days, and the transcript, when printed in single-side A4 paper, would be 5 centimetres thick.

Beale's charge to the jury had two purposes – directions on principles of law in the case, and the issues they needed to decide on, which included the evidence relating to those issues and the arguments made by the prosecution and defence. His charge was painstakingly detailed, balanced and meticulous and, as a highly experienced judge, probably constructed with an eye to minimising reasonable grounds for an appeal by either side.

Among the many important matters Beale spoke of, a few stood out, and he listed them as the calculated deceptions put forward by the prosecution. First up was the unusual invitation offered to the Wilkinsons – Erin had never invited them to her house before, and the claimed premise was fake. The second was poisoning the guests' beef Wellingtons, deviating from the recipe (which called for a whole Wellington, not individuals) and using 'smelly' mushrooms. Thirdly, Erin's doctors didn't observe her experiencing diarrhoea and at no time did she tell them she'd vomited. Lastly, Beale spoke of 'the sustained cover-up', telling them to 'reject the innocent foraging mishap defence. The only evidence for it comes from her mouth. The children didn't know of her foraging, neither did Simon, no mention of it to the Facebook group, no books on foraging found at her home.'

Beale then moved on to the lack of evidence of motive, saying motive is sometimes internal, known only to the person. From years working in crime, I can confirm this is spot-on. For some killers, murder is simply to remove an obstacle or a step toward a particular goal. The average person considers murder abhorrent, whereas a dangerous few give it seconds of thought – some even brag.

Beale said that while the defence had no burden of proof, 'a significant portion of her case relies only on her evidence, that's the foraging for wild edible mushrooms, binge eating and vomiting, taking Imodium and stopping to have diarrhoea on the side of the road when she took [her son] to Tyabb. You should reject all of that.'

The judge also dealt with one of the investigation's early eureka moments – the evidence of death cap sightings in Outtrim and Loch, and Erin's phone being pinged in the vicinity. While compelling for the investigators, that evidence, which had been probed at length during the trial, wasn't to be considered by the jury, simply because there was no evidence Erin had checked the iNaturalist site in April/May 2023. While her phone may have later been in the vicinity, the science putting it there wasn't definitive, and even if she had been, what she was doing there would be an assumption. The prosecution had lost a tasty piece of their case, but they'd lost it in the interest of fairness.

Beale then turned to the defence, and what Mandy had argued to be a flawed approach. He said there were two key issues: 'Is there a real possibility the death cap mushrooms were included accidentally? Is it a reasonable possibility that she didn't intend to kill or cause really serious injury?' The defence, the judge said, reckoned the prosecution had been selective in their evidence, and 'they haven't drawn your attention to bits of evidence they don't like'. He went on, 'They've assumed she's guilty, they've cherry-picked, they've disregarded inconvenient truths. They've ignored the nuances of human behaviour.'

Beale said, 'She's not on trial for being a liar. Views about what's morally correct don't have any place in this trial. As for the alleged incriminating conduct, nothing she did afterward changes what her intention was at the time of serving the meal. She'd served a meal responsible for people dying and the custody of her children was on the line. She had an innocent motive to tell a lot of lies.' The judge observed that according to the defence case, Erin had organised the lunch to 'reconnect with everyone for the sake of her children'.

As his charge to the jury drew to a close, Justice Beale said, 'Don't be influenced by sympathy or prejudice, use your heads not your hearts. It's a tragedy that three people died and one nearly died. It's natural for you to have been moved when the family of the deceased were giving evidence. You would have felt a deep empathy for them and their loss. There can be an instinctive response to punish the person responsible. We know Erin Patterson caused their deaths because she cooked and served the meal.'

Justice Beale had completed his charge to the jury. Next came the ballot to reduce the number of jurors from fourteen to twelve. Two male jurors departed the courtroom, accompanied by members of the Jury Commissioner's office, to collect their baggage. All fourteen had come with clothing, toiletries and other essentials, prepared to spend however long sequestered in accommodation an easy distance from the court.

At 1.01 pm on Monday, 30 June – day forty of the trial – the jury of five women and seven men retired to begin their deliberations.

The judge told the jury that if they hadn't reached a verdict by 4.15 pm that afternoon then they'd completed their day of work.

Next stop: their new temporary homes.

Jury sequestration is rare. In city trials it usually only occurs where there is a potential issue to the probity or safety of jury members – in terrorist or organised crime trials, for example. In a city, jurors can usually go home aware of their responsibilities and the likelihood of being followed, or bumping into people who know what they're doing and want to chat about it. The risk of a problem is low. In a country town, however, the risk of encountering people who know you're on the jury is significantly higher, especially in a trial that has garnered the remarkable coverage that this one had. This jury would be in accommodation, eating together in a communal dining room or relaxing in the rooms. No gyms, no tennis games or a quick nine holes of golf – just twelve jurors and their minders. It's a genteel form of temporary imprisonment.

Each day they were bussed to and from the courthouse. Their work days would be structured as they had been over the weeks before, beginning at 10.30 am and finishing at 4.15 pm each day, but in this phase of the trial, Friday would be a full day and they'd also deliberate on Saturdays. If they came to a decision on a Saturday, the court would resume to take that decision straight away – courts don't linger when the jury has decided.

The judge, court staff, lawyers, police, victims' families and friends, the still-large media contingent and the public then all settled down to wait while the jury did their work. Sometimes a decision is returned within hours. At the other end of the scale, juries can take weeks, sometimes sending notes to the judge with questions or seeking guidance. Sometimes they'll send a note to the judge telling them the jury is deadlocked and can't reach either a unanimous decision – required in Victoria's murder trials – or even a majority. At that point, the judge may offer some advice in the hope of a resolution. However, if the issue persists, the judge will discharge the jury and a retrial may or may not follow – that's a decision for the government's prosecutors. It's a terrible position, for the accused and for the victims, their families and friends – finality is thwarted or delayed.

The carefully made plans for the jury did hit a small hurdle, courtesy of something relatively simple – the temporary accommodation required. When a massive criminal trial is run in a regional town, and it goes a bit longer than planned – almost double the time originally planned – things can get tricky. With school holidays looming, as well as the National Table Tennis Championships, held at the Gippsland Regional Indoor Sports Stadium in nearby Traralgon, accommodation in the area was in short supply.

On the Saturday afternoon of 5 July, court officials became aware that Detective Eppingstall and two of the prosecution solicitors had been staying at the same motel as the jury. The jurors were moved to another motel in another town. Justice Beale informed the lawyers for both sides that the jurors had been on another floor of the hotel and ate in a common room on that floor, with both areas being separate from other hotel guests.

However – there is usually a however – all hotel guests had to use a common entrance. Beale also noted the accommodation shortage in the region, that the jury relocation was a coincidence, and confirmed that neither Eppingstall nor the solicitors had come into contact with the jurors. Having noted the situation two days before, Eppingstall had taken steps to avoid any interaction. The issue came about when the prosecution team's earlier accommodation had been booked out. When they discovered they were now in a hotel along with the jury they had tried to find alternatives, but with no luck.

By the end of Saturday, 5 July, the jury had been deliberating for five and a half days. We'd been told that if they decided on a Saturday, the judge would take their decision in Morwell. Like most of the players in this case, he was nearby, waiting. If it came on another day, there would be around an hour's notice before court convened.

The next day, the jury, oblivious to the accommodation challenges, were given a bit of fresh air on their Sunday off, with court staff taking them to a winery, making sure there was no interaction with staff or other wine tasters. It would be pure speculation to suggest that the combination of fresh air, a change of scenery and some of the pinot noir and chardonnay for which the region is noted, may have helped provide a clarity of thought to bring them to consensus.

Nearly six days is quite a long time for deliberations, but the jury had a vast amount of evidence to consider. In addition to Justice Beale's charge to them, there were over 3500 pages of transcripts, plus exhibits such as CCTV, statements, reports, photos and so on.

By Monday, 7 July, I suspected the judge might be considering a chat to the jury to see how they were progressing. Many of us who've been around a while – being worldly or, as some might suggest, cynical – speculate that the prospect of a looming long weekend, festive period or school holidays may also stir a jury to decide. Victoria's school holidays had started on Friday, 4 July. All things considered, I knew it would be prudent to be in Morwell on Monday.

At 10 am, the usual suspects – the media and members of the public fascinated by the case – were waiting outside. The media were there in droves – probably forty or so, and a mix of print and TV, several dressed and ready for their piece to camera. Selfies were being snapped by the waiting public. Some media, short of anything new to report, were interviewing each other. But there was a buzz in the air.

The lawyers and police arrived, all looking quite tired – a stark contrast to day one, when they'd looked fresh and ready for battle. In the media overflow room on the first floor we were speculating – after this long, would there be an acquittal? A hung jury seemed more likely. Getting twelve people to agree on anything, let alone something of this magnitude, would always be a challenge.

We had no idea what the jury were thinking. Twelve anonymous people plucked from obscurity to make a decision that would impact on so many, and would be reported around the world. We knew absolutely nothing about their lives or experiences, nor would we ever. Unlike in the United States, jurors shouldn't be interviewed by media about their experiences, nor should they offer themselves for interview. The Australian Institute of Criminology in 2007 noted, 'the secrecy of the jury room is a sacrosanct principle in the Australian common law tradition'.

Just before 1 pm the courthouse cleared for lunch. The nearby Daily Cafe and Foodstore had been doing a brisk trade throughout the trial, and this Monday was no different. Stephen Eppingstall and three colleagues were at one table, with members of the media sprinkled at several others. The police left around 1.25 pm. Ten minutes later, the Supreme Court media emailed us – the jury had reached their verdicts and they would be delivered at 2.15 pm.

Toasted sandwiches and half-drunk coffees were abandoned, bills quickly paid and then it was back to the courthouse – a few even broke into a trot – to get through security and set up. Outside the courtroom there was already a queue of around fifty people waiting to get in. Many would be disappointed. Many of the media, including me, were in the nearby media room, watching on video.

Shortly after 2 pm the lawyers and police arrived. A couple of people – probably family members or those close to the family – were taken into court. A court worker was on hand to make sure they were okay. Ian Wilkinson and Simon Patterson were not in court. There were plenty of court security officers and police from the adjacent station, all calm but watchful.

At 2.15 pm Justice Beale was back on the bench, and then the jury filed into the jury box, taking their seats for the final time in what had become an epic trial.

The foreperson was asked to read the jury's decision. She took each of the four charges individually, announcing each as guilty. There were no shouts, loud gasps or claps, as you occasionally get.

And with that, Erin Patterson ceased being the accused. She was now the prisoner – for what will be a very long time.

Erin Patterson, standing in the dock at the rear of the court, looked calmly at the jury. No tears, no emotion, nothing. *The Australian*'s John Ferguson, who'd been writing about the case since the very first days and was in court, watching her closely as the foreperson announced the verdict, summed up Erin's demeanour aptly. He wrote, 'You had to be sitting close to see it, but Patterson's throat moved ever so slightly, almost as if she was about to gulp, when Gail's name was raised. But not even the guilt of killing a kind old soul like her children's grandmother was enough to make her break out in proper, heaving – humane even – emotion.'

Ferguson went on, 'Remember, there were often times in court when Patterson cried or tears welled as she went through her evidence or listened to the words of others. No, what the court got on Monday was the full Erin. Cold, mean and vicious.'

Beale thanked the jury for their 'excellent work', saying 'you've been an exceptional jury'. He finished by delivering what was probably great news for most of them – an exemption from jury service for the next fifteen years.

Just ten minutes later, the judge and jury had departed and the courtroom was slowly clearing, with everyone trying to snatch a glance at the ordinary looking middle-aged woman who'd just been convicted of mass murder. Erin Patterson was now that rarest of creatures: a female mass murderer.

As the court emptied, Erin remained outwardly devoid of emotion. Her lawyers spoke quietly with her before she was taken, for the last time, through the underground tunnel and back to the police cells to await transport back to the Dame Phyllis Frost Centre.

The media crowd didn't get commentary or statements from the key players as they left the court, preferring, as they'd done throughout the trial, to keep a dignified silence. As the afternoon light diminished, the media pack loitered outside the police station, hoping for pictures of Patterson as she headed back to prison.

The Patterson/Wilkinson family didn't comment. In a statement, Victoria Police said, 'Our thoughts are with the respective families at this time and we acknowledge how difficult these past two years have been for them. We will continue to support them in every way possible following this decision.' On the family's position, they said, 'The Patterson and Wilkinson families will not be supplying a statement via Victoria Police and have asked for privacy at this time.'

30

FAREWELL, MORWELL

The jury's decision was followed by an early evening exodus from Morwell, the temporary boost to the local economy going with it. The Supreme Court's media provided some figures on coverage of the case, which were close to eye-watering. There had been 252 journalists registered with them, including fifteen outlets from the United Kingdom, the United States and New Zealand. Among them were nine authors, seven podcasts and podcasters, seven documentary crews and one crew producing a drama. One hundred and ninety of that total number also had real-time audio access via Vimeo. Seven further international outlets made contact after the jury's decision. The court said it was the largest media event they've managed in recent history. I think it's a fair bet that the Patterson case was one of the biggest, if not the biggest, courtroom events in Australian history. The only other case that attracted such global interest was the Lindy Chamberlain case.

The coverage was detailed, fast and extensive. Audience interest usually flags during a long trial, but in this case it didn't. The public's demand for information was rapacious and well fed by the media. And the media were closely monitored, not only by the court but also by lawyers – the prospect of a mistrial being something that loomed large in the minds of all involved.

Fortunately, there were only sixteen directions issued by the court to remove content, mostly because it breached sub-judice rules. Four of those were social media types, and then there were NSW broadcasters Kyle Sandilands and Jackie O on Kiss FM, who found themselves in strife. The inevitably outspoken Sandilands decided to offer his views on air during the case. One of his comments was, 'Hasn't she done something like this before, with the mushrooms?' This was followed with, 'But the rest of us already know, yeah, you fuck ... come on, bro. You can tell by looking at her, just lock that bitch up.'

While Sandilands may have got his wish, thanks to the work of the jury, comments like that during a live trial are utterly inappropriate – something any journalist or broadcaster should know. Justice Beale took aim at them the morning of the broadcast. Having read a transcript of the comments, he said, 'I encourage all commentators to engage their brains before they open their mouths, as they may otherwise land themselves and their organisations in hot water. I will be referring this morning's matter to the Office of Public Prosecutions for contempt proceeding.'

Others finding themselves potentially on the wrong side of the law included influencer/blogger Constance Hall, who told her 1.3 million fans she'd had to take a post down, explaining, 'I had to remove the post about the mushroom trial because I received an email from the Vic government telling me to immediately delete it and that numerous comments on the post breached "the principles of sub justice [sic] contempt",' adding, 'I'm not quite sure what [sub judice] means but it sounded legit.'

When reporting or commenting on a live trial, it's handy to come to grips with sub judice – true crime is an incredibly popular genre, but it can be a minefield for the unaware, with ramifications for a live trial and for both the victims and the accused.

Online news outlet Crikey published an article about the 'media circus', then quickly cast themselves in the role of the clown by breaching a suppression order, resulting in some hasty editing. Other offenders included the ABC, Network Ten and Mamamia.

With many of the constraints lifted, though an interim suppression order remained in place on some matters, the media wrapped its time in Morwell with the predictable, and in many instances utterly reasonable, stories noting what they really thought of Erin. Photos and vision that had formed some of the exhibits in the trial were now released for publication, accompanied by a slew of opinions, from the expert to the observational. For variety, there were also articles about the experience of covering a long trial and some tourism tips on Morwell.

*

In the middle of all this, a bombshell dropped, and it came from an unexpected source. At 5 am on 8 July, the *Herald Sun* grabbed the top spot in the morning media, publishing an interview with Doctor Chris Webster, one of the original treating doctors in Leongatha, who'd given evidence in the trial. No longer legally constrained, the doctor opened fire, his comments giving voice to the thoughts of many.

When Ian and Heather Wilkinson arrived at Leongatha Hospital, Doctor Webster thought they'd been deliberately poisoned. His thoughts darkened when Doctor Beth Morgan from Dandenong Hospital, who was treating Don and Gail, rang, telling him they both had grossly abnormal liver function tests, and there were concerns they'd been poisoned by death cap mushrooms.

For Chris Webster, the pieces of the medical investigation were quickly coming together. When he saw Erin at Leongatha Hospital on the morning of 31 July, he immediately asked her where the mushrooms were from. As he told the *Herald Sun*, 'It was a single word response. Woolworths.' He said that for him, that one single word confirmed the suspicion that had been growing in his mind: Erin was a killer.

Doctor Webster had presented in court as what Australians would call a knockabout bloke – no pretence, no prevarication, colourful in language and straight to the point. When Erin delivered her one-word answer, he recalled thinking, 'If she said she picked them, it would have been a very different mindset for me because there would have been an instant assumption it was all a tragic accident. But once she said that answer, my thoughts were, "Holy fucking shit, you fucking did it, you crazy bitch, you poisoned them all."'

What also troubled Webster was Erin's attitude to the welfare of her children. He said, 'She wasn't freaking out about the safety of her children. Looking into her eyes,

I thought, "I don't know what planet you're on but you're not on earth. If it was an Agatha Christie novel, this is how one of her characters would have done it."' Rather astutely, he realised his actions may be closely scrutinised later, and that included his call to 000 when Erin decided to leave the hospital within five minutes of arriving. Her actions, he thought, were very strange for someone who may have been exposed to what he described as a 'potentially fatal toxin'.

Webster's colourful view, which provided a perfect media grab, was that Erin was 'a disturbed sociopathic nutbag'.

He then moved on to his regrets, and his views on the trial. He noted that while it was a 'once in a lifetime opportunity' to be part of such a thing, it was laced with problems. He regretted not asking Heather more after she'd told him the lunch wasn't for a birthday celebration but didn't elaborate. He recalled, 'If I had my time again I'd be asking more about the mushrooms. It seems ridiculous because now we know the whole story.' He went on, 'Every fibre of the Sherlock Holmes detective part of my doctoring wanted to keep exploring, but part of me thinks if I got onto the fact it was death cap mushrooms earlier I would not have had that interaction with Erin.'

Doctor Webster said he felt that during the trial what was lost was just how 'humble and decent' the victims were, noting that Heather's last words, as she was being loaded into the ambulance for her trip to Monash, were, 'Thank you Doctor Webster for all your care'. He said the moment would 'haunt me forever'.

On Erin at trial and her fate, he was similarly colourful, saying that when he entered the witness box to give evidence, she gave him 'the stinkiest of stink eye'. 'I looked over and searing daggers shot out of her eyes and went into my brain.'

While many were nodding their heads in agreement, some were less than delighted by his comments, and complaints about his character and professionalism joined the rumour mill. After taking some advice, Webster closed the incident down, telling the *Daily Mail*, 'I stand by what I've done, this is very important. I'm happy to do all the media but it's become all too much now and I have engaged a lawyer and [am] now gagged from any future media [in the short term].'

*

Doctor Webster's forthright comments weren't the only revelations that followed the convictions. On the day after the decision, we were all back in Melbourne for an afternoon hearing on suppression orders – which were broadly what the jury didn't hear. Both defence and prosecution lawyers were in accord, however a lawyer for some major media organisations was also at the bar table arguing for most of the interim suppression orders to be lifted in the interests of open justice. The notable exception on which they were all in agreement was ensuring the children could not be identified until the youngest turned twenty-one. Justice Beale reserved his hearing decision for a month. For media types, it was a tense few weeks wondering what could and couldn't be used in upcoming books and documentaries. We'd sat through all the preliminary hearings, gathering information, but couldn't use anything we'd heard.

On Friday, 8 August, Justice Beale was back on the bench and the suppression orders largely lifted. Journalists, with stories of 'what the jury didn't hear' already prepared, published immediately. The primary chunk of what was now available was all the evidence that had been heard in the pre-trial hearings but not at the trial, and so they couldn't be reported until the verdict was in and the order was lifted. One reason for this was that some evidence may have been unfairly prejudicial to the Accused – Erin. Trials need to be conducted with conspicuous fairness and judges also, I suspect, have an eye cast to any potential issues that could lead to an appeal. Simon's hospitalisations and dramatic near-death experience and his suspicion, shared with family members and Doctor Chris Ford, that Erin had been trying to poison him was the biggest revelation. But there were others, including the jar of vomit Don had taken to hospital with him and handed to Doctor Ford.

Erin's inquiry to the Facebook page 'Poisons Help; Emergency Identification for Mushrooms and Plants', which had arisen during the trial but not in the presence of the jury and ruled inadmissible by the judge, also got a mention. Erin had posted on the page in 2020, under the profile Erin Erin, that her cat had eaten a mushroom that was growing under a tree and 'he's having a vomit'. She included photos of the mushrooms in her post. As prosecutor Jane Warren told the judge, 'the Accused has never owned a cat'. We also had a story confirmed.

During the trial, the tantalising but elusive evidence of a second visit to the Koonwarra tip remained just that, but it was spot on. In the hours following the lunch Erin drove to the tip and paid to dispose of cardboard and the contents of a 120-litre bin. Again, the visit was captured on CCTV but it wasn't possible to identify what was being disposed of, so it was inadmissible. These revelations were stunning and refreshed the global media frenzy a month after the trial's end.

*

Simon's story was still on the top of the media wishlist, but in the face of allegedly lucrative media offers, the Patterson family and friends have continued to maintain a dignified silence. I've worked with victims of crime for decades, and while media attention to stir interest in a cold case is essential, in a case like this one, feeding the media beast has little value. With the trial concluded, for the family and loved ones of the victims, and for those connected in some way to Erin or the Patterson and Wilkinson families, it's time to get on with the slow process of healing.

31

THE VOICE OF THE VICTIMS

Erin Patterson returned to court on Monday, 25 August 2025, and this time not to the Morwell courthouse, but to Court 4 of the Supreme Court in Melbourne, with its ornate plasterwork, polished timber, crimson carpets and dramatically large chandelier lighting.

She entered the packed courtroom just before 10.30 am, flanked by security officers and escorted through to the dock, which looks across the bar table to the judge's seat on the bench. Erin was plainly dressed and wearing her usual sandals. Not a skerrick of emotion or engagement was on show.

The day's proceedings began at 10.30 am, with the arrival of Justice Beale. Two days had been set down for submissions on sentencing – and they would factor into Erin's fate. And for the first time in this long case, those impacted by her crimes would get the chance to tell their stories through their Victim's Impact Statements. These statements also play a part in the judge's consideration of the sentence to be imposed.

There were twenty-eight statements tendered to the court, of which seven were read directly in the courtroom. The statements that were heard were from Martha Patterson, Don's mother; Colin Patterson, Don's brother; Tim Patterson, Don's nephew; Ian Wilkinson; Ruth Dubois, Ian and Heather's daughter; Lynette Young, Heather and Gail's sister; and Simon Patterson. Simon's was read out by his cousin Naomi Gleadow, and Naomi also read out Martha's, Colin's and Tim's. Nanette Rogers SC read out Lynette's.

Ian Wilkinson was dignified, compassionate, considered, brave and resolute. His voice on this day was strong – the voice of an orator. He began by speaking of his wife, Heather, a 'compassionate, intelligent, brave, witty, simply a delightful person who loved sharing life with others'. They'd been married for 44 years, she was mother to four children 'and believed her greatest work was to raise them to be good people with values of care for each other in the family and for other people beyond the family'. He spoke of the loss of Don and Gail, close friends for nearly 50 years – 'my life is greatly impoverished without them,' he said. On a few occasions the emotion would cause his voice to waiver, and he'd pause briefly to collect himself.

Of Erin, Ian said, 'I'm distressed that Erin has acted with callous and calculated disregard for my life and the life of those I love. What foolishness possesses a person to think that murder could be the solution to their problems, especially the murder of people who had only good intentions towards her. Erin has brought deep sorrow and grief into my life and the lives of many others.' Then he said something that took the air out of the courtroom, 'In regard to the many harms done to me, I make an offer of forgiveness to Erin. I bear her no ill-will; my prayer for her is that she will use her time in jail wisely to become a better person.'

It was an incredible moment of grace. But there was a sting in the tail for Erin: 'In regards to the murders of Heather and Gail and Don, I am compelled to seek justice.'

Ian ended his statement, saying, 'Now I am no longer Erin Patterson's victim and she has become the victim of my kindness.'

Ruth was next, speaking from her wheelchair with her father at her side. She spoke of her mother and her uncle and of her aunt. She said, 'We grew up in a home being shown love, empathy, compassion, and to always look for the best in people. It is horrible to know that it's these good attributes that were used to lure these kind people with the intention of causing harm. The world seems colder and harsher knowing this, then for the offender to sit and watch over casual conversation while these people, who showed nothing but love and care for her, ate a meal that would kill.'

Ruth captured the gravity of Erin's crimes, saying, 'on 29 July 2023, four generations of our families, ranging from newborn to 99 years old, countless friends, and wider community, were handed a lifetime of carrying this unimaginable horror.'

Simon Patterson wasn't in court, but his statement was delivered by his cousin Naomi. He had written that, 'Mum and Heather's father outlived them, reaching one hundred with a sharp mind but failing lungs. Dad's mother has reached one hundred, too, and his grandmother reached 101, all with sharp minds and loving hearts throughout.'

He observed, 'I will be aware for roughly the next 30 years, presuming I live that long, that they could still be alive had Erin not chosen to murder them.'

He also took the chance to call out some of the media and their behaviour that he said was 'callous' and 'deplorable', as they, strangers, menaced 'our home, brandishing notebooks, phones, cameras and microphones'.

It was a sobering moment for anyone whose job entails chasing down a story, no matter what.

Of his two children, he wrote, 'The grim reality is they live in an irreparably broken home with only a solo parent, when almost everyone else knows their mother murdered their grandparents. None of these hurdles that my children face are easy for them to overcome. The fact these foreseeable hurdles were actively put in front of them by their own mother is an impact we will wrestle with for the rest of our lives. Despite this, both children are incredibly strong, loving, intelligent, observant, and wise beyond their years.'

After the reading of all the statements the court adjourned until 2.15 pm, resuming with evidence from Jennifer Hosking from Corrections Victoria, who is the Assistant Commissioner for sentence management. She appeared by video-link and gave evidence about Erin's time behind bars at the Dame Phyllis Frost Centre. Hosking said Erin had spent most of her time in the Gordon unit, which housed prisoners 'who need protection or closer supervision from the main population of the prison'. Erin was in a cell on her own, with limited access to a courtyard around 1.5 metres or so square. In her cell she had a television, a computer and personal items, including a hair straightener, books, a fan, crochet needles and wool. We learned that Erin had crocheted herself a blanket for her bed.

Hosking, when questioned by Mandy, accepted that Erin spent at least 22 hours each day in her cell. Erin, she said, didn't pose a risk to other prisoners, but it was her safety that was their concern.

After Hosking came submissions on sentencing from the defence and the prosecution, and they all agreed on one point – life imprisonment for the murder convictions. But, Mandy said, 'unless the court considers that it's in the interest of justice not to do so, the court must fix a non-parole period of 30 years if the relevant term is the term of the offender's natural life. Even the imposition of a 30-year non-parole period would see Ms Patterson reach the age of 80 or so before she became eligible to apply for parole.'

Ms Warren, for the Crown, had a different view, and it was the question of mercy and whether it could be applied to sentencing. She quoted former Victorian Supreme Court Judge Lasry who said, 'Sometimes a crime is so horrific, so cruel and so callous that a step towards mercy becomes too difficult to take'. Warren said Erin Patterson's crimes were so cruel and horrific she didn't deserve mercy and that fixing a non-parole period wasn't appropriate.

Justice Beale agreed 'the offending here is horrendous', and then adjourned the case until 8 September 2025 for sentencing.

There was a mixed bag of reports about Erin's demeanour during the submissions, with some saying she had been moved to tears and others reporting she was impassive. I saw her as she was escorted from the dock that afternoon and there was no emotion at all on her face, aside from a brief flicker of recognition when she saw her friend Alison Prior in the public gallery. Aside from that, her eyes were mostly slightly downcast and then she was whisked out of the courtroom. Back to the Dame Phyllis Frost Centre to wait fourteen days before she knew if she would die in custody or ever have the chance of freedom again.

*

On Monday, 8 September 2025, the Erin Patterson case was back in Court 4 of the Supreme Court in Melbourne for sentencing. For the first time in Victoria, a television camera was allowed into a courtroom to broadcast live. Justice Beale's decision for allowing the broadcast was to 'increase understanding of the work of the court'. He said, 'Given the intense public interest in the case, the broadcast will provide an opportunity to inform the public of the reasons for sentence promptly and completely'. The camera was focused solely on Justice Beale.

Erin Patterson was in the dock. She'd arrived in court wearing a paisley shirt, tan jacket, black pants and her usual sandals. At the bar table were Nanette Rogers SC, Ms Lenthall and Ms Warren for the Crown, and Colin Mandy SC and Ms Stafford for Erin Patterson.

Justice Beale walked onto the bench at 9.30 am sharp. When everyone had resumed their seats, including Patterson, he began to detail his sentencing decision. He said, 'Erin Patterson, after a long trial, during which you gave evidence that the poisoning of your four lunch guests on the 29 July 2023 was an accident, the jury found you guilty of three counts of murder and one count of attempted murder'.

Reporters with a view of Patterson said she had her eyes shut and appeared to be meditating.

Justice Beale recapped the case, canvassing her litany of lies. He said she'd deliberately served her guests with beef Wellington on grey plates and hers was on an 'orangey tan' plate to make sure she didn't eat a poisoned meal. He said that her crimes involved 'substantial premeditation', and he was satisfied that by 16 July 2023, when the lunch invitations were made, that 'you did so with the intention of killing them all'.

Erin, he said, had shown 'no pity' towards Gail, Don, Heather and Ian and 'instead of informing those treating the Pattersons and Wilkinsons that you had used foraged mushrooms (which you could have done without having to admit that you had deliberately poisoned their meals), you repeatedly denied foraging'. That denial meant medical treatment that may have made a difference was not commenced as quickly as it could have been if the cause of the illnesses was known immediately. Erin Patterson had that power.

He said her crimes 'involved an enormous betrayal of trust' and traumatised four generations of the Wilkinson and Patterson families and 'inflicted untold suffering on your own children who you robbed of their beloved grandparents'.

Justice Beale was measured and methodical and said Erin Patterson's failure to show remorse, 'pours salt into all the victims' wounds'.

On sentencing considerations, he noted her case fell into the 'worst category' for the offences of murder and attempted murder. The gravity of her crimes meant rehabilitation 'has taken a back seat' when considering sentencing purposes. Erin Patterson knew the protracted suffering that serving death cap mushrooms to Gail, Don, Heather and Ian would bring. She showed 'no pity for [her] victims' and followed through on her 'lethal plan' with pre-meditated callousness.

In hearing Justice Beale's summation, we were reminded of the horrific deaths that Gail, Don and Heather endured and the ongoing health impacts that Ian will carry forever. He underlined the betrayal of trust that cut short three lives and caused lasting damage to the man who survived her appalling crime. The fact that Erin Patterson also had the gall to tell the police that she had been very helpful again underlines the brutality and deliberate nature of her crimes. She has demonstrated no remorse for her actions.

Justice Beale said the fixing of a non-parole period would not 'undervalue the horrendous nature of your offending'.

He instructed Erin Patterson to stand. She did. Justice Beale then said, 'For the attempted murder of Ian Wilkinson, I sentence you to 25 years' imprisonment. For the murder of Heather Wilkinson, I sentence you to life imprisonment. For the murder of Gail Patterson, I sentence you to life imprisonment. For the murder of Don Patterson, I sentence you to life imprisonment.'

Beale went on: 'All sentences are to be served concurrently. The total effective sentence is life imprisonment and I fix a non-parole period of 33 years'.

With his job done, Justice Beale said, 'Would you please remove Ms Patterson'.

At 10.18 am the sentencing was over. An emotionless Erin Patterson was led from the courtroom. Back to a prison cell, which will be her home until she is in her eighties.

Let's leave the final word to Ian Wilkinson, who addressed the media outside the court. He thanked police, prosecutors and all the health workers involved in the case. He said, 'I want to say thank you to the many people from across Australia and around the world who through their prayers and messages of support have encouraged us. I thank the people of the Leongatha and Korumburra communities in particular. Your thoughtfulness and care has been a great encouragement to us. That is all I wish to say for now. Please respect our privacy as we continue to grieve and heal. Thank you for listening. I hope you all have a great day.'

EPILOGUE

The jury found that, beyond reasonable doubt, Erin Patterson knew precisely what she was doing when four good people, Don, Gail, Heather and Ian, sat at her dining table in her 'forever home' in Gibson Street, Leongatha, on 29 July 2023. She knew that mouthful after mouthful of her special beef Wellington would likely result in a slow and dreadful death for these four family members. She'd researched and planned this terrible crime but, like so many others now in prison, had failed to consider that she would be caught. Lies followed and they sealed her fate.

Erin's mental health was never raised as an issue in the trial or in the sentencing. She knew what she was doing, and was competent to instruct her legal team. Tim Watson-Munro is Australia's leading criminal psychologist. He's delved into the minds and crimes of some of the most notorious criminals in Australia and around the globe, and his assessments have been frequently used in court. Though he hasn't examined

Erin, he said that mental health issues may have an impact on the gravity of her guilt.

Given her long period in prison awaiting trial, Tim thinks Erin would by now have adjusted to prison life, but it wouldn't have been smooth sailing. With conviction comes the reality that the accused won't be going home. As Tim said, 'The majestic distraction of dealing with lawyers and the demands of a trial are gone. Fewer legal visits, off the front page. It's a stark reality and now it's time to start adjusting to the magnitude of what her sentence is.'

The media and global audience remain obsessed by the case, and that won't diminish until sentencing is done.

Jury decisions aren't provisional, and it's only after sentencing that Erin Patterson can lodge an appeal. No matter what happens for her, the diabolical deeds she committed will stay with the families of her victims for all their lives, and while the jury's decision is a step toward finality, it won't bring closure – the pain will always be there. In cases like this, the wounds never heal, they only become less raw. For them, as for most who have followed this case, the fact a family lunch could cause such heartbreak is almost beyond comprehension. But the cold, hard truth is … Erin Patterson did indeed cook up a recipe for murder.

ACKNOWLEDGEMENTS

My thanks to my agent Lyn Tranter and publisher at Hachette, Vanessa Radnidge – we started talking about a book on the Erin Patterson case as that story turned from a mystery to murder.

My thanks to both of them, and to the exceptional team at Hachette who make books happen from draft through to the finished product at the bookshop. Special thanks to Chrysoula Aiello, Jenny Topham, Jessica Harvie, Kate Taperell and all the publicity, sales and marketing team. And to Christa Moffitt, Vanessa Lanaway, Pamela Dunne and Graeme Jones.

Thanks also to the media team at the Supreme Court of Victoria for their patience, professionalism and help.

RAISING READERS
Books Build Bright Futures

Dear Reader,

We'd love your attention for one more page to tell you about the crisis in children's reading, and what we can all do.

Studies have shown that reading for fun is the **single biggest predictor of a child's future success** – more than family circumstance, parents' educational background or income. It improves academic results, mental health, wealth, communication skills and ambition.

The number of children reading for fun is in rapid decline. Young people have a lot of competition for their time, and a worryingly high number do not have a single book at home.

Our business works extensively with schools, libraries and literacy charities, but here are some ways we can all raise more readers:

- Reading to children for just 10 minutes a day makes a difference
- Don't give up if your children aren't regular readers – there will be books for them!
- Visit bookshops and libraries to get recommendations
- Encourage them to listen to audiobooks
- Support school libraries
- Give books as gifts

Thank you for reading.
www.JoinRaisingReaders.com